Creating the
Literature
Portfolio

Creating the
Literature
Portfolio

A Guide for Students

Alan C. Purves
Joseph A. Quattrini

NTC Publishing Group
Lincolnwood, Illinois USA

Dedication

We wrote this book together, but no one really writes one alone. Writing, like reading, is informed by all of one's language experiences and all of one's colleagues, teachers and students alike. We thank the colleagues who have informed our work.

Acknowledgments for literary selections can be found on page 247, which should be considered an extension of this copyright page.

Sponsoring Editor: Marisa L. L'Heureux
Design management and cover design: Ophelia M. Chambliss
Interior design: Lucy Lesiak
Production Manager: Rosemary Dolinski

ISBN 0-8442-5950-0 (student text)
ISBN 0-8442-5951-9 (instructor's edition)

Library of Congress Cataloging-in-Publication Data

Purves, Alan C.
    Creating the literature portfolio : a guide for students / Alan C.
Purves, Joseph A. Quattrini.
        p.   cm.
    Includes index.
    ISBN 0-8442-5950-0
    1. Literature—Study and teaching (Secondary)   2. Portfolios in
education—United States.   3. English language—Composition and
exercises—Study and teaching (Secondary)—United States.
    I. Quattrini, Joseph A.   II. Title.
PN59.P78   1996
808'.0668—dc20   96-14224
                                                                CIP

Published by NTC Publishing Group
© 1997 NTC Publishing Group, 4255 West Touhy Avenue
Lincolnwood (Chicago), Illinois 60646-1975 U.S.A.
All rights reserved. No part of this book may be reproduced,
stored in a retrieval system, or transmitted in any form or by any means,
electronic, mechanical, photocopying, recording, or otherwise,
without prior permission of NTC Publishing Group.
Manufactured in the United States of America.

67890VL987654321

Contents

3 Perspectives for Interpreting Meaning   75

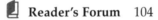

4 Using the Language and Devices of Literature 107

Preface

The book you are holding in your hand is the result of a seven-year collaboration of two people, each of whom started out wondering what the other was up to. Alan Purves was a university professor studying ways of evaluating student work in literature; Joe Quattrini was a high-school teacher of English who wasn't sure that researchers should be studying anything about what he was doing. For some reason, we found out that we liked each other, generally thought alike, and really believed in using portfolios as part of teaching and learning.

Portfolios have been used a lot in writing courses and in courses in the arts. Together with a number of teachers around the country, we became interested in seeing what it would be like to invite students to create portfolios of themselves as readers and students of literature. These portfolios help people show the world their skills at reading difficult prose and poetry, their ability to formulate and defend hypotheses concerning what they read, and their ability to create interesting representations in art, music, drama, and other media of the various works of literature that they encounter. This kind of portfolio is just as important as a writing portfolio; in fact, the two go hand in hand.

Most importantly, we both believe that it is important for you, the student, to be part of the act. You are not simply a customer or a consumer of the lessons you get in class. You have reason to understand what is going on, what you are studying, why you are studying it, and how to do well at it. We both recognize that each of you is an intelligent human being, a person with your own goals for what it is you want to get out of studying literature.

The study of literature in schools brings together an art form—the poems, plays, stories, novels, and other words you read—and a set of inquiring minds who seek to make some sort of disciplined sense out of what they read. People study literature to find out what the writers have to say about the world in which they live, to find out how artists put together beautiful combinations of words or screw them up, to find out why readers like or don't like things they read, and to find out whether the various individual pieces add up to anything. People also study literature because they are interested in developing their own writing. In fact, we do not separate reading from writing, which is why you will find a bucketful of writing assignments in this book. We hope to introduce you to some of these activities and to help you take part in them on your own.

It is our idea that you should become an independent operator, not simply a person going through a cookie-cutting machine that turns out a particular kind of reader or critic. That is why we have invested so much of our careers in portfolios. We think that your being able to create a portfolio of who you are as a reader (including a demonstration of what you know, what you are able to do, and what sorts of habits of reading, writing, and thinking you have developed) is important for you and for the educational system. We don't have any firm idea of what you should put in your portfolio, although we will tell you some of the things that instructors generally like or dislike. They are one of the groups of people who will look at your portfolio, and they are important, but other people are interested as well—prospective employers, admissions and honors committees, friends and relatives, and editors and publishers, to name but a few categories. We suggest something of what they like and dislike, but the real person you need to satisfy is you.

ORGANIZATION OF THE BOOK

This book is not organized according to the normal structure of a course in literature; rather, it is organized to lead you through the stages of building a literature portfolio. We begin with an introductory chapter about literature and portfolios and then move on to discuss the nature of you as a reader; some of the issues in reading and interpreting literature; the ways in which people link literature to the world of the writer and the reader; how people evaluate what they read; and how to fashion the final portfolio.

Each chapter begins with an overview (called "Looking Ahead") and ends with a retrospective look at what you have done (in "Portfolio Progress Report"). Each chapter has suggested assignments ("For Your Portfolio Notebook") and hints on how to build a portfolio systematically through the course of a semester or a year. Each chapter contains references to keeping a portfolio as a physical collection of papers and artifacts and as a set of spaces on a disk or hard drive. We use computers ourselves, and we see their potential in helping you create an attractive and interesting portfolio.

Although we include some selections of literature in this book, we expect that you will use it with a library of books or a literature anthology of some sort.

Above all, we hope that you will find each chapter stimulating and helpful. We had fun making the book, and we enjoyed working with three fine editors, Marisa L'Heureux, John Nolan, and Marianne Quinn. We hope you will enjoy using it.

1 Portfolios, Literature, and You

▶▶▶LOOKING AHEAD

This is an ambitious chapter. We set out to give answers to these questions:

- What is a portfolio?
- What is literature?
- What kinds of thinking are involved when you read? What kinds of gaps do you fill when you read between the lines?
- What is critical reading? How can you show your skill at it in literature courses?

Besides seeing some answers (not *the* answers) to these questions, you will also have a chance to give your own views on the nature of literature and to prepare a "Great Moment in Literature" for a "Reader's Forum" presentation. By the end of the chapter, you will have started defining the kind of reader you want to make of yourself. Your portfolio will be under way.

THE BASICS OF PORTFOLIOS

This book is about portfolios and literature classes. You have probably been reading literature in your classes since kindergarten, and some of you may have been making portfolios of your writing or of other work connected with class work or with a hobby. Now we are going to put the two together. Let's start with portfolios in general, then turn to literature, the kind of reading required to get meaning from literature, and on to the literature portfolio.

What Is a Portfolio?

The word *portfolio* comes from the Italian and means literally "carrying sheets of paper." It refers to a case for holding loose, unfolded sheets of paper. In one meaning, these sheets are important government papers that are carried from one part of the government to another, so that a portfolio refers to the particular branch of government whose papers are being carried. A government official, for instance, might have a portfolio in labor, or health, or economics, or foreign affairs. In another meaning, a portfolio is a repository for the commercial papers of a bank or a particular customer—stock certificates, mortgages, deeds, and wills.

In both these meanings, a portfolio suggests that the papers are important. Artists of various sorts also carry portfolios of their work and these, too, are important, for they represent all of the important creations of an artist and a record of his or her artistic career. Today, artists' portfolios may not contain sheets of paper, and they may not be carried in a big flat case. Instead, an artist's portfolio may hold tapes or CDs, videos, photographs, and computer disks. It all depends on the kind of work the artist does and the kind of material he or she uses.

The importance of the papers or other materials in a portfolio lies in the fact that the portfolio is a public presentation of an artist's work. Through the materials in their portfolios, people get jobs or commissions to make new works, have their work selected for publication or exhibition, or receive prizes for the excellence of their work.

In classes around the world, students are creating and keeping portfolios, too. Having a portfolio means that the work you do is important and respected. It also means that it is yours, not simply stuff you hand in to an instructor and then never see again. You can take your portfolio to the next course, use it in applying for a job or getting into a different school or program, save it for your kids, or put it in the attic so that you can take it down years later and gloat over how intelligent you were way back when. A portfolio can represent your work in a single course such as English 144, or it can represent your work over the course of your whole educational career. In this book, we will focus on the course portfolio, but what we have to say could apply to a larger and longer-term portfolio, as well.

An academic portfolio is a public presentation, a presentation of you as a student to the outside world: your instructor; an instructor in another course; a jury of students, faculty, and parents; or an admissions or graduation committee. A portfolio is the means by which you are judged to be a great student, a mediocre one, or one who is a basic clod. The work that is in the portfolio represents you; it is how you present yourself. No one else is going to be judged; you can't shift the blame. You succeed or not depending on the portfolio. We will try to help you make your portfolio the best it can be, but the job is yours.

What Does a Portfolio Look Like?

Some people think of a portfolio as a big, black cardboard case. That is certainly one kind, but we have seen a lot of other kinds of portfolios. Some are presentation binders, some are plastic milk cases, some are computer or CD-ROM disks. Your portfolio can really be whatever is most convenient for you (assuming that your instructor doesn't have any specific requirements).

What Is in a Portfolio?

Just about anything and everything. It can have formal tests and notebook entries. It can have papers you have written for class, perhaps both early drafts and final versions. It can have papers you have worked on with other students. It can have pieces you may have written for other courses—or just on your own. It can have records of what you have read, watched, or done. It can have tapes—audio and video—of presentations or performances you have been involved in, alone or with others. It can have pictures you have made or other art works. In short, it can have all the things you have done that show who you are as a reader, writer, and student of literature.

How Do I Manage a Portfolio?

The best way to begin is to make a distinction between your working portfolio—the place where you will keep all the things you are working on or have finished and may put in your final portfolio—and the final or presentation portfolio itself. The final portfolio is what you are going to show the world. It is a rather formal look at you and what you have done.

Your working portfolio is not simply an early version of your presentation portfolio; it is the place where you keep together the work you do toward producing the final version. One part of your working portfolio will be the file where you keep papers that have been marked and returned for revision, as well as projects and records of projects that you think you want to use in your presentation portfolio. Another part will be what we will refer to as a "Portfolio Notebook." This is where you keep a variety of exercises, ideas for papers, answers to response starters, and other items that will provide evidence of your daily work with literature. It is the place where you will "rehearse," or practice, for your final portfolio by trying out new techniques, writing different kinds of interpretations, completing reflective pieces, and working on any other kinds of activities that will make you a stronger reader and writer.

You manage a portfolio by setting yourself some goals, an outline of what it is you want to say or show about yourself. Then you gather material that you think might back up your claims about your accomplishment of those goals. Periodically you should sort through the material to see what it is you want to keep and what you need to add. This step of gathering and sorting the material may take weeks, months, or even years (depending on the sort of portfolio). At the appropriate time, you assemble what you have done into a final portfolio, arrange it in the order you want, prepare an introduction, table of contents, or autobiographical statement, and then send it out to whoever it is that is going to review or judge your work or you.

That's all there is to it. Simple? In some ways, yes. But doing a good job of creating and assembling the parts can be challenging, and this book will help you through the process.

FOR YOUR PORTFOLIO NOTEBOOK

Name the Portfolio Owner

Play Sherlock Holmes with a set of clues. Below are the lists of things three students put in their portfolios. What can you tell about each student from an examination of the list of entries? In your "Portfolio Notebook," write a sentence or two characterizing the kind of literature student you can infer from each set of evidence.

Student A
Portfolio Notebook
Drafts of six original poems
Final versions of four of those poems
Tape of an oral poetry reading
Two critical essays on novels
Program and review of a play production
Photos to go with a selection of Shakespearean sonnets
A research paper on Dickens's London
Reader's autobiography of new writers read

Student B
Portfolio Notebook
Three short critical essays on European short stories
A long critical essay involving psychological analysis of the main character in a Faulkner novel
A research paper on Keats and Greek mythology
A critical essay on African American alienation in 1960s fiction
A critical bibliography of four Asian American poets

Student C
Portfolio Notebook
Translations of five poems each by two Puerto Rican poets
A bibliography of Caribbean plays in English translation
A research essay on the fiction of Miguel Asturias
A taping of readings of three Nuyorican writers
A critical essay on magic realism

TOWARD A DEFINITION OF LITERATURE

Literature can be an individual poem, play, story, novel, or essay. But the word can also be used to define the whole body of poems, plays, stories, novels, and essays that have ever been written or recorded all over the world. All different sorts of people have taken a stab at defining literature. Here is a handful of definitions gathered from over the years:

It's what people read:

- It's what makes the hair on the back of your neck stand up.
- It's what pleases and teaches us by its pleasing.
- It's what strikes the readers as the wording of their own highest thoughts and appears almost as a remembrance.

It's what people write:

- It's the precious lifeblood of a master spirit.
- It's the spontaneous overflow of powerful emotions.
- It's the record of the best and happiest moments of the happiest and best minds.

It's something special in and of itself:

- It's what oft was thought but ne'er so well expressed.
- It's the best words in their best order.
- It's the best that's been known and said in the world, containing high truth and seriousness.
- It's the wedding of form and content into an organic unity.

It's part of something else.

- It's the verbal expression of a culture, taking its place with dance, music, painting, sculpture, and drama.
- It's the sum of those individual works that people around the world and over the years have considered worth holding on to.

- It's each poem or story as a part of that larger universe called *literature.*

As these examples show, literature has been defined broadly and narrowly. It has been defined from the perspective of both the reader and the writer, as well as from the perspective of those who want to distinguish a work of art from what is not art (or trash). It has also been defined from the perspective of those who see each piece as part of a larger whole or tradition. All of these definitions are right—or partly right. Often the people making the definitions are people who want to distinguish literature from something else. Often they want to separate "good" or "real" literature from everything that is false or bad. Within all of these different definitions, though, most people agree—or nearly agree—on some parts of a definition of literature.

The Medium

Most people agree, for example, that literature uses words. How many words does it take to make a piece of literature? At least one, some people would say. But others would argue that literature can be made from other sorts of symbols—letters for instance, or the various typewriter marks such as the sideways smiley face :)—or from pictures such as those in a wordless picture book or a cartoon strip. Others would say that there must be some words. There is also the argument that the words must be written down somewhere. But some people have pointed to poets like Homer, who carried *The Iliad* around in his head and never wrote it down. People also now talk about film as literature, arguing that it is not just the script but the actual film that is the piece of literature.

Still, it is generally agreed that words and language are a necessary part of literature. They are the medium of an author, who may compose orally or may write them down or otherwise record them. And the writer uses words alone or combined with pictures, action, animation, or music. The writer knows how words work, and if the piece of literature is printed, he or she knows about how spelling, punctuation, and grammar may be used to help the words work their magic. The words are then combined using various techniques such as simile and metaphor, rhythm and rhyme, and even typeface to form some sort of artistic impression.

The Form

Literature may use words, but many critics have also argued that there must be some sort of shape to the whole thing. A random group of pretty words isn't a piece of literature, just as a set of colors in a paint box isn't a picture. There must be *something* about the words, the ideas, the characters, and the actions that gives them some sort of coherence.

What that something is has been a problem. For instance, people have said that a piece of literature must have a beginning and an end. But some of the recent fiction, particularly pieces composed to be read on computers (called *hypertexts*), have no clear beginning or end. The reader can start and stop anywhere and at any time. Yet the piece still has a form. When we read it, we get a sense of its being complete.

People have also argued that the something lies in the fact that each piece of literature falls into some sort of a clear type, known as a *genre*. The major genres are poetry, prose fiction, prose nonfiction, and drama. These have been divided into subgenres time and again, as we shall see in Chapter 2. Some would say that every new work must be able to be put in a genre pigeonhole to be a piece of literature. The problem with genres and their various subgenres is that they are sometimes defined so rigidly that an author who writes something a little bit different doesn't fit. A novel, for example, is often said to be a long piece of fiction written in prose. That means it is a made-up or imagined story. In the 1960s, Truman Capote wrote a book called *In Cold Blood.* It is the true account of a murder, but Capote used a great many of the devices of novel writing to tell his story. He added detail about characters and reconstructed certain scenes as he imagined they must have been. Was the book a novel? Was it nonfiction? People decided that the new hybrid was a genre called a *nonfiction novel.*

A similar case is the *prose poem,* a term that seems like a contradiction, but a number of distinguished writers in several languages argue that that is what they are writing, poems that are not verse (that is, without a regular rhythm or rhyme) but an extension of free verse to a format that looks more like the prose paragraph.

Armchairs

Who ever thought a warm neck would become an armrest, or legs eager for flight and joy could stiffen into four simple stilts? Armchairs were once noble flower-eating creatures. However, they allowed themselves too easily to be domesticated and today they are the most wretched species of quadrupeds. They have lost all their stubbornness and courage. They are only meek. They haven't trampled anyone or galloped off with anyone. They are, for certain, conscious of a wasted life.

The despair of armchairs is revealed in their creaking.

—Zbigniew Herbert

Is this a poem or a short paragraph followed by a sentence? What is its genre? We will come back to form later in this book, but at this point, form is determined partly by what a piece of literature looks like, partly by what it sounds like, partly by what the writer decides it is, and partly by what the reader thinks it is.

The Purpose

Over the ages, there has been general agreement that one of the major distinguishing features of literature is that it seems to have as its main purpose that of giving pleasure to the people who read it while they are in the act of reading it. This is not to say that literature cannot also give us information, make us think, inspire us to great (or not-so-great) actions, or strike up other responsive chords. But most poems, plays, stories, or even essays are written with the primary goal of having us enjoy the experience of participating in the reading at the time.

There are also pieces of writing that did not start out to be pieces of literature, but we now read them as if they were. Lincoln's Gettysburg Address is a good example. We often read it as an example of good speechmaking or even simply good prose, using a serious, elegant style and just the right turns of phrase to make it appealing. We don't read it as the people at the graveside might have heard it, not as literature but as an appeal to the best instincts of a people torn apart by war.

The Content

Literature has to be about intense moments of beauty or moments of heightened consciousness. At least that's what some people say. They also say it has to be made up and imagined. A laundry list can't be literature, nor can an instruction manual for assembling a deck chair. Newspaper articles can't be literature either. Literature has to be a work into which the writer has invested imagination.

What if the imagination decided to take something that was simply picked up and treat it as a piece of literature? There is a whole form of literature called "found" or "pop" literature. Here is an example:

test
1. Distinguish between morning and afternoon.
2. Define familiar objects in terms of use.
3. Copy a diamond shape.
4. Count 13 pennies.
5. Distinguish between ugly and pretty faces.

—Bern Porter

We don't know where Porter found this (or even if he really did), but he has placed it on the page where a poem might be and put it in a book called *Found Poems.* Does that make it a poem? Many people would say that it does.

From all of this, what can we say about literature? What definition would you come up with? Does your definition include nearly every example you can think of? What's the dividing line?

FOR YOUR PORTFOLIO NOTEBOOK
Your Own Literature Definition

Consider the following question: What is literature? You've read some answers from other people. Now get your own ideas down on paper. Just write, as quickly as you can, your responses to these questions. Fifteen to twenty minutes of writing should give you a few pages of text to work with.

Keep what you write in your "Portfolio Notebook." At the end of your work in creating a literature portfolio, it should be interesting to come back and compare notes with yourself.

- What is literature? What does it mean? to you? to other writers and readers? to society?

- How does it mean—what is meaning, anyway, and where is it?

- What is it for? Who is it for?
- When it's good, what makes it good? What do you like about it? Why do you care? *Do* you care?

FROM READING TO CRITICAL READING

Nearly every literature course we have ever come across involves people reading. It's one of the necessary steps in studying literature, since most of the material in the class assignment list is printed or published.

There are many different kinds of reading in the world and many different approaches to the act of reading. There is the reading you do when you go down the aisles of a supermarket and check the items on the shelves against a shopping list. There is the reading you do when you are given some pieces of wood and some screws and a piece of paper explaining how to turn them into a chair. There is the reading you do when you are driving along looking for a place to stay or eat. There is the reading you do when you've got an exciting mystery story and no other distractions. There is also the reading you do in literature classes. This reading must be looked at differently from the other types because you are not allowed to be passive about it. Not only do you interpret a selection to find out what it means. You might also

- determine how your understanding of the selection relates to a particular part of your life or experience;
- see what other selections it resembles; and
- analyze how the selection is put together to see how it is trying to affect you and then judge how well the writer has accomplished his or her goals.

To read with this much insight it is helpful to have a clearer understanding of just what goes on when you read.

Reading as a Gap Filler

Reading is based on a major mental activity: filling in the gaps of the text so as to make meaning. What this really involves is reading between the lines.

Suppose you are asked to complete the series: 3, 6, 9, ___. If you came up with a number, you just filled a gap—not just with a number but also with a justification for choosing that number. You brought to the task your own contexts for creating meaning. If you chose *12* to fill in the gap, you must have reasoned that the +3 differential would continue.

But maybe it wouldn't. The series could just as well be 3, 6, 9, 9, 6, 3 or 3, 6, 9, 3, 6, 9 or 3, 6, 9, 2, 4, 6 or something else. The point is that any one gap can be filled in a number of justifiable ways, depending on the contexts brought to the task.

We're always filling in, even when there don't seem to be any blanks. The symbol "+" might be read as an addition signal by one student, a positive valence by another, the cross hairs of a rifle scope by a third, and the cursor for a computer drawing program by a fourth.

In its most basic form, we can think of writing as marks on a surface. (We normally think of the result as black and white, but that is simply a result of the nature of inks and paper.) The marks form patterns on the surface, and it is in those patterns that we make or decipher meaning.

Take this most simple example. In the frame are three boxes. They are in a line, and they are separated by white space. They appear to be aligned horizontally and to be spaced nearly so as to be equidistant:

The three form a pattern. That pattern has a potential meaning, even though you may not be sure what it is. The meaning is derived from the boxes and the space between them. Both are integral to the meaning.

Let us take another example:

A
B
C

Here we have three letters in a column. But we understand this as more than three letters. The letters are vertically spaced and are the first three letters of the alphabet. The type is in a style called Considine Shadow. It is a display style, used often for signs and advertisements. The arrangement, size, type, and spacing all help us to determine meaning. Meaning comes from the pattern. We can look at these three marks and assume that they signal an ordered list.

And here is another example:

We now have a combination of marks and spaces that form into three groups. The marks are a sans-serif type (that is, without little curlicues). The individual marks are letters, and each group of them is formed into a chunk that we see as having meaning. When we look at them, we think of them as words. The words themselves are arranged in a column, centered in a frame. The size of the first word in relation to the next two indicates its greater importance. The use of the sans-serif type makes the words seem strong and important, as if they constitute a sign or warning. The first word is a member of that group that we call adjectives and could be either a modifier of the second or third words or a predicate adjective (as in "Be quiet, you!"). The size and placement indicate that it is probably the latter.

The point of these three examples is that the very display of the letters and marks contains a great deal of information that we have learned to understand as meaningful patterns. We have used not only the marks as cues, but the space around them. We have read the lines, and we have read between the lines.

The written English language is a complex system of icons. Icons are not exact pictures of things but abstract pictures that stand for things, sounds, words, ideas, and relationships:

- The smiley face on that pin on your shirt is an icon; it isn't a picture of anyone.
- So is a light bulb in a balloon over the drawing of someone's head.
- So is the letter *A*.
- So is the group of letters *The*.

- So is this group of groups of letters that you are looking at between the large *S* and the dot.

Writers use the icons and the space in between them to create a pattern of meaning. Readers look at the icons, but they also fill in the space between them to make meaning. There are four kinds of gaps that need to be filled in.

Physical Gaps.   These are gaps in the visual space of a text. A comic strip gives a good example of how visual gaps work. When we look at a comic strip containing four pictures strung out in a row, we could see them as four separate pictures. But instead we use the spaces in between (called gutters) to make links between the pictures. We may see a link in time or in sequence; we may see a link in point of view; we may see a link in mood.

When we see a group of words like the following on a page, we also use the spaces to help us make connections:

The limits of language are no greater than the limits of imagination.

We have learned that we are to look at these words from left to right, beginning with the capital letter. We make connections by using the gutters between words as well as the words themselves. The gutters indicate that each word is separate. The final gutter after a dot indicates that the unit of meaning, like the panel of a comic strip, is over. Then we begin again.

A poetic use of this space is seen in the following concrete poem:

silence silence silence
silence silence silence
silence   silence
silence silence silence
silence silence silence

—Eugen Gomringer

The words don't form a sentence, but we see them in a pattern with a set of small breaks (like gutters) and a larger one. We try to make some sort of meaning out of the whole grouping as well as out of the relationships between the individual groups of words.

Just as we use words and spaces to make up sentences, so we use groups of sentences to make up larger sets of relationships. These usually come in units that we call *paragraphs*:

> The woman rolled over. "Isn't anyone going to help?" She groaned.
>
> A young, dark-skinned man came walking along from the direction of the "section." He heard a groan. Looking in, he saw a woman obviously in pain. Rushing to her, he held up her head. He felt something wet in his hand. "What can I do for you?" he asked.
>
> "Help."
>
> He looked around. There didn't seem to be anyone around. He looked for a phone but saw none. Carefully he lifted the woman and helped her stand up, and then, when he realized she could walk, helped her out on to the sidewalk.
>
> "I'll get taxi for you, lady," he said.
>
> A taxi came by and he waved, but it didn't stop.

The first break indicates a shift of focus from the woman to the man. The second indicates a shift from one person talking to another. The third and fourth indicate person shifts, and the last a shift from talk to action. We assume that the he and she are the same person across the breaks, and so we make a little story of this exchange.

A similar kind of gutter appears in the breaks between speeches in a play and between stanzas in a poem.

> Tyger! Tyger! burning bright
> In the forests of the night,
> What immortal hand or eye
> Could frame thy fearful symmetry?
>
> 5 In what distant deeps or skies
> Burnt the fire of thine eyes?
> On what wings dare he aspire?
> What the hand dare seize the fire?
>
> —*from* William Blake, "The Tyger"

Poems have two sorts of gutters that you have to leap in order to make meaning: one at the end of each line and one between stanzas. In the first stanza of Blake's "The Tyger," the poet asks a question of the tiger; in the second, the questions continue, and we are set to wondering whether they are also asked of the tiger or of someone else.

There are also larger sections of many pieces of literature that we have to cross in order to make connections. In novels, for example, there may be a gutter between chapters, so that we have to fill in what happened in a day or a year. Sometimes the chapter break can also mean a change in narrators or in scenes, as well as a change in time.

One of the major gaps is that which comes at the beginning or end of a piece of literature. Often a story will start or stop abruptly and beg the readers to use their imagination to fill in the blanks on either end. Notice how the technique is used in this poem:

Child on Top of a Greenhouse
The wind billowing out the seat of my britches,
My feet crackling splinters of glass and dried putty,
The half-grown chrysanthemums staring up like accusers,
Up through the streaked glass, flashing with sunlight,
5   A few white clouds all rushing eastward,
A line of elms plunging and tossing like horses,
And everyone, everyone, pointing up and shouting!

—Theodore Roethke

We are not sure how the child got on top of the greenhouse or what happened next, but we are asked both to concentrate on the moment and to build it into a scenario.

Filling in the physical gaps in the literature we read is a good part of critical reading. It is the way in which readers make sense of the collection of words, phrases, sentences, and sections. The kind of reading that focuses on these gaps is often called *close reading*, since we are asked to pay very careful attention to joining together the pieces of a work of literature.

FOR YOUR PORTFOLIO NOTEBOOK

Fill in the Gaps

Choose a group to work with and form two teams. Then take a sentence like, "They first saw the donkey standing on the roof." One team is to write the paragraph leading up to that sentence; the other is to write the paragraph following it. Then put the two together to see what sort of story emerges. Some other sentences you might use are these (or make up others if you want):

- They walked backwards into the post office.
- "Oh, no," she said. "The dog has locked us out of the car."
- If we can't talk because of the phone strike, what shall we do when it's over?
- They looked out the window onto Third Avenue and stared into the eyes of the rhinoceros.

Mental Gaps.   We spend a lot of time looking across various sorts of physical gaps to connect the various sections that we read. But sometimes there is another sort of gap that we have to connect. That gap or gutter is between what we see on the page and what it may mean. Suppose we read these lines:

> Tomorrow, and tomorrow, and tomorrow
> Creeps in this petty pace from day to day
> To the last syllable of recorded time,
> And all our yesterdays have lighted fools
> 5   The way to dusty death. Out, out, brief candle!
> Life's but a walking shadow, a poor player
> That struts and frets his hour upon the stage
> And then is heard no more. It is a tale
> Told by an idiot, full of sound and fury,
> 10   Signifying nothing.
>
> —*from* Macbeth, Act 5, Scene 5

We can put together the words to make sentences, but there is another kind of gap that we have to cross. How can tomorrow *creep*? How could yesterdays *have lighted* something? In what way is *life* a shadow or a play actor? The writer must have had some connections in mind, and we have to figure out what they are. This kind of gap is what literary people call *metaphor*, a general category for language that appears to be talking about two things at once. To understand such language, we have to work out an explanation that makes a day *(tomorrow)* like a person or animal that *creeps* along the ground. We have to cross the gutter between *life* (an abstract concept) and an actor *(player)* that is on the stage for just an hour.

All sorts of writing uses metaphor—the bringing together of two dissimilar pictures or a picture and an abstraction. A metaphor is like a comparison, but it goes further than saying something is like something else. It asks us as readers to make a close connection between two worlds, the one that's on paper and the one we create from our imagination or experience. We have to see the writer's picture of an actor strutting on a stage for an hour between the raising and the lowering of a stage curtain and then connect it to our picture of what life is like.

There is a whole variety of kinds of metaphors that writers use. Life strutting on a stage is a kind called *personification*, in which human qualities are given to nonhuman things. Another is *simile*, in which we are told directly that one thing is like another, as in "O my luve is like a red, red rose." Another is the *symbol*, in which we are told about a cross or the stars and stripes and are left to make a connection to Christianity or to the United States.

A relative of the symbol is the *allegory*, which occurs when a second story or meaning can be seen in a story. One example is a tale about a group of pigs that stage a revolution and take over a farm, first driving out all the people and running things themselves. Slowly, however, they become more and more oppressive to the other animals and begin doing business with humans and then acting more and more like them. The story is called *Animal Farm*. You can read it simply as a story about animals. But you can also make a connection to another story, the story of the Russian Revolution of 1918 and the ascendancy of the Communists and finally the Stalinists. The two stories appear parallel, and we say that the animal story is an *allegory* of the Russian experience. There have been many literary allegories, often to political events but sometimes to the stories of various religions: the slave narrative *The Drinking Gourd*, for example, is seen as an allegory of the Biblical book of Exodus. A *fable*, a short tale about an animal or human, is also usually an allegory, with the moral making the connection at the end. But most allegories don't come out and make the connections for you. You as a reader have to do this yourself.

Another kind of gap or gutter between what you read and what you understand occurs when writers use *irony*. Irony is somewhat like allegory in that there are two parts, the part you read and the part behind it that gives added meaning. Often irony involves the contrast between something that happens and its significance in light of other occurrences. It is ironic, for example, that in O. Henry's "The Gift of the Magi" the wife sells her hair to buy her husband a watch chain while he sells his watch to buy her combs for her hair. In other cases, irony is written so that you, who know how the story is going to come out, are reading the thoughts and statements of someone in the story who doesn't know what is going to happen. This is called *dramatic irony*, and a famous example is in the Greek tragedian Sophocles' *Oedipus Rex*, when we know that Oedipus is the person who killed his father and married his mother, but he does not and vows to catch and kill his father's murderer.

Another kind of irony occurs when a writer tells a story using a narrator that we guess we should not trust. In the short story "Haircut," Ring Lardner has a barber tell the story of a cruel trickster who teases a retarded youth until the youth kills him. The barber all the while speaks admiringly of the trickster, but we guess that Lardner wants us to see him as cruel and vindictive, not as funny. You have to decide how reliable or trustworthy the narrator is. Another famous ironic piece is Jonathan Swift's "A Modest Proposal," in which the narrator suggests that the best way to deal with the population problem in Ireland is to raise the babies of the poor to be used as food. We guess that his suggestion must be ironic because Swift was a clergyman who clearly did not advocate murder or eating other people.

Irony does not have to run throughout a whole work. Jane Austen begins her novel *Pride and Prejudice* with this sentence:

> It is a truth universally acknowledged, that a single man in possession of a good fortune, must be in want of a wife.

When we begin to read that sentence, which sounds like it will tell us an important truth, we expect an important ending like "all human beings are victims of pride." But, on the other side of the gutter from what we expect, we find out that the "truth" is really quite trivial. The difference between the buildup and the punch line is the kind of gap we call ironic.

FOR YOUR PORTFOLIO NOTEBOOK

Finding Ironies

As the Jane Austen example shows, writers often use irony to create a gap between the expected and the found. Here are more examples, these from Alexander Pope. The first is from one of his moral essays; the second refers to the Queen of England:

> But thousands die without this or that,
> Die and endow a college or a cat.
> —*from* "An Essay on Man," Epistle II, lines 95-96

> Here thou, great Anna! whom three realms obey,
> Dost sometimes counsel take—and sometimes tea.
> —*from* "The Rape of the Lock," Canto III, lines 7-8

A number of other writers use this device of leading readers up a cliff and then dropping them off into the mud. Some of the famous ones are Jonathan Swift, Jane Austen, Lord Byron, William Makepeace Thackeray, James Thurber, Lewis Carroll, and Dorothy Parker, as well as many modern comedians. Find three or four examples and put them in your "Portfolio Notebook." Then try writing a few of your own.

Physical/Mental Gaps. On page 16 we mentioned that gaps may have a physical signal on the page with nothing on the other side of them; the gutter has become an empty space that we must fill in. A famous story by Frank Stockton is called "The Lady, or the Tiger?" In it, a man who has dared woo the king's daughter is condemned to go into an arena. There are two doors: behind one of them is a tiger that will eat the man; behind the other is a beautiful woman who will be his wife. The king's daughter finds out what is behind each door and signals to her lover to choose a certain one. He chooses a door. Which did he choose, the lady or the tiger? The author does not tell us.

How do you fill in the gap? What do you put on the other side of the gutter? Many stories, plays, and poems stop and leave us to draw the conclusion, to make an ending or draw another picture. Even stories that have an ending such as "They married and lived happily ever after" invite us to wonder whether they really did live happily—or did they have a horrible time, and what about the stepsisters? What happened to them?

There are a number of kinds of questions that a piece of literature may leave us asking:

- "What happened to the people?" is one.
- "But what if, instead of _____, they had . . .?" is another.
- "I wonder if the author wants us to _____ ?" is another.
- "How can we relate that story to our lives?" is another.

The questions may be *whys* or *whethers* or *ifs*. They may also be whether the story is a good one or not, whether it is one worth reading or seeing again. Each of these questions comes after we have read. It is as if the writer had drawn the next to last panel of the comic strip and left us another square to fill in. At the end, we have to decide what really ended, what kind of closure there was.

When we fill in these kinds of gutters, we are doing what is usually called *interpreting* or *evaluating* the work. It is something most authors want us to do. We may have finished reading, but something stays with us.

Text/Context Gaps.   The last kind of gap we want to discuss is the one between the writer and the text. What is on the page or contained in it may stand alone, but we often need to learn about the circumstances of the writing of the text. We read a poem:

Humpty Dumpty sat on a wall. . . .

We know that the poem was written by someone who lived at a particular time in a particular place. That person must have had a reason for writing what he or she wrote. Can we bridge the gap between what we have read and what we know of the writer or of the writer's time?

In the case of this poem, perhaps we can. We know that the poem was written in the late 1600s, even if we don't know who wrote it. In England in the 1680s, about the time that this was written, there was an attempted coup against King James II, and James unsuccessfully tried to rally support for himself. The poem says that the army was unable to put Humpty Dumpty (whom we generally picture as an egg) together again. It is possible that this was a political poem referring to the events.

Oftentimes we read a book or a poem and think we see something of the author in what we are reading. Charles Dickens wrote *David Copperfield*, and many of the incidents are very close to incidents in his life. How much of an autobiography is it? That depends on how big a bridge you want to build across the gutter.

Some writers like William Wordsworth are personal; others like Jane Austen seem almost anonymous. But all writers write in their time and culture. When we read a book like *Black Boy* by Richard Wright or the poems of Langston Hughes, we tend to remember that the writers were African Americans, and so we look at the books and make connections between what we read and what we know of the African American experience. The same is true when we read a poem by an Irishman like William Butler Yeats or Seamus Heaney, a woman like Sylvia Plath or Adrienne Rich, a Hispanic like Sandra Cisneros or Rodolfo Anaya, an Asian like Amy Tan or Lawrence Yep, or a seventeenth-century aristocrat like Richard Lovelace or John Suckling. When we know something of the background of the writer, we make connections between that knowledge and the words and spaces on the page.

We often do this sort of connecting when we read a story containing a reference to something from another time or another part of the world. We connect what we know with what we are reading. When we read in Shakespeare's *Julius Caesar*, for instance, that Caesar "...doth bestride the narrow world/Like a Colossus," we may remember or look up the reference to Colossus and then make a connection between the size of that ancient statue and the importance being attributed to Caesar.

In all these cases, we are making a connection across a gap between the work we are reading and something we know about its author, the time it was written, or the references it makes to other works.

There is another kind of gap we often cross as we read. D. H. Lawrence begins his story "The Rocking-Horse Winner" as follows:

> There was a woman who was beautiful, who started with all the advantages, yet she had no luck. She married for love, and the love turned to dust. She had bonny children, yet she felt they had been thrust upon her, and she could not love them. They looked at her coldly, as if they were finding fault with her. And hurriedly she felt she must cover up some fault in herself. Yet what it was that she must cover up she never knew.

Many people who read this may say to themselves, "Hmm. This sounds familiar." What they may be sensing as they read is that Lawrence has opened his story very much like a fairy tale. That may lead the reader to wonder what to make of this similarity. Is there a gap here to be bridged?

As a result of our prior reading, we have a sense of different types, or genres, of stories. Writers have also read a lot, and they often have the blueprint of a genre in their minds as they write. What they write, the particular poem, story, or play, may be seen in terms of the blueprint or a blend of blueprints.

Defining Critical Reading

What then is critical reading? In its most basic form it is looking at the marks on the page and making links across the various gaps that are there. It can also involve making links between what we read and what is off the page—things we know about life, the world of the author, the world described in the work, and other works we have read. The number of kinds of links that can be made may well be in the billions, so don't worry if you haven't made too many the first time you read something. You can always go back and try again.

Talking or writing about those links in a coherent and reasonable way is what is known as *criticism*. It involves presenting a clear statement of the connections you have made and the understandings you have reached at a particular time. Different kinds of links are seen as different kinds of criticism, and in this book, as in many literature classes, you will be invited to try different ones.

Critical Reading and the Literature Class

The literature class is the place where you most often are asked to give evidence of your critical reading. A number of people have shown that, as a course subject, literature can be divided into three interrelated aspects: *knowledge, practice,* and *habits.*

Knowledge includes understanding the basic elements of various selections you read, such as the characters, plots, and settings. It also includes understanding references to myths and folk tales and the like and having a knowledge of the world surrounding the pieces—who wrote them, when those writers lived, what the world was like then.

Practice is putting into effect—or showing what you can do with—what you know. It may be divided into (1) reading, watching, and listening with understanding and (2) speaking and writing about individual texts or about literature in general.

Speaking and writing form the key to the literature curriculum in many ways. Like any school subject, literature involves public acts in which you must be articulate about procedures and strategies as well as about any conclusions you have drawn. You are not just reading in a closet but bringing an impression of what you've read out into the open. More is expected than in your private reading: essays evaluating a text are not required after reading a library book, for example.

The particular kinds of speaking and writing about literature taught in literature classes constitute what is called *literary criticism.* Though we've seen that any coherent interpretation of a work can be labeled criticism, there are a number of specific kinds of literary criticism practiced and taught around the world. Often these are referred to as *schools of criticism.* No one of them is the right or only way of being a critic. We briefly summarize a few of the more popular ones here:

- *Cultural criticism* looks at the way the work and the author represent groups of people or cultures and their values, particularly what the work says about such cultural issues as the oppression of others, cultural conflict, or cultural customs.

- *Deconstruction* focuses on the language used in the work. It looks for gaps or contradictions, what is omitted as well as what is talked about. It assumes that the meaning of a work shifts in relation to the particular time or particular place in which it happens to be situated.

- *Feminist criticism* looks at the work from the perspective of the feminine consciousness and focuses on the issues of gender that are depicted or implied.

- *Formal criticism* looks at the way the work is put together, how the language is used to create a pleasing work of art. Formalist critics are not concerned with the background or context of a work; they look only at what is on the page.

- *Historical criticism* looks at the work from a historical perspective and to see how it is representative of the time in which it was written.

- *Reader-response criticism* looks at the work from the perspective of how the reader reacts to it. It deals with what the reader does or might do in getting meaning from the text.

- *Psychological criticism* explores the psychology of the author, the characters in a selection, or the response of the audience. It may use one of a variety of psychological approaches such as Freudian, Jungian, or Adlerian.

- *Structural criticism* looks at the work as an organization of parts and also in the context of a broader concept such as its genre or the set of themes and myths that the work deals with. It views the individual work both as a whole made up of parts and as a part of a larger whole called literature.

All of these types of criticism—and more—are valid ways of looking at a text. You may be asked to practice one or more types in your class or over your life as a student.

Habits, as applied to learning, refers broadly to the set of attitudes, stances, and beliefs that you develop through instruction, whether formal or informal. As a literature student, you become a creature of habit, with a set of ways of reading and then talking and writing about your reading. You may have developed the habit of skimming a book and then going back into it. You may have learned that it works better to let others talk first before you give your opinion or that it is better to jot down notes before you write an evaluative piece. You may have developed the habit of looking for a character in a novel who you think is speaking for the author or of judging what you read by whether it deals with important issues, takes a position you approve of, or simply uses language in an exciting way.

Studying literature—being a critical reader and writer, being a consumer of literature or a producer of it—involves many habits. Some of these you work to develop; others you may develop unconsciously. As you will see throughout this book, we happen to think that it is important for you to consider what your habits are and see whether they are productive or not.

FOR YOUR PORTFOLIO NOTEBOOK

Twenty-Seven Ways of Looking At What You Are Looking At

Here is a short poem to read. Try to keep mental notes of the thoughts you have as you read it. Jot down your thoughts in your "Portfolio Notebook."

Nothing Gold Can Stay
Nature's first green is gold,
Her hardest hue to hold.
Her early leaf's a flower;
But only so an hour.
5   Then leaf subsides to leaf.
So Eden sank to grief,
So dawn goes down to day.
Nothing gold can stay.
                    —Robert Frost

Now, a quiz. How many of the following did you think about as you read the poem? Make a note of each one that occurred to you:

- the age, gender, race, or political agenda of the author
- other works by the same author
- the author's purpose for writing it
- when the poem was written (1923), and what was happening then

- the present date: what is happening now
- the meanings of individual words such as *hue* and *subsides*
- nature as a personification (Mother Nature)
- your prior knowledge of things that are green, things that are gold, things that won't stay
- typical associations in myth and literature and culture for the colors green and gold
- the reference to the Garden of Eden
- the idea of the Fall from Innocence
- alliterations such as "**h**er **h**ardest **h**ue to **h**old"
- the rhyme, rhythm, and meter of the poem
- the most important word or words in the poem
- cause and effect: what causes things to sink to grief
- the structure of the poem
- associations for words like *sank, down, subsides*
- the contradiction of "Nature's first green is gold"
- whether it is a good poem
- what an earlier draft of the poem might have looked like
- what a story about this idea might look like
- pictures in your head, what you visualized as you read
- how you would read this aloud
- whether you agree or disagree with the ideas in the poem
- whether you are rereading as you go through the poem
- to what degree you understand the poem, the questions you have
- how you would explain this poem to someone else

The above activity demonstrates some of the things to consider and ways to think about a work of literature. It wasn't really a quiz, because there is no one way or set of ways that is right or better than others. One of our goals with this book is to get you think about the ways you think about what you read.

PULLING THINGS TOGETHER

If a portfolio is a showcase of your best work and a literature portfolio is a demonstration of the knowledge, practice, and habits you have developed as a literature student, what exactly can you do to create a strong, effective portfolio? This is a question we will be dealing with throughout this book, but as you may have guessed, there are no hard and fast answers. What you might do, though, is begin to set some preliminary goals for yourself—establish some ideas of where you want or need to go with your reading.

A Checklist of General Goals

In Chapter 2, you will go through a rather formal process of establishing reading goals in connection with your portfolio. Here we will ask you to begin thinking in that direction by considering some of the general literature goals most instructors are working toward. For each goal in the chart on page 29, there are five possible levels of accomplishment, from basic to rather sophisticated. When you go through the chart, you should decide at about what level you rank in the accomplishments column. That way you can get an early idea of how far you still need—or want—to progress.

Materials for Your Portfolio

The way that you will demonstrate, to yourself and others, that you are making progress as a literature learner is through the materials you put into your portfolio. Since literature as a course subject deals with what you know, what you can do, and what habits you have developed, it makes sense that your literature portfolio should reflect these three facets of your life and work as a student. You will need to develop materials—artifacts—that demonstrate the *knowledge* about literature you have gained; the *skills* that you have mastered in reading literary works and in talking, writing, or otherwise expressing yourself about them; and the *habits* of reading and using literature that you have developed.

These materials are the stuff of your portfolio. Into it may go a great number of individual items. Here are some of the things that might count as evidence:

Knowledge
- Catalogs of books read with some way of establishing that you did read them

CHART 1-1 General Literature Goals

Goals	✔ Levels of Accomplishment
Seek various forms of knowledge	Of personal experience Of genres Of terminology Of background and culture Theoretical
Select appropriate literary material	Written rather than oral Dealing with varied subjects Complex Mature Classic
Show understanding of literary texts	Clear but literal Elaborated and detailed Presenting a consistent viewpoint Acknowledging alternatives Generalizing to abstract understandings
Reflect on literary texts from personal and critical perspectives	Relating literary texts to personal experiences Seeing personal implications in the theme of a selection Recognizing difference between personal implications and broader themes Discussing critical issues arising from the text and the reading Placing the text in the broader context of literature and culture
Select from varied types of literary text	Personal favorites and course requirements Literary and other kinds of texts Varied genres Works read intensively and works read to broaden acquaintance Works from own and other cultures
Participate in a community of readers	Sharing responses Accepting responses of others Modifying responses in the light of those of others Summarizing responses of a group Taking group responses and reformulating them
Share in public values concerning the role of literature and the arts in society	Distinguishing between personal and public criteria for judging texts Recognizing levels/types of taste Recognizing cultural contributions Recognizing issues concerning arts policy Supporting literature and the arts in active ways

- Reading notes on books read
- Summaries of histories of literature and biographies of authors
- Results of tests on literary terms
- Papers on history or illustrating critical positions

Practice
- Papers criticizing or analyzing single works
- Papers comparing works
- Papers on humanities topics
- Audiotapes of oral interpretations
- Videotapes of play performances
- Book-jacket designs
- Illustrations or photographs of scenes from novels
- Discussion tapes
- Research papers
- Tapes of musical settings

Habits
- Logs of activity related to literature
- Logs analyzing and critiquing your methods of reading
- Book reviews you have written
- Summer reading lists
- Papers or tests demonstrating the sort of critical writing you do on short notice
- Ticket stubs or programs from films, theatrical performances, or concerts you have attended

Here is a specific example. You read a novel that has been assigned in class, William Golding's *Lord of the Flies*. You assemble in your portfolio the following artifacts, some required by your instructor, some representing your own ideas and goals:

- a reading response journal
- the sketches for a jacket cover and the final design for the cover illustrating the historical time at which Golding wrote the novel

- a taped discussion with another student of the role of symbols in the novel

- a composition discussing the relationship between *Lord of the Flies* and other shipwreck literature

- a list of other works you're planning to read in which children are left in control of a situation

Does this list sound like the sort of material you would assemble? Maybe, maybe not. Your literature portfolio is limited only by your imagination, your past activities, and your ability to establish why the item belongs in the portfolio and what it says about you.

Assembling material is only a part of what you will have to do in creating the literature portfolio. You are going to have to show people who will look at or judge your portfolio why each piece belongs there and what it says about you as a student of literature. What does each piece tell your audience about your knowledge of literature, your practices as a reader and critic of literature, and your habits of reading and viewing literature? If a piece cannot be justified, you may not want to include it. A great term paper in political science may say something about your writing and your skills in a social science, but it may not shed any light on your strength as a student of literature. Great as it may be, don't use it.

The way of showing why something you have selected belongs in the portfolio is through an introduction to your portfolio, a letter of justification and explanation, an autobiographical statement, a table of contents, and/or an annotation. We will go into greater detail about the arrangement and annotation of your final portfolio in Chapter 8, but you should plan at the outset of the course why you think you might include something you have done and tentatively where it fits into your portfolio.

BUILDING YOUR PORTFOLIO

Now that you know something about what a literature portfolio is and how it might look, you are ready to begin on your own portfolio. You know that you will have a working portfolio to begin with, a temporary storage place for your materials. As you start shaping it, you might follow a few simple steps in getting started. A portfolio is as much a journey as a destination, as much a reflection as a journey.

Usually in this section of a chapter we will give you some specific methods or techniques to try. Here we will simply ask you to rough out a very general plan of attack by writing answers to the following questions in your "Portfolio Notebook."

1. Take stock of yourself:
   - What sort of a reader of literature are you?
   - What sort of a writer and talker about literature are you?
   - What do you know about literature or about the material in this course?
   - What do you think you can do with the particular texts or the particular kinds of ideas that the course is about?
   - What habits of reading, discussion, or writing have you developed? For instance, do you keep a reading log? Do you take notes? Do you underline or write in the margins?

2. Set some goals. Refer to the chart on page 29 or to your own notes:
   - What sort of reader do you want to become?
   - What do you want to get out of the course?
   - What sort of writer do you want to become?
   - Do you want to work with others or develop your independence?
   - What sorts of habits do you want to develop?

3. Mark out a path to get from here to there:
   - How can you best achieve your goals as a reader?
   - What steps should you take in voluntary reading?
   - What kinds of notes or log should you keep?
   - Who should you work with? On what?
   - What sorts of projects should you try?
   - What outside activities might help you?

Keep your answers to these questions in your working portfolio. Review them periodically to see if you want to change your ideas or approach.

READER'S FORUM

Although we might think of reading as a solitary activity, there's a sense in which no one reads alone. First, there's the writer, always present, even if not physically. Then there are all the other readers, past and present, of the same text. Go to a large library and look for materials that have been written about any famous work. The list may be longer than the work itself. There is always a community of readers, even if we're not aware of its membership.

Like dancing, singing, running, and other human activities, reading can be done without other people physically present. But aren't those activities sometimes more interesting when they are shared with others? That opportunity to share is what the various activities in "Reader's Forum" will offer you. When you discuss your reading with others, you are sure to notice

- differences in meanings: a work has as many meanings as it has readers;
- the meaning of differences: the importance of there being differences in the first place.

For your first "Reader's Forum" activity, get ready to present a "Great Moment in Literature." Sports shows on television have long featured "Great Moments in (*fill in the name of the sport*)." You see a film clip of an athlete performing an outstanding feat, and you hear the commentator tell you what it all means. "Great Moments in Literature" is a similar feature, except that it is live rather than televised and about a text instead of a sport.

Choose one piece of text that hit you between the eyes, made you go "Hmmm," knocked you out, grabbed you by the throat, or otherwise engaged you in speculative thought about issues of consequence. The text can come from any literary work, a song, a speech, a poem a friend wrote, a letter you found in your textbook, or just about anything else that has words.

You're not necessarily saying the work is good or that you like it. You might hate it, in fact. You're saying that this particular text—perhaps only a small part of a work—had a powerful impact on you.

For your audience, read this striking text. You might also want to display it. Tell listeners what was so significant about the text—how and why did it grab you? Try to explain what features of the text and of you as a reader made this powerful connection.

Three to four minutes should be enough for you to make your point. A minute or two of text and a minute or two of explanation should do it. Be sure to write out your explanation so that you don't lose track of what you wanted to say. Decide whether you should use your comments before or after the text. Rehearse your "Great Moment" aloud before you try to present it.

When you are listening to others make their presentations, don't just wait for your turn. Try keeping notes of which features of the texts and which characteristics of your classmates produced these powerful connections.

PORTFOLIO PROGRESS REPORT

The "Portfolio Progress Reports" at the end of each chapter will help you to keep track of what you have accomplished as you work toward your goals as a reader. These records form an important part of your working portfolio, which continues through the entire course. When it comes time to prepare your presentation portfolio, you will have more to draw from than just a list of works read and techniques tried. You will have a series of reflections about your work, about your knowledge, practice, and habits as a reader. You will also have a draft of your presentation portfolio.

Although the questions will be applied to different activities, the same three questions will be the basis for these "Portfolio Progress Reports":

1. **Knowledge:** What *do you know* that you didn't know before?
2. **Practice:** What *can you do* that you couldn't do (or do as well) before?
3. **Habits:** What *do you do* that you didn't do (or do as much) before?

For this first "Portfolio Progress Report," review your work with the activities below. Then write at least a few paragraphs in your "Portfolio Notebook" to answer each of the three questions above:

- your writing about "What Is Literature?"

- your responses to "Twenty-Seven Ways of Looking at What You're Looking At"

- your first thoughts about yourself, your goals, and some possible activities

- your "Great Moment in Literature"

- your experiences as a speaker and listener in "Reader's Forum"

MOVING ON

In the next chapter, you will be moving on—from general comments about portfolios and literature and reading to ways of giving specific shape to your goals as a reader. You will see where you've been as a reader and where you're going.

2 Keeping Tabs on Your Reading

▶▶▶LOOKING AHEAD

This chapter will take you from general reading practices to setting specific goals for yourself as a reader. These goals will be the blueprint not only for your portfolio, but also for the reader you want to become. Along the way, you will complete a reading autobiography that shows where you have been as a reader as well as a number of activities that will show you how you read—what you tend to look for, what you tend to see, what you tend to think about it.

You will see a number of ways literature collections and reading lists and portfolios can be organized, and you will complete a preliminary self-assessment to serve as a benchmark for later assessments of your growth as a reader. Completing another "Portfolio Progress Report" will provide documentation for the development of your knowledge, practice, and habits.

GETTING A SENSE OF WHO AND WHAT YOU ARE AS A READER

How do you know how you read? *Do* you know how you read? How many kinds of readers are there, anyway?

The Basics of Written Text

As readers, most of us who read English have certain expectations and practices in common. We expect to read from top to bottom, from left to right. We expect end punctuation for each sentence, capital letters at sentence beginnings, spaces between words, indentation for paragraphs, and so on. Yet all of these are conventions—agreements that are as arbitrary as speed limits and local ordinances about dog collars and bagging trash for collection.

thisparagraphwillnotobservesomeoftheseconventionsoragreementsanditwillbeharderforyoutoreadimaginereadinganentirebookthisway

Perhaps samples like this explain the agreements. Conventions make reading more predictable and, therefore, easier to do. Some writers, though, especially modern writers, have played on our expectations for conventions and deliberately moved away from the conventional. The French writer and literary critic Roland Barthes, for example, liked to ignore the one-idea-per-paragraph convention. In some works, every paragraph he wrote was one sentence long. In other works, he went to the opposite extreme and eliminated most of the breaks between sentences and paragraphs. The result is writing composed of huge run-on sentences. So things may not always be as predictable as we would like.

The term *print media* used to refer to books, magazines, newspapers, and other things to read. Print media had some predictable characteristics:

Linearity	Print in English is meant to be read from left to right, from top to bottom, from beginning to end.
Repeatability	Print is easy to reproduce in quantities through printing presses and photocopiers. Every copy of a book or newspaper should be the same.
Uniformity	Conventions such as spelling and paragraphing are fairly standard for a given language or culture.

Fragmentation   Because of the wide variety of materials available, a single community can have information about hundreds of different viewpoints on a topic.

Nowadays, computers and other electronic media are allowing new forms of text that are not linear, either in form or in process, and these forms are having an effect on the writing and reading processes. Not only can different people form communities of sorts through computer networks, but works can be composed by a number of authors at the same time.

Reading Practices

Just as varied as the ways text is presented are the practices of individuals as they read. Let's consider five students who are all assigned to read and respond to questions about the same literature selection but approach the assignment with different practices. Which of them, if any, sounds like you?

Brenda reads the short story on the bus on the way home from school. She reads it once just to see what happens. She reads it again to get a clearer picture of the parts she didn't notice or understand the first time through. Later that night, she reads the questions she was supposed to answer about the story: "What was the main conflict in the story? How did the main character resolve this conflict?" Without looking back at the story, she writes a few paragraphs to answer the questions.

Paulo starts reading after dinner. He reads the story once, reads the questions, and goes back to mark two places in the story to use as quotes or examples: one for the conflict and another for the resolution. He copies these passages and numbers them as his responses to the questions.

Fifteen minutes before the assignment is due, *Ron* reads the questions to see what he has to write about, skims rapidly through the story until he finds what he needs, and writes his answers. Although he ignores the rest of the story, he uses quotes about the conflict and resolution to support his answers to the questions.

Risa glances at the questions and then reads the story. Dissatisfied with the assignment, she answers the questions by saying that they're not very good ones. Her answers, which run several pages, suggest that there are at least three important conflicts in the story and that characters use various means to try to resolve them. One of them, she says, is resolved by forces beyond the characters' control.

Tara reads most of the story, falls asleep near the end, and forgets to finish the story and do the writing assignment.

These five people read the same story—or do they? Their practices differ with respect to timing, order of operations, character and quality of responses, and so on. This is a situation we might call "academic" or "school-oriented" reading, but individual practices and habits vary just as widely with any other kind of reading. Do all people read an instruction manual the same way? Or a map? A memo? A greeting card verse, a contract, a best-selling novel, *Macbeth*, the libretto of an opera, or anything else?

One question you will need to deal with in creating your literature portfolio is, "How should I read?" Clearly, there are no right or wrong ways, only ways that work for you.

A Reading Autobiography

The question "What should I read?" becomes equally important when thinking about a portfolio. You have been reading things, some assigned, some by your own choice, some by accident, for years. Later in this chapter we will look at possible organizational patterns for your reading choices. But for now, concentrate on beginning to understand those choices, as well as your reading practices and habits, by looking back at your early reading experiences. A reading autobiography detailing your history and development as a reader can be the first step in creating your literature portfolio. Here are some excerpts taken from one student's reading autobiography:

> A very special and important part of my childhood was reading and listening to the magic of books.
>
> I had many books that I begged my mother to read over and over again. Bedtime favorites or selections for a public library sharing often included Dr. Seuss or Richard Scarry books. I was so mesmerized by the words and the illustrations. I also remember how the warm, soothing voice of my mother made these books that much more fantastic. Before bed was the ideal time for me to listen to a story. I could go to bed with all the magical characters and dream of the adventures they would take.

Reading as a child was extremely vital to me. It helped develop my likes, dislikes, and feelings. My favorite books included Dr. Seuss's *The Lorax* and Washington Irving's *The Legend of Sleepy Hollow*. To me, *The Lorax* is a book not only for youngsters but for all humankind. It teaches a very strong and important lesson, that nature has to come first . . . once it has been destroyed, it can't be replaced. This belief has been carried with me as I've grown, partly as a result of the book.

Irving's classic has also affected my literary likes and dislikes. His *Sleepy Hollow* story was probably my all-time childhood favorite. It had such variables as mystery and darkness that I found it frightening and captivating. When I have a chance to choose the books I want to read for leisure or pleasure, I usually select a mystery or drama, one that gives me that same feeling I experienced as a child.

. . . I still look for books to entertain and inspire me. I was inspired by Dr. Seuss and I continue to be amazed by writers. Whenever I heard a story as a child, I wanted to be a writer so I could give that same feeling to someone else. Those feelings haven't changed. Even though I want to be a teacher, the dream of writing a book remains.

—Philip Horender

FOR YOUR PORTFOLIO NOTEBOOK
Your Reading Autobiography

Begin your own reading autobiography by answering the questions that follow. Consider these responses to be your working draft. Then, organize and present your answers in a few pages of unified writing—your personal "story" of your own reading. Your instructor might ask you to read these aloud or to share them with portfolio group members or the rest of the class.

1. What were your earliest experiences with stories? Who read to you (or told you stories)? When and where? What stories or books do you remember as being first?

2. What stories or books made a strong impression on you? If you selected three favorite books or stories from your younger days, what would they be?

3. What do you choose to read now? How do you choose works or genres or authors or topics? What are the last three books you read? Why did you read each one? What are you reading right now? What are you looking forward to reading—specific works or types of works?

4. Besides books, what else do you read? What poems, essays, articles, scenes from dramas, or other forms do you choose to read? How do you choose which ones to read? Whose recommendations do you follow?

5. When and where do you read the works you are reading by choice? What surroundings do you prefer for reading?

6. What features of the things you read do you find most interesting? What features are you most likely to notice?

7. What kinds of things do you like to write or discuss about what you read? To whom do you usually talk or write about books and other works you read?

8. How would you describe yourself as a reader (don't say *bookworm*, please)? What does reading do for you—or to you?

Projections and Interpretations

Different methods of reading, different reading choices. Here's one more difference to ponder: What makes your interaction with what you read unique from anyone else's?

To answer this question, it helps to see reading as an event. Until a reader interacts with a written text, there is no reading. We sometimes think of reading and listening as receiving activities and of writing and speaking as sending activities, but this is oversimplifying. A communication act is not as simple as tossing a ball from one person to another. All four of the language processes require that meaning be constructed and interpreted. So someone must do the interpreting. And, of course, our interpretations are not always "right."

Let's say you are driving down the street. You see a woman on the sidewalk. You can't quite identify her, but she is smiling and waving. As you start to wave back and return the smile, searching your memory and straining your eyes to try to recognize the woman, you realize she's waving to someone else. You don't know her at all, and you wonder what she thinks you were doing, waving and smiling at her.

We're not always right, but we're always interpreting—trying to make sense of events and experiences. One way we try to do this is by "seeing" (or imposing) patterns. We stare at clouds and decide that one looks like a duck and another like a whale. Those who spend time alone in the woods or at sea sometimes report suddenly seeing a pattern in the waves or in the leaves of trees.

With a reading event, both your stance and your stand as a reader help to determine what you are going to "see" in a given work. To understand what this means, let's start with some general tendencies of human thinking. The three principles that follow, derived from Robert Potter's book *Making Sense,* are principles of *projection.* Here projection means attributing one's own ideas or feelings to another person or group.

- *You are likely to see what you expect to see.* If you have heard
  that your new instructor is brilliant but a little absent-minded, you will probably "notice" one or both tendencies in the
  instructor's behavior. You will be interpreting in accordance
  with your expectations. We tend to project interpretations
  on the world around us, including objects, people, places,
  and, of course, books and other artistic creations. Some
  artistic creations have made fun of this tendency to find
  what we expect to find in others. In a movie called *Being
  There,* the main character is a simple person who has spent
  most of his life watching television. Suddenly thrust out
  into a world that baffles him, he wanders through the film
  like a lost child, understanding little that happens to him.
  Other people understand him even less. Because he is quiet,
  they think he is thoughtful, even secretive, maybe brilliant.
  His most popular comment is, "I like to watch." Although
  he's talking about liking to watch television, listeners find
  all kinds of meaning in this comment, including predictions
  about the stock market.

- *You are likely to see what suits your purpose at the time.* When you are hungry, especially if you are dieting, every advertisement on television seems to be one for food. You pick up a magazine, and food ads stand out. Books on living within a budget advise people to avoid shopping when they are hungry. Everything in the store looks better, so people spend more when they are craving food. Similarly, the main thing that interests you when you are rushing through the final chapters of a compelling mystery story is to find out "whodunit." You probably aren't paying much attention to the writer's evocative descriptions of the locale. Good as they may be, they don't fit your purpose at that moment.

- *You are likely to see what your background has prepared you to see.* Every reader comes from somewhere. Your particular background and experiences, unique among the five billion or so people on the planet, predispose you in a number of powerful ways. We all bring different maps to any one book.

Our expectations and the way we relate to a written text are important because reading is a transaction, and the reader is an active player in the game. It may be more obvious that no two writers are identical, but it is just as true that no two readers are alike. One of the purposes of this book is to help you to see what kind of reader you are, where you are coming from. Then you can decide how to develop yourself further to become the reader you want to be and then how to present that reader in your literature portfolio.

FOR YOUR PORTFOLIO NOTEBOOK

Making Music

Try an experiment. Ask twenty friends and relatives of different ages to answer the following two questions. Write the answers in your "Portfolio Notebook":

1. What is music?

2. What are the three best and worst music groups (or individuals)?

Now make up a chart to help you evaluate the answers. How many of the "best" from one list are on the "worst" of another list? What other contradictions can you see? What other patterns can you find? If all twenty of these people were to go to performance of any one group, how many different sets of expectations and predispositions would you expect to find?

WAYS OF LOOKING AT LITERATURE

What is your "map" for literature? How will you choose to see the territory of literature?

The Triangle Approach

One traditional view (or map) of literature is based on a triangle. At its points are the three basic aspects of literature:

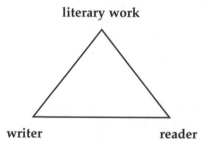

The history of literary criticism (or interpretation) and much of the ongoing argument about the nature and purpose of literature might be seen as disagreements over which of these elements is most important. Some critics have favored the writer, noting that the writer's intent is what matters most. Humpty Dumpty would agree with such critics. In *Through the Looking Glass*, he said, "When *I* use a word, it means just what I choose it to mean—neither more nor less."

Others, such as reader-response critics, have elevated the reader to the position of judge: The reader decides what a work means. What the writer intended is less important than what the reader inferred or concluded about the meaning of the work. If you read a letter—one that was intended to compliment you—as an insult, then the letter "means" an insult.

Still others, formalist critics, have said the work itself is the key. Meaning is in the work, and we do not need to pay much attention to writers and readers. We would better spend our time on a close reading of the work, to see what meaning it contains.

So, writer, work, and reader (or audience) are the "big three." If you think of the many essays and other interpretive pieces you have been asked to write about literature, most of them have probably asked you to do one or more of the following:

- Show how the *writer* accomplishes his or her purpose by using A, B, and C.
- Show how A, B, and C develop the *meanings or themes of the work.*
- Show how a *reader* would respond to A, B, and C.

If you have taken almost any formal examination in literature, you might recognize the wordings, since they appear in so many essay questions. All roads lead to meaning, of course. And which road(s) you take will determine what meanings you arrive at.

Our purpose is not to settle the argument of which element is most important. (Indeed, we doubt it will ever be settled, or even should be). We have come to believe that the purpose of creating a literary portfolio—or of reading in general—is not so much to finish a conversation as to be involved in one, less to answer someone else's questions than to ask your own and use methods of inquiry to develop answers to them.

We should tell you now that we think "more is better." More ways to read, more perspectives to use, more ways to think about a work are better. You will mark yourself as a reader not only by the materials you choose to read, but also by how you choose to read them. As you create your portfolio, you will be adding to your list of works read. You will also be adding to your repertoire of ways to read and interpret. Eventually, you will draw from your working portfolio your presentation portfolio, and this public portfolio will be more than a list of works read, although that will be part of it. Your presentation portfolio will present *what you can do as a reader.*

Beyond the Triangle

Although the triangle shows some necessary ingredients of critical reading, we would like to offer another, more articulated map of literature and reading experiences, as in the diagram that follows. The intersecting circles show different kinds of features that may be involved in the reading of a work of literature:

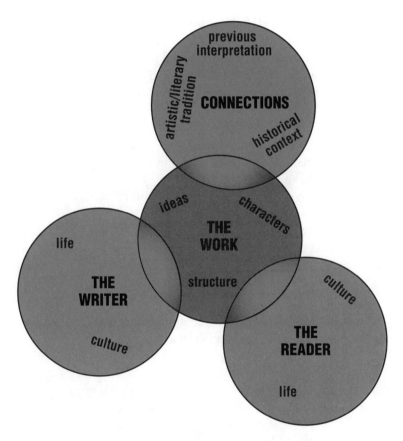

Critical Perspectives on Literature

Try to imagine this picture in three dimensions, each circle representing a sphere that intersects with other spheres—something like a molecular model you might have used in chemistry class.

Each sphere is the site of particular questions or issues related to the work being read. If we look at a single short poem from each perspective, we will find that different issues are put into the foreground or background because of the perspective chosen.

Mirror

I am silver and exact. I have no preconceptions.
Whatever I see I swallow immediately
Just as it is, unmisted by love or dislike.
I am not cruel, only truthful—
5 The eye of a little god, four-cornered.
Most of the time I meditate on the opposite wall.
It is pink, with speckles. I have looked at it so long
I think it is a part of my heart. But it flickers.
Faces and darkness separate us over and over.

10 Now I am a lake. A woman bends over me,
Searching my reaches for what she really is.
Then she turns to those liars, the candles or the moon.
I see her back, and reflect it faithfully.
She rewards me with tears and an agitation of hands.
15 I am important to her. She comes and goes.
Each morning it is her face that replaces the darkness.
In me she has drowned a young girl, and in me an old woman
Rises toward her day after day, like a terrible fish.

—Sylvia Plath

Now here are some of the different questions that might be asked
about the poem from the various perspectives:

The Writer	
The Writer's Life	What was Sylvia Plath like? Was she a happy person? How did she feel about growing older?
The Writer's Culture	What were dominant cultural views about women and aging at the time this was written?

The Work	
Structure, Techniques	Why is the poem divided into two sections? What is the effect of words such as *liars* and *swallow?*

Characters or Speakers	Who is talking here? Is *I* the same speaker everywhere in the poem? Who is *she?*
Ideas, Lessons, Philosophy	Why are candles and the moon *liars*? What do they lie about? Is it *not cruel, only truthful* to be *unmisted by love or dislike?*

The Reader

The Reader's Life	How does the poem make you feel? Does anything here remind you of a similar experience?
The Reader's Culture	How does your society view women and aging? How do women view themselves?

Connections

Historical Perspectives	What happens to aging women? How have they been treated because of their age? How have they viewed themselves?
Artistic/Literary Tradition	What other works use mirrors as key features of the text? What *terrible fish* in art or mythology or literature can be connected to this work? What other works are similar in form?
Previous Interpretations	How has this work been received? What is the "usual" interpretation of this piece?

It's not so much that the answers will be different; it's more that the *questions* will be different. We asked a group of readers to look at "Mirror" and record some observations under the following headings:

What you are looking at (words, lines, features)	What you're thinking about it (issues/ questions)	What you would call that thinking (labels)

Here are some responses from different readers:

"Searching my reaches for what she really is"	I don't understand— looking at one's reflection in a lake would show only the outside. Reflections don't show what's inside.	speculating about this contradiction

* * * * *

The title	Is the author looking in a mirror or remembering a certain experience?	looking at the author's past

* * * * *

"flickers" is striking	The word draws me— spurts of emotion.	acknowledging words, attention-getters

* * * * *

"I am not cruel, only truthful"	I like this line—good line.	judging the poem

* * * * *

"I am not cruel, only truthful"	Life seems cruel sometimes, the truth can be cruel.	agreeing with the ideas

* * * * *

I am not cruel, only truthful—/The eye of a little god, four-cornered."	Personification made me forget what I was dealing with— a mirror. Is this what God is supposed to be like?	Makes me wonder: does God look at us in the same unjudgmental way?

* * * * *

"The eye of a little god"	Who is this—the person looking or the mirror?	Wondering how to interpret

* * * * *

"Like a terrible fish"	Poem sounded gentle and pure until this ending makes it turn sour. Why end it like this?	Observing irony, surprising ending

* * * * *

"Like a terrible fish"	Moby-Dick? Jaws? The whale in Pinocchio? Jonah's whale?	Looking for the right kind of fish

* * * * *

"In me she has drowned a young girl"	She is obsessed, looking for something she can't find, that she is "drowning" her youth.	Drawing a conclusion about the speaker's mental state

* * * * *

The poem in general	Cool poem. It sent a message. I understand how the woman feels.	Sympathizing, judging

These are single observations from different readers. From these, you can see that each noticed and commented on different features of the work. Even when readers commented on the same line or lines, their comments were different. If we had space to print all the responses, you could see that no two "readings" were identical. In some cases, the "features" lists were totally different. One person found the title to be a significant feature and kept relating everything else to the title. Others didn't mention the title at all. The "terrible fish" was noted by about half of the readers, but only one reader took that line and went fishing for "terrible" associations.

FOR YOUR PORTFOLIO NOTEBOOK

Your Own Response

Part 1. This is the next step in analyzing and developing your personal reading method. For the poem that follows, complete a response sheet by making at least six or seven observations. Set up your paper in the three-column format used for "Mirror":

What you are looking at (words, lines, features)	What you're thinking about it (issues/ questions)	What you would call that thinking (labels)

Gretel in Darkness

This is the world we wanted.
All who would have seen us dead
are dead. I hear the witch's cry
break in the moonlight through a sheet
5   of sugar: God rewards.
Her tongue shrivels into gas. . . .

Now, far from women's arms
and memory of women, in our father's hut
we sleep, are never hungry.
10   Why do I not forget?
My father bars the door, bars harm
from this house, and it is years.

No one remembers. Even you, my brother,
summer afternoons you look at me as though
15   you meant to leave,
as though it never happened.
But I killed for you. I see armed firs,
the spires of that gleaming kiln—

Nights I turn to you to hold me
20   but you are not there.

Am I alone? Spies
hiss in the stillness, Hansel,
we are there still and it is real, real,
that black forest and the fire in earnest.
                                    —Louise Gluck

Part 2. Now you have a sample of your reading style—every bit as important as your writing style. Analyze your responses and try to discover what you do most often when you read. Which of these categories (one or two of them) best describe your main interests or observations?

Categories of Observations	Kinds of Questions and Comments
The Writer	
The Writer's Life	Who wrote this? What kind of person was he or she? How old was the writer when the poem was written? What happened before and after he or she wrote this?
The Writer's Culture	In what place and time was it written? What was going on at the time? What events and ideas were important? What was the world view?
The Work	
Structure, Techniques	How many parts are there to this work? How are they related? What key words, images, figures of speech (metaphors and so on) are important?
Characters or Speaker	Who is talking here? To whom? What is their relationship like? What motivates them? What conflict do they have?

Ideas, Lessons, Philosophy	What ideas or lessons are expressed or implied here? What values? What forces have determined these events? What are we supposed to learn?

The Reader

Yourself as a Reader	How does it make me feel? What features of the work stand out? What in *me* makes those features stand out? What happens to me when I read this?
Your Culture	What is the present world view in the place where I am situated? What events and ideas are important? How do we tend to view things?

Connections

Historical Perspectives	Does this refer to historical events? Is it about something or somebody in the past?
Artistic/Literary Tradition	What does this remind me of? How is it related to other works, story lines, characters, or myths?
Previous Interpretations	What have other readers and critics had to say about this poem? How is it usually read?

If you have identified one or two areas of interest or focus, you have a little idea of your reading perspective. In a later chapter, you can make some selections of techniques to add to your repertoire, and thus develop yourself into the reader you want to become.

POSSIBILITIES FOR PORTFOLIO ORGANIZATION

When you create a portfolio of literature, you are, in effect, designing your own collection of things to read and showing how you think about them—that is, you are organizing things according to your personal perspective. Just as there are many ways to organize a collection of literary selections, there are many ways to organize materials in a portfolio. Further, there is no one best organization. As you determine the purposes for your own portfolio, you can select or invent a system that works for you. Although you might not adopt any one system completely, you should know what some of the typical choices are.

Methods of Organization

Anthologies and other literature collections are organized in a variety of ways, including by genre, theme, style, author, literary period, and culture. Since your portfolio will deal with various responses to literature, you might consider using some of these organizational methods.

By Genre. In collections organized by genre, there are typically sections for poetry, nonfiction, fiction, and drama. In such a collection, "Mirror" and "Gretel in Darkness" would both be included in the poetry section or unit. When the essential means of classification used is the genre or form of the work, "What *is* it?" is the main question dealt with. Many collections, of course, are also divided into subgenres: detective novels are not the same as romance novels, although they are both fiction.

By Theme. Love, war, death, time, family, growth—these are typical themes around which a collection—or your reading purposes—can be organized. In such a system, the topics or themes of the works are the organizing principles. A play, poem, essay, and short story would be in the same section if each dealt with a similar theme. The question here is "What is it *about*?"

By Style. Collections organized by style would include categories based on stylistic aspects of works. Just as there are "easy listening" and "heavy metal" or "hard rock" or "alternative" categories for radio stations, there are categories for literature that depend primarily on style as the differentiator. Satirical works, regardless of genre, might be included in the same category. Works that feature metaphor or allegory could be grouped together. There might be other categories for formal and informal writing or writing of a personal nature. The question here might be "What is the intent?" or "Who is the audience?"

By Author.   This is one of the simplest systems. Every work by Poe included in the collection—poems, stories, and letters—would appear in the same section. In this system, "Who wrote it?" is the fundamental question.

By Chronology or Literary Period.   Some collections of American literature are organized chronologically, beginning with something like "The Colonial Era." English literature collections organized to present a survey through time tend to start with a category called "The Anglo-Saxons" or "The Precursors" and work their way up to "The Modern Age"—which probably won't include contemporary works. Stops along the way, depending on the collection, might include "The Medieval Period," "The Renaissance (or Elizabethan Age)," The Romantic Period," "The Victorian Period," and so on. You might even find a "Pre-Modern" period, populated by writers who didn't know they were premodern at the time. The key question here is "In what era or literary period was the work written?"

By Culture.   Collections organized by culture must consider both space (place) and time. If you want to emphasize distinctions between works from Africa, Asia, North America, South America, and Europe, you can group the works by these continents. If you want to include works written by different cultural groups in North America, you can organize your collection according to those cultural groups. The main question is "What culture produced this writer and this work?"

Organization within the Organization

Here is a small complication: After you organize by one of the systems we have just looked at, how do you arrange works within each area of classification? For example, in a collection organized by genre, how do you arrange the poetry? By themes? By style? In a portfolio built around cultures, will you present each culture chronologically? By some other method?

When you think about it, every literary, social, and political movement in the United States could design a collection of literary works to serve a specific agenda. Gender, color, religion, and a host of other issues could be the organizing principle. Toni Morrison and Maya

Angelou are both African American, both women, both twentieth-century writers. Although both write in varied forms or genres, Toni Morrison is probably best known for her fiction; Maya Angelou, for her poetry. Should they be included in the same category because of heritage or gender or time period, or should they be separated by genre? It depends on where the lines are drawn, and it matters who gets to draw them. We think you should be aware of the existence (and the potential existence) of many systems of classifications, but we also think that you and your instructor should negotiate, within the framework of your literature course, the system you will use to organize your goals for *what* to read and *how* to read.

Eclectic Reading

One final alternative is to make your reading approach *eclectic*—that is, drawn from a wide range of sources. Are you eclectic if you fire a shotgun in a bookstore and then read everything that has a hole in it? Well, no. There is a difference between eclecticism and aimlessness, and the difference is the sense of purpose you bring to the making of choices. An eclectic reader is not restricted by traditional or conventional categories but is guided by personal motives and perspectives. Perhaps a true eclectic is also willing to examine his or her own motives and perspectives now and then.

If you read only one kind of thing, there's a danger of becoming *inread*—a little like being inbred but with intellectual consequences. There's nothing wrong with specializing, but don't forget to work on range and flexibility too.

Your Approach

If you don't have a better method in mind, if your course requirements don't specify anything different, or if you don't want to be entirely eclectic, you might begin by working across the categories we have been discussing. You could start by selecting a certain number of works from each genre or literary period. You might then read works by a favorite author or go on to explore a theme or style or culture. Eventually you might find that one category or another will hold your interest, and you can pursue that direction wholeheartedly.

FOR YOUR PORTFOLIO NOTEBOOK

Design an Anthology

Find a literature textbook or anthology that is organized by one of the methods explained above. Then, using materials from the anthology's table of contents, design a different kind of collection, a smaller one based on a different method of organization. Use one of the methods we have discussed or your own method (be sure to explain what it is). For example, you might find a book organized by genre but decide to select from it twenty titles based on three themes.

Your collection should have twenty to twenty-five titles. Complete the activity by making a new "Table of Contents" page showing the titles you have selected arranged by the methods you have chosen.

DETERMINING YOUR GOALS AS A READER

How you might organize your portfolio reading is one thing to consider. The goals that you might pursue to become a mature, critical reader are another.

Four General Purposes for Reading

Although there are many ways to set goals for reading, the most useful and comprehensive model we have found is to set reading goals by language purposes or outcomes. The system will encourage you to work toward breadth and depth of reading, toward building your reading repertoire, and toward connecting your reading to writing, listening, and speaking, as well as to other areas of study and to your life experiences.

The model, derived from Roseanne DeFabio's detailed model in her book *Outcomes in Progress*, includes four purposes for reading:

- *Reading for information and understanding:* activities involve collecting data, facts, and ideas; discovering relationships, concepts, and generalizations; and using knowledge generated from oral, written, and electronically produced texts.
- *Reading for literary and aesthetic response:* activities involve reading literary texts, relating texts to your own life, and

developing an understanding of the many social, historical, and cultural dimensions the texts represent.

- *Reading for critical analysis and evaluation:* activities
  involve reading literary and other texts; analyzing experiences, ideas, information, and issues presented by others
  using a variety of established criteria; and forming opinions and judgments on experiences, ideas, information,
  and issues.

- *Reading for social interaction:* activities involve using language for effective social communication with a wide
  variety of people; using the social communications of
  others, such as letters and journals, to enrich your understanding of people and their views.

It may not seem as if all of these purposes are directly connected to literature, but consider what we might do with a work besides
read it from beginning to end. As an example, we will use *The
Crucible* by Arthur Miller. For information and understanding, we
might read about the Salem witch trials and the McCarthy era in
U.S. history to understand some of the background to the play. For
literary and aesthetic response, we might relate one of the issues of
the play—a decision of conscience, perhaps—to our own lives. For
critical analysis and evaluation, we might attend a production of the
play and write a review of the performance. For social interaction,
we might, after reading and enjoying the play, send a copy to a
friend with a letter that tells why he or she *must* read it.

Of course, these four categories overlap. To analyze a work
effectively, you must give some information. To use language for
social communication—say, in a group discussion—you will probably need to give your own personal views on a work. Each category
is really an area of focus rather than a separate and distinct language purpose. In an apology, the personal feeling may be more
important than the information you convey. In a sales call, persuad-
ing the listener to buy something is the focus of the conversation.

Later in this chapter, you will write personal goals for your
work with this book by defining one goal for each of these four categories. Your completed portfolio can include at least one project
from each category as evidence of your ability in reading and working with literature.

Criteria for Measuring Progress

In order to measure how well you accomplish the various reading goals, we now suggest some criteria for mapping and monitoring improvement in your reading practices. Reading is a kind of performing, and these are some characteristics of performance. Think of each characteristic as a scale or continuum along which you might progress—from less to more.

Range. This is the scope of your reading expertise, including depth and breadth. Exploring a broad range of materials is as important as depth in chosen areas.

Evidence of range: Various disciplines and subjects and topics within disciplines; various cultures, historical periods, and genres of literature; various modes and forms of writing.

Less	More
limited subjects, genres, periods cultures, writing forms	variety of complex, sophisticated subjects and genres; numerous writing forms

Flexibility. This is your ability to read and interpret in varied and changing conditions. Flexibility can only be developed or assessed when you have opportunities to use and analyze language in various contexts. A flexible reader can function as many kinds of "audience."

Evidence of flexibility: Awareness of demands of different audiences and purposes; ease of adaptation; consistency of quality of interpretation regardless of audience and purpose.

Less	More
limited variety of forms and purposes for reading and interpreting	many forms, purposes, and analyses from varying critical perspectives

Connections. Connections involve your ability to see commonalities in apparently unrelated experiences or contexts and to apply already learned concepts to a wide range of works.

Evidence of connections: Use of analogies—logical connections with similar or closely related concepts; use of metaphors—imaginative connections with dissimilar concepts; comparisons; concrete examples of abstract concepts.

Less	More
ability to apply new information to immediate context, but not from one context to another	ability to apply information and understandings to many contexts and to judge the usefulness of such applications

Conventions.   These are the forms that literature takes as well as the traditional practices, rules, and devices involved in those forms.

Evidence of conventions: Experience with specific forms (sonnet, scientific journal, and so on) and the typical structure, strategies, and intents of those forms; ability to recognize how forms accommodate demands of audience, purpose, and customary features of the work.

Less	More
limited strategies for dealing with forms	creative range of strategies for understanding and appreciating forms

Independence.   Your ability to select, plan, carry out, and monitor your own performance without reliance on the direction of others.

Evidence of independence: Control of purpose—decide what to do and how to do it; use of resources—find the help needed to accomplish the purpose; evidence of an individual perspective—personal view, language, and style.

Less	More
limited ability to discover relationships among sources or to make generalizations and conclusions	insight and originality in discovering and establishing relationships among sources, and in making generalizations and conclusions

The four reading goals and the five evaluation criteria will function as the measures of your own reading progress and portfolio work. We will use them to do the following:

- continue to develop a picture of where you are now—portrait of a reader
- help you set goals for the kind of reader you want to become

- keep track of your progress through "Building Your Portfolio" and "Portfolio Progress Reports"
- express your achievement of your goals through your portfolio presentation

Assessing Where You Are

Before you can set reasonable goals, you need to assess where you are in relation to your reading purposes. For the moment, let's distinguish between grades and growth, between evaluation and assessment. Grades or evaluations are generally measures of achievement. The main question is this: How well did you do in the course compared with other students? Assessment, as we use the word here, is less concerned with grades and more concerned with growth, which is a matter of change. For assessment, the main question is this: How much did you improve? A person who scores 100 percent on every test achieves 100 percent. A person who raises a bowling average from 145 to 175 shows growth or improvement. Which is more important?

There's no easy answer to this, but the best answer might be "both." Your grades will be the measure of your achievement on the course activities. Your instructor will have a system for evaluating your work to determine your course grade. Your portfolio, on the other hand, can be a measure of your growth as a reader and writer and speaker. Learning means change. If you want to be able to manage your own development as a communicator after the course is completed, you need to have the tools and experience with which to assess your growth.

One way to assess yourself is to think of one or more things you have done that would be examples of each of the four language purposes, then rate your accomplishment of the task against the various criteria. In the sample below, notice that a typical example is identified and that each rating is accompanied by an explanation. The rating scales themselves range from "least" to "most" competent.

Sample Self-Evaluation

Language Purpose: reading for information and understanding

Example: I was using the computer in the library to do research, and I was able to find several useful sources for my paper on genetic engineering.

Range

least————————————————XX————————————————most

1   2   3   4   5   6   7   8   9   10   11   12

(I don't have a wide range of topics or subjects I can read effectively.)

Flexibility

least————————————————————XX————————————most

1   2   3   4   5   6   7   8   9   10   11   12

(I can apply what I read in most contexts or situations.)

Connections

least————————————XX————————————————————most

1   2   3   4   5   6   7   8   9   10   11   12

(I usually just read, not looking for comparisons to other processes or situations.)

Conventions

least————————————XX————————————————————most

1   2   3   4   5   6   7   8   9   10   11   12

(I'm not that familiar with the features to expect from different types of works.)

Independence

least————————————————————————XX————————most

1   2   3   4   5   6   7   8   9   10   11   12

(I can work well on my own if it's something I'm familiar with or know how to do pretty well.)

To interpret this example, think of the whole procedure as a sort of game. If the various purposes define the game, the five criteria define levels of play. A change in the direction of "more" on any of these criteria means growth as a reader. Let's tie the numbers on the rating scale to some benchmarks for levels of play. On this scale, a rating of 6 is the level of the average high school graduate. A rating of 9 would be appropriate for the average college graduate. And a 12? This top rating would be appropriate for an outstanding professional. When you use these ratings, remember that they are not grades. A 6 is not 50 percent of a 12. There is no passing or failing. We are looking for meaningful assessments of your growth as a reader and language user.

FOR YOUR PORTFOLIO NOTEBOOK

Preliminary Self-Assessment

With the sample above as a guide, complete a preliminary self-assessment of yourself as a reader. Using the language purposes and assessment criteria (listed below for your convenience), give a typical example for each purpose; then rate your performance against each criterion and give an explanation of each rating in a sentence or two. The result will be a total of twenty ratings, five each for the four language purposes.

Purposes

- Reading for information and understanding
- Reading for literary and aesthetic response
- Reading for critical analysis and evaluation
- Reading for social interaction

Criteria

- Range
- Flexibility
- Connections
- Conventions
- Independence

Writing Goals

Now that you have completed the preliminary self-assessment, you are ready to set some goals. You will be writing a goals statement of between two hundred and five hundred words for each of the four reading purposes. The following suggestions may help you.

Questions to Consider. Start by writing rough responses to these questions:

- What are some strengths on which you can build?
- What are some weak areas in which you would like to improve?
- For each area you have identified, what specific growth or achievement do you seek? Think of materials, contexts, audiences, purposes, forms, and so on.
- What activities could help you? What materials, practice, and other resources would you need?
- How important is each area you have identified? What will change or growth in this area mean to you?
- How can you relate the area to your earlier experiences in reading, writing, speaking, and listening? The four reading purposes? Your future work?
- How will you determine progress toward or achievement of this goal? What measures will you use? What measures will others use?
- What do the various areas you're considering say about you?

Formulate Goal Statements.   Next, review your notes to see if any patterns begin to emerge. Determine the major things you want to accomplish as a reader—the specific abilities you want to develop and achievements you want to reach. Then begin to put together goal statements. Do the following for each goal:

1. State what you want to accomplish as specifically as you can. It may be helpful to use the language of the assessment criteria: "I want to increase my range. . . ."

2. Suggest some reading, writing, listening, and/or speaking activities that will help you to reach this goal. You might skim through this text for ideas and examples.

3. Tell how you will determine to what extent the goal is reached. Give some measures of accomplishment to show how you will know if you're making progress.

Here is an excerpt from one student's statement of her reading goals. It deals with reading for literary and aesthetic response:

In reading for aesthetic purposes, my goal is to increase my flexibility with respect to interpreting what I read.

To achieve my goal, I will read a wide variety of prose and poetry and I will keep a notebook which will include entries about each piece of work I read. Since I want to be a writer, the entries will focus on different techniques and styles that catch my eye as I read. Examples of these techniques might include the manner in which a story is composed (problem-solution) or the structure or tone of the work.

I will determine that this goal has been reached when I am able to use the techniques I will have acquired to write my own poem or short story that is unlike anything I've ever written before. I am looking for a change in the expression of my audience, a more enthusiastic response. Once I have written a piece, I will not only note the responses I receive but I will also ask for additional ideas for revisions.

—Jaime Sajeski

Organize Readings and Activities.   Finally, begin to select the actual works of literature you will read to achieve your goals. Even though your goals are set up according to reading purposes, you can organize your work within each category according to what you read. For example, depending on your specific goal and the requirements of your course, you might select and organize readings (and activities) within the category of "Reading for Information and Understanding" using any of these patterns:

By genre: add to your knowledge of forms of lyric poetry such as the villanelle and the ode

By theme: investigate how literature has treated the topic of passion in human relationships, or belief in a deity, or the possibility of heroism

By style: explore the forms of satire, from *Satyricon* to Swift to *Saturday Night Live*

By author: learn about Zora Neale Hurston or Chaucer or Lope de Vega

By time: trace the development of the sonnet or the song, through the centuries or through one decade.

| By place or culture: | conduct a broad survey of American Literature or a narrow one of contemporary Native American poets |

FOR YOUR PORTFOLIO NOTEBOOK
Write Goal Statements

In your "Portfolio Notebook," write at least one goal for each of the four reading purposes. Then conduct a "presearch" of your library and other resources to see what materials might be available to help you achieve those goals. Your instructor can suggest to you how many works, as well as how many activities, you should select for each goal.

Finding materials at this stage is much like completing a preliminary bibliography for a research project. You may change your plan later, but at least you will have an idea of the kinds of materials available.

By writing your personal goals for reading, you have also taken an important step toward building your portfolio: You have begun to define the repertoire of skills you want to develop. You will be returning to your goal statements each time you write a progress report.

BUILDING YOUR PORTFOLIO

Keeping useful records of your reading involves more than just listing the works you read as you proceed through the course. Think of each reading record as a tool for later use. The better you make the tool, the better it will work for you.

Perhaps we should note here what we *don't mean* by "reading record." We don't mean plot summary. Although you may have been required to do plot summaries, or just done them by accident, plot summaries are not particularly useful unless you're working toward becoming a plot expert, perhaps to help you in plotting your own writing.

And we don't mean prove that you read the work. Although you do need evidence in order to prepare your portfolio, you need evidence of what you did, how you did it, and what it means to you. Proving that you read from beginning to end is not enough, nor is it even the point.

We offer you here several types of reading records we and our students have found useful in building reading portfolios. You and your instructor will have to decide which ones will be most useful within the contexts of your course and your goals. If your instructor does not give a specific assignment for using these reading records, we suggest that you try at least two or three of them before you go on to later chapters. You need some basis of comparison before you can tell what will work best for you.

Response Journal

A response journal or reading log is a record of your reading and your thinking about that reading. Each time you read, you also write your comments and reactions: what you liked or didn't like, connections you made to your own life or to other reading or viewing experiences, predictions about what might happen, hypotheses about interpretations, questions you have, what you expected or didn't expect, observations about techniques, and anything else you find interesting or important. Besides writing your comments, you should also include a quotation or citation from the work to show what specific feature(s) caused your response.

Your response journal can be in a separate place, but it also makes sense to have it as a special section of your "Portfolio Notebook." You may set up the journal in paragraphs or in a column format. The examples that follow, based on "Gretel in Darkness," show journal entries of each type.

Paragraph Format
"Now, far from women's arms/and memory of women, in our father's hut/we sleep, are never hungry"—Should they be happy or sad to be far from women's arms? I can't remember if it was a stepmother who caused Hansel and Gretel to go into the forest in the fairy tale. In fairy tales, stepmothers aren't usually characters we admire. If Gretel is free now from the stepmother and the witch who would have eaten them, why isn't she happy?

Double-Column Format

Elements of the Text	Your Comments, Questions, Speculations, Associations
"we are there still and it is real, real,"	I like the repetition of *real*. It seems to highlight that her past is more real to her than her present. But why? *Is* it real?

Triple-Column Format

You saw this format earlier in the chapter. The third column is to try to label the kinds of thinking you are doing as you proceed through the work (see pages 49–51 for some specific examples).

What you are looking at (features of the text)	What you're thinking about it (issues, questions, speculations, associations)	What you would call that thinking (labels for your thought processes)

Dialogue Journal

To use a dialogue journal, you need a reading partner. After you complete some or all of your responses, you switch journals with your partner, who is also reading the same work and keeping a journal. In the third column of the dialogue journal, you write your responses to your partner's responses. You might write questions, comments, or anything you might write in response to the work itself. With a dialogue journal, you are conducting a "reading" of your partner's reading of the work. When your journal is returned with your partner's comments, you will have another observer's view of your reading. You will have in progress a written conversation of dialogue about the work and your reading of it.

As with the response journal, a dialogue journal can be a section of your "Portfolio Notebook." Set up the dialogue journal according to the example below:

What you are looking at (features of the text)	What you're thinking about it (issues, questions, speculations, associations)	Partner's response
"This is the world we wanted."	If they wanted it, then why isn't she happy or content with it, even at the end of the poem? What else does she need besides safety and food and shelter?	I read that line as sarcastic or ironic, to show that now that the earlier threat is gone, the trouble isn't over.

Burke's Pentad

Kenneth Burke has devised a scheme for investigating actions and motives, a scheme that can be applied to both people and literary characters. His pattern for analysis is called the *pentad* because it has five areas of questions. Like the facts in a case of law or the news questions in an article, these areas allow for easy comparison from one work to another. The question areas are these:

Act   The event—whatever was done
Scene   When and where—the time and place of the act
Agent   The actor—who did it
Agency   The means—how the act was done
Purpose The reason or motive—why the act was done

At first glance, the pentad might seem to be a detective's method of investigation to be employed at the scene of a crime. The pentad *is* a method of investigation, and it can be applied very well to a work of literature. The *act* can be the action—what happens—within the work, or the work itself as an act of communication. In "Mirror," for example, bending over the lake can be an act, and so can talking about bending over the lake—that is, the entire poem—be an act. In fiction, telling a story is an act, and the event within the story is also an act.

You will have to decide whether to use the pentad to describe the action within the work or outside the work to describe the communication act of the work itself. In either case, the rest of the pentad terms apply. For example, if you were dealing with *Gulliver's Travels* from inside the work, Lilliput would be one scene. From outside the work, the publication of the book in England is an act, and England at the time of the book's publication there is the scene. Here are more detailed questions for your reading record:

Act   What is happening (or being said)? In how many steps or stages? In what order? With what results?

Scene   Where and when is this action taking place? Who is present? Is there movement or change in the setting or audience?

Agent   Who is doing the acting (or talking)? How many are involved in the act? What is this character (are these characters) like? From what stance does the (each) character speak?

Agency Through what means is the action performed—intellectual, psychological, physical, other? (In a speaking act, what techniques does the speaker use?)

Purpose Why is the action being performed (or why is the speaker speaking)? What is the anticipated payoff or result? Is this the actual result? To what extent is the actor's (speaker's) purpose actually achieved?

Study Guide

When you are reading a long work, you might want to prepare a study guide for later use. The study guide requires you to pay attention to specific features of a work, the features often asked about on examinations and interpretive papers. You complete the study guide by making entries in whatever category is appropriate for the part of the text you are reading at the time. You will probably have a number of entries for each part of a study guide. Here are some headings for a study guide, along with questions to consider for each category:

Titles   What does the title come to mean during the course of the work? How does it connect with characters, settings, themes, and other elements?

Form   How do the genre and the structure—parts or divisions or episodes—help to develop the meanings of the work?

Conflict   What internal and external conflicts are part of the
central conflict? *Is* there a central conflict? If so, how
is it developed? What is the climax or turning point?
How is the conflict resolved—through what agency
or power? How do the characters, circumstances,
and society within the work change as a result of
this resolution?

Characters   What characters are important? What are their most
significant features? What are their motives? How
do they interact? How do they relate to the world
within the work? How do they change? What do
they learn about themselves and others?

Settings   What is the world of the work? What are the significant features of the landscape and society of the
work? How are these related to the world outside
the work? How are time, space, and place treated
within the work?

Narration   Who is the speaker or narrator? Is there only one?
How does this choice affect your understanding of
the work? Does the narrator make direct comment
on the action and on characters? Is the narrator a
character or an unnamed speaker? What is the tone
of the narration?

Language   What are the most important words in the work? What
are the most important images or symbols in the
work? How are they used? How do they relate to
the setting, character, and other elements of the
work?

Contexts   Who wrote this work? During what time of his or her
life? In what time and place was it written? What
was the world view or spirit of the times? How has
this work been "read" in the past? How has it been
interpreted?

Ideas   What is this work about? What views and ideas about
people and events are offered here? What values are
advocated or implied? In what ways do I agree or
disagree with these ideas?

READER'S FORUM

There is much to learn from listening to others involved in the same process as you. "Reader's Forum" activities in the remaining chapters of this book will give you a chance to hear the plans and views and performances of other portfolio makers.

In this chapter you have completed several activities that begin to define you as a reader—the reader you were (reading autobiography), the reader you are (responses to "Gretel in Darkness"), and the reader you want to become (your goals as a reader). Select one of these activities and prepare a one- or two-minute presentation to your classmates.

Be clear and specific in your presentation. Nobody reads (or lives) "in general." For example, "I loved children's books when I was a kid" tells us almost nothing about you. "I used to chant 'I think I can, I think I can' each time I stepped up to bat" paints a little clearer picture. Details, details.

When you are listening to others' presentations, keep a pencil handy. You can jot down ideas for your own goals, new works you might want to read, and names of classmates you might want to work with because your goals or interests are similar—or because they are different.

PORTFOLIO PROGRESS REPORT

Here is another "Progress Report" to help you to keep track of what you have accomplished as you work toward your goals as a reader. Remember that these reflections form an important part of your working portfolio, which continues through the entire course.

Although the questions will be applied to different activities, the same three questions are the basis for this "Progress Report":

1. **Knowledge:** What *do you know* that you didn't know before?
2. **Practice:** What *can you do* that you couldn't do (or do as well) before?

3. **Habits:** What *do you do* that you didn't do (or do as much) before?

Review your work with the activities below and then write at least a few paragraphs in your "Portfolio Notebook" to answer each of the three questions:

- your reading autobiography
- your responses to "Gretel in Darkness" and areas of concentration
- your Preliminary Assessment and your four reading goals
- your reading record experiments with the response journal, the dialogue journal, the pentad, and/or the study guide
- your experiences as a speaker and a listener in "Reader's Forum"

MOVING ON

You have written your goals and completed a "Portfolio Progress Report" about your first steps. In the next chapter, you will add to your repertoire a number of ways to read, interpret, and write about literary texts—any of which could be used for your portfolio presentation.

3 Perspectives for Interpreting Meaning

▶▶▶**LOOKING AHEAD**

In this chapter, you will see that more is better: the more choices you have about ways into a reading, the more rich and informed your work is likely to be. You will gain some experience with a formal method of constructing literary interpretations and learn a number of ways to mark up and make notes about a text you're working with.

In addition, we will talk about contexts and their importance to determining meanings, and you will try some activities to illustrate this idea. You will also have a chance to try an array of interpretive activities centered on a single short work.

Also featured here are guides for interpreting works from various critical perspectives. You will learn to use some of the tools of literary criticism. At the "Reader's Forum," you will have a chance to present one of the activities you did in the chapter.

THE MEANING OF MEANING

"What does it mean?" That's probably the question asked most often about the works you read in literature courses. It's also the question we have in mind when we look at an X-ray, a financial report, a valentine, a grade transcript, a newly unearthed artifact, an obituary, and the Big Bang theory. Where *is* meaning, anyway? We know that words are not thoughts, or we would never have trouble putting our thoughts into words.

In Chapter 2, we suggested that meanings—not *the* meaning, but meanings—exist not in messages but in the senders and receivers of those messages. If you have ever played a game with friends in which you created a secret code, you know that language users assign meanings to signs and symbols in ways that suit the users' purposes at the time. A poem written in Latin won't mean anything to you if you don't understand Latin.

Sometimes students describe their work with literature as "finding the meaning" or "uncovering the real meaning" or "getting the deeper meaning." These expressions make it seem as if authors bury (deep) nuggets of real meaning in a field of less important words. The reader's job, then, would be to use a shovel or meaning-detector to go over the field and retrieve the hidden meanings. In this view, reading is seen as a scavenger hunt, with the prize being a bag of themes, symbols, and other nuggets of meaning.

We suggest that meaning isn't a place or in a place. Meaning *happens*. And writers and readers make it happen. "Deeper" meanings happen with more complex arrangements of words (from more sophisticated writers) and with more complex processes of constructing meaning (more sophisticated readers). The text of this book is flat, two-dimensional. The third dimension, depth, must come from people—the writers and readers.

Contexts as Determiners of Meaning

We would like you to consider more than just the meaning. We would like you to consider the who, what, when, where, why, and how of meaning. Meaning has time, place, and human contexts, and these contexts help to determine what meanings can be derived. An X-ray film of your leg has a different meaning for the radiologist than it has for you. During a consultation about your X-ray, it is not the radiologist who will be thinking, "Will I have to wear a cast for eight weeks?" Meaning changes as perspectives change; meaning changes as time goes by. The X-ray that meant "fractured tibia" at the time it was taken no longer has the same "meaning" five years later.

When George Orwell's *1984* was published, it was a futuristic novel. Today, both time and technology have caught up with what was the future for Orwell. Word for word, the book has not changed; what has changed is the context, and so the views of the book have changed, as have the possibilities of meanings. It might be helpful if you think of any literary text as a note written and sealed up in a bottle. It might not wash up on your shore for a thousand years.

Place is another important feature of the context that helps to determine meaning. A simple expression such as "What's up?" has different meanings in different English-speaking places. In most of the United States, that expression means something like "What's new with you?" An acquaintance from Australia once pointed out that, in his part of the world, the same expression means "What's *wrong* with you?"—a challenge, if not an insult.

For any single work of literature, a multiplicity of human contexts exist. The work was composed by a person (or persons) at a specific time in a particular place for an audience—perhaps for a certain person or in response to a special event. There are personal and historical contexts. There are also physical contexts. The work was produced in a certain way: say, sitting at a desk writing with a quill pen on foolscap, the desk lit by a candle, each installment of the work to be printed in a monthly magazine.

Over time, readers have interacted with the work. If it is a popular work, much will have been written about it, adding to its historical context. When you pick up the work and start to read, you are adding another set of contexts: your own. Readers don't come from *Readerland*. There is no such person as "the reader." There are only readers. Each reader, as we have seen, will come from a time and a place and a set of life experiences, and these contexts will be powerful determiners of meaning.

Reading is a matter of constructing the meaning of something made of words, so making interpretations of literary works is not a simple process. We need to consider time, place, and human contexts in order to develop *possible meanings* and then to explore those possibilities in fashioning an interpretation. How to begin?

One Method for Constructing Meaning: Claim, Data, and Warrant

Let's begin with an example and a basic method. We will give some formal names to the process used earlier with "Mirror" and "Gretel in Darkness." The names are *claim, data,* and *warrant.* These are terms developed by Stephen Toulmin in his book *The Uses of Argument.*

A *claim* is a conclusion or assertion of meaning made by a reader/observer/interpreter. *Data* refers to evidence, often a word or group of words from the text being considered. The *warrant* is the justification for drawing the conclusion from the evidence, the logical link between the data and the claim. To demonstrate your ability to read and interpret, you will have to make claims about the meanings of works. You will have to use data or evidence to support those claims, and you will need to justify the connections you make—state warrants—between the data and your claims.

FOR YOUR PORTFOLIO NOTEBOOK

Applying the Method

Read the poem that follows, using one of the reading record forms from Chapter 2 to keep track of your thoughts. When you have finished reading and writing, make an interpretation by writing a paragraph that includes the ingredients listed below. Your instructor may ask you to present your theory to your classmates.

A claim: your theory (or hypothesis) of a meaning
Some data: some evidence from the poem to support your claim
A warrant: your reasoning for developing your theory from the data

Inverse
When I reflect
on the why of your origin,
I am startled by your
transformation.

5   I see no point,
     follow no line,
     draw no parallel.

     I cannot translate
     lost
10 as I am
     in this endless rotation,
     dilating to infinity.

The Effects of Context. What did you say about the meaning of "Inverse"? After looking at the poem, readers of different ages have said the following:

- "It's about lost love, a relationship that changed for the worse."
- "A scientist is baffled by the mysteries of the universe."
- "A father looks at his child, remembers the child's earlier years, and realizes he no longer recognizes the child he used to know."
- "The most important things to say are just impossible to communicate."

No one of these meanings is right or wrong, even though they differ from each other. In fact, they differ from the writer's thoughts at the time he was writing the poem—which still does not make any of the interpretations wrong or incorrect.

It happens that the writer of the poem, an English instructor, was observing a math class. As he watched, he was struck by two thoughts. First, he used to love the "architecture" of mathematics (he had earlier intended to be a math major). Second, though he had a vague sense of familiarity with the terms on the board during this lesson, the mathematical processes involved seemed alien to him. He started to play with the terms the math instructor was using in her lesson, stringing phrases together, just doodling with words, really. After a while something like a poem started to take shape. With some revisions, that something became "Inverse." Here is the poem again, this time with the math terms in boldface:

> **Inverse**
> When I **reflect**
> on the why of your **origin,**
> I am startled by your
> **transformation.**
>
> 5   I see no **point,**
> follow no **line,**
> draw no **parallel.**
>
> I cannot **translate**
> lost
> 10   as I am
> in this endless **rotation**
> **dilating** to **infinity.**

The other "readings" listed above, and perhaps your reading, do not mention math in this poem. This is not surprising, since readers did not know the personal and physical contexts of the writing. However, the readers did see loss, change, confusion, and bewilderment, responses the poem seems to generate even when the boldfaced words aren't seen as math terms.

There is an event in *The Adventures of Huckleberry Finn* that will help to show how contextual and personal interpretations can be. Huck and Jim are traveling down the Mississippi River on a raft. They are separated when a fog closes down on the river, reducing visibility to nothing. Huck is in a canoe, and Jim is on the raft. After a night of whooping and hollering to try to find each other, and also of blindly crashing into the banks of the river, Huck finds the raft again. Jim is asleep, so Huck decides to play a trick on him: Huck will pretend they were never separated, tell Jim it must have been a dream, and enjoy Jim's interpretation of the dream:

> So Jim went to work and told me the whole thing right through, just as it happened, only he painted it up consider-able. Then he said he must start in and "'terpret" it, because it was sent for a warning. He said the first towhead [tree-covered

island] stood for a man that would try to do us some good, but the current was another man that would get us away from him. The whoops was warnings that would come to us every now and then, and if we didn't try hard to make out to understand them they'd just take us into bad luck, 'stead of keeping us out of it. The lot of towheads was troubles we was going to get into with quarrelsome people and all kinds of mean folks, but if we minded our business and didn't talk back and aggravate them, we would pull through and get out of the fog and into the big clear river, which was the free states, and wouldn't have no more trouble.

It had clouded up pretty dark just after I had got on to the raft, but it was clearing up again now.

"Oh, well, that's all interpreted well enough as far as it goes, Jim," I says, "but what does *these* things stand for?"

It was the leaves and rubbish on the raft and the smashed oar. You could see them first-rate now.

Jim looked at the trash, and then looked at me, and back at the trash again. He had got the dream fixed so strong in his head that he couldn't seem to shake it loose and get the facts back into its place again right away. But when he did get the thing straightened around he looked at me steady without ever smiling, and says:

"What do dey stan' for? I's gwyne to tell you. When I got all wore out wid work, en wid de callin' for you, en went to sleep, my heart wuz mos' broke bekase you wuz los', en I did-n't k'yer no mo' what become er me en de raf'. En when I wake up en fine you back ag'in, all safe en soun', de tears come, en I could 'a' got down on my knees en kiss yo' foot, I's so thank-ful. En all you wuz thinkin' 'bout wuz how you could make a fool uv ole Jim wid a lie. Dat truck dah is trash; en *trash* is what people is dat puts dirt on de head er dey fren's en makes 'em ashamed."

—Mark Twain

In just a few seconds, Jim is able to apply a new context, and thus a new interpretation, to the same set of details or events. He goes from a dream that has mythic significance and portent to a personal rebuke for Huck's trickery. When you get ready to start interpreting, you need to consider the contexts you bring to the reading experience.

Literature instructors sometimes tell students that they should not use the expression, "The author *was trying to say....*" In a way, though, the expression does suggest that what writers "say" and what readers "hear" are unlikely to be identical.

FOR YOUR PORTFOLIO NOTEBOOK

Making an Interpretation

You have just seen Jim change his interpretation because the context changed. Now here's an event for you to interpret—in fact, interpret in three different ways. One interpretation of the event is provided for you, along with a context. You write three more interpretations and explain the contexts that justify them.

Event:	A person holds up the first two fingers of one hand.
Reading #1:	The event means that the answer is "two."
Context:	Bobby's arithmetic teacher just asked, "What is twenty divided by ten?"

Reading #2:
Context:

Reading #3:
Context:

Reading #4:
Context:

GETTING INTO A TEXT

You now have a format to use as a blueprint for interpretations, as well as a sense of the relativity of meaning. In this section, we will be looking at techniques you might employ in close readings of text.

Some Basic Understandings

Here are two more ideas to consider as you begin to interpret a work. They have to do with how our minds work as we read.

Reading Is Recursive. One idea is that reading is a recursive process—that is, a process that runs back on itself. We keep going back over what we have read and projecting ahead of where we are in a text. This process happens within a sentence and also through an entire book. When you stop reading in a certain sense goes on.

Did that last sentence seem to be a mistake? After you read the first few words of the sentence, did you anticipate a different ending? Did you go back and read it over again to see if you had missed something or misread the beginning? This going back and forth is what good readers do all the time.

Because of our experience, our reading processes are so sophisticated that we are never reading at only one place in a text. When you are in the middle of *West Side Story*, you may be thinking back to the opening scene of the play and also imagining how the play might end. If you know this play is an analog, a modern version of *Romeo and Juliet*, you have more to think about. If you recall that *Romeo and Juliet* is a tragedy and are familiar with the structure of a tragedy, you have even more to think about—all while you are on the first page of Act II.

As you read on, you will also be reformulating your earlier expectations and meanings in the light of what you just read. When you get to the end of the work, you will need to reflect on earlier events and ideas. As important as endings are, "meaning" doesn't just happen at the end of a work, so you can't wait to finish a work before you start to think about it—no more than you would expect to finish a meal before you started to taste it.

The Effects of Psychological Time. You should also be aware that as you read there are different time schemes operating. Clock time, of course, is measured by how many minutes it takes you to read the work. *Dramatic time* is the amount of time that supposedly elapses during the course of a work: *One Day in the Life of Ivan Denisovich* covers one day; *Huckleberry Finn,* a few months; and so on.

Psychological time, a third time scheme, is much harder to measure. This is the mixture of past, present, and future that exists in your head as you read, as you are looking forward and backward, inside and outside the work to construct meaning.

There's a saying that you can't step into the same river twice: by the time you try to step back in again, some new water will have entered and some old water will have left. You can't read the same work twice either. By the second reading, you will have changed, just as the river did.

Each reading of a work, then, is really a draft, just as is each version of a writing. You can never get "everything" when you read, even if you read a work twenty times, so don't try to get everything. Instead, try to get one coherent view of the whole piece.

Marking Up the Text

When you read a work for your portfolio, you should already be planning how you want, or will need, to reread it. Make each reading productive by keeping some kind of record, either within the work or in your "Portfolio Notebook."

Written record forms such as those discussed in Chapter 2 are one approach you can use, but if you own the book you are using, a simpler, more direct method is to mark the text you want to return to, either by underlining, highlighting, drawing brackets, or making notes and comments in the margins. We have seen readers who have devised systems with colored pencils (red is for the setting, blue for character A, and so on) and symbols ("x" is for something important, "*" is for something really important, and "#" is for something absolutely crucial). Before you buy those colored pencils or devise the code, a few warnings:

- *Don't overdo it, or you might not get the effect you want.* One college roommate had a habit of using a highlighter to mark almost every line of his books. Besides bringing out the homicidal tendencies of his roommates (from the steady *screeking* of the highlighter), he had made stand out only those three or four lines of text per page that were *not* highlighted.
- *Don't overcomplicate things.* With an overly elaborate system, you might spend more time and energy trying to

interpret what you meant than using the system to help you understand the text.

You can also mark a text less permanently by inserting removable adhesive notes on pages you want to reread. Each note can contain brief comments about the passage and its interest or significance—a short-hand reading log, in effect. Whatever method you use, make sure to key your markings to the activity or project you're working on. This way, each draft of your reading can also be a draft of the thinking you're doing for your writing or other activity to follow.

The poem that follows has been marked to show three different close readings. In the first version shown, the reader marked references to the concepts of *time* and *love*. The boldfaced words show direct references to these two concepts:

To His Coy Mistress
Had we but world enough, and **time,**
This coyness, Lady, were no crime.
We would sit down and think which way
To walk and **pass** our **long love's day.**
5   Thou by the Indian Ganges' side
Shoulds't rubies find; I by the tide
Of Humber would complain. I would
Love you **ten years before the Flood,**
And you should, if you please, refuse
10 **Till the conversion of the Jews.**
My vegetable **love** should grow
Vaster than empires and **more slow;**
An hundred years should go to praise
Thine eyes and on thy forehead gaze;
15 **Two hundred** to **adore** each breast,
But **thirty thousand** to the rest;
An age at least to every part,
And **the last age** should show your **heart.**
For, Lady, you deserve this state,
20 Nor would I **love** at lower **rate.**

But at my back I always hear
Time's winged chariot hurrying near;
And yonder all before us lie

Deserts of vast eternity.
25   Thy beauty shall **no more** be found,
    Nor, in thy marble vault, shall sound
    My echoing song; then worms shall try
    That long-preserved virginity.
    And your quaint honor turn to dust,
30   And into ashes all my lust:
    The grave's a fine and private place,
    But none, I think, do there embrace.

    Now therefore, **while** the youthful hue
    Sits on thy skin like morning dew,
35   And **while** thy willing soul transpires
    At every pore with instant fires,
    Now let us sport us **while** we may,
    And **now**, like **amorous** birds of prey,
    Rather **at once** our **time** devour
40   Than languish in his slow-chapped power.
    Let us roll all our strength and all
    Our sweetness up into one ball,
    And tear our pleasures with rough strife
    Through the iron gates of life:
45   Thus, though we cannot make our sun
    Stand still, yet we will make him run.
                    —Andrew Marvell

In this next version, the reader was concerned with the ideas of unity and separation, so the pronouns are marked to see at what points *you* and *I* become *we* and *us*:

    Had **we** but world enough, and time,
    This coyness, Lady, were no crime.
    We would sit down and think which way
    To walk and pass **our** long love's day.
5   **Thou** by the Indian Ganges' side
    Shoulds't rubies find; **I** by the tide
    Of Humber would complain. **I** would
    Love **you** ten years before the Flood,
    And **you** should, if **you** please, refuse

10   Till the conversion of the Jews.
My vegetable love should grow
Vaster than empires and more slow;
An hundred years should go to praise
Thine eyes and on **thy** forehead gaze;
15   Two hundred to adore each breast,
But thirty thousand to the rest;
An age at least to every part,
And the last age should show **your** heart.
For, Lady, **you** deserve this state,
20   Nor would I love at lower rate.

But at **my** back I always hear
Time's winged chariot hurrying near;
And yonder all before **us** lie
Deserts of vast eternity.
25   **Thy** beauty shall no more be found,
Nor, in **thy** marble vault, shall sound
My echoing song; then worms shall try
That long-preserved virginity.
And **your** quaint honor turn to dust,
30   And into ashes all **my** lust:
The grave's a fine and private place,
But none, I think, do there embrace.

Now therefore, while the youthful hue
Sits on **thy** skin like morning dew,
35   And while **thy** willing soul transpires
At every pore with instant fires,
Now let **us** sport **us** while **we** may,
And now, like amorous birds of prey,
Rather at once **our** time devour
40   Than languish in his slow-chapped power.
Let **us** roll all **our** strength and all
Our sweetness up into one ball,
And tear **our** pleasures with rough strife
Through the iron gates of life:
45   Thus, though **we** cannot make **our** sun
Stand still, yet **we** will make him run.

In the third version, the reader marked verbs to see the kinds of words used to describe the action in each of the three parts of the poem:

Had we but world enough, and time,
This coyness, Lady, **were** no crime.
We would **sit** down and **think** which way
To **walk** and **pass** our long love's day.
5   Thou by the Indian Ganges' side
Shoulds't rubies **find;** I by the tide
Of Humber would **complain.** I would
Love you ten years before the Flood,
And you should, if you please, **refuse**
10   Till the conversion of the Jews.
My vegetable love should **grow**
Vaster than empires and more slow;
An hundred years should **go** to **praise**
Thine eyes and on thy forehead **gaze;**
15   Two hundred to **adore** each breast,
But thirty thousand to the rest;
An age at least to every part,
And the last age should **show** your heart.
For, Lady, you **deserve** this state,
20   Nor would I **love** at lower rate.

But at my back I always **hear**
Time's winged chariot **hurrying** near;
And yonder all before us **lie**
Deserts of vast eternity.
25   Thy beauty shall no more be **found,**
Nor, in thy marble vault, shall **sound**
My echoing song; then worms shall **try**
That long-preserved virginity.
And your quaint honor **turn** to dust,
30   And into ashes all my lust:
The grave's a fine and private place,
But none, I **think,** do there **embrace.**

Now therefore, while the youthful hue
Sits on thy skin like morning dew,
35   And while thy willing soul **transpires**

At every pore with instant fires,
Now let us **sport** us while we may,
And now, like amorous birds of prey,
Rather at once our time **devour**
40 Than **languish** in his slow-chapped power.
Let us **roll** all our strength and all
Our sweetness up into one ball,
And **tear** our pleasures with rough strife
Through the iron gates of life:
45 Thus, though we cannot **make** our sun
Stand still, yet we will **make** him **run.**

FOR YOUR PORTFOLIO NOTEBOOK

Your Own Interpretation

Get a clean copy of "To His Coy Mistress" and mark up the text to demonstrate your own view of the poem.

FOR YOUR PORTFOLIO NOTEBOOK

Creating Warrants

Part 1. Read the following piece, marking or tabbing the text if you need to, and then write answers to the questions that follow it. Each answer will be a claim. The evidence from the passage on which you base your answer will be the data. The link you make between the data and the claim will be the warrant. Question 1 shows an outline you can follow in responding.

A hawk once flew over the hut of a king. It held in its talons a piece of human flesh, which inadvertently it let fall into the cauldron in which the king's soup was being prepared. The king was so enchanted with this soup that he ordered his cooks to repeat the same taste every day. Nonplused, since they had not seen what had fallen out of the sky, they tried every fish and fowl and even added reptiles and insects to the broth; all to no avail. In a rage, the king slew his head cook and told the others to cut him in pieces and throw them into the soup he could not make. When the king began to eat his soup that day, a broad grin of contentment spread over his face; he then told the surviving cooks to kill a slave each day and throw him into the cauldron. The king eventually ate every member of the tribe who had not fled, until one day he found himself all alone, with no more subjects to devour. Such was his passion for human flesh that he at once began to tear pieces from his own body; at last nothing of him remained but the parts he could not reach, and so he died.

1. What does this story say about human motives?

   Claim (from you):
   Data (from text and/or your knowledge beyond the text):
   Warrant (from you):

2. Whose fault is the outcome?
3. How might the hawk function as a symbol in this work?
4. What do you think was the writer's intent in composing this story?
5. Can you connect this story to any other story in literature, myth and religion, or history?
6. What is the effect of there being no females in this story?

Part 2. The claims you have written for the preceding questions may be seen as direct attempts to explain meanings in an expository way. There are other responses to the text that you can make that are not as direct as making and explaining claims but are as interpretive (and perhaps more interesting). These responses require you to interpret the text and then present your interpretation in a more creative or literary way, by doing something with the text itself.

Your instructor may assign you to one or more of the activities, or you may choose one or more on your own.

Activity 1: Write five possible titles for the story. Select the two you think are best and explain how these are appropriate to the story.

Activity 2: Retell the story from the first-person point of view. Try writing the king's interior monologue, for example.

Activity 3: Tell more of the story. Write either some antecedent action (events that took place before the story opened) or some consequent action (events that might take place after the story closes). Or do both.

Activity 4: Develop an event in the story into a scene to show detail. You might write the scene in which the cooks try to find the secret ingredient.

Activity 5: Retell the story from an observer's point of view, perhaps that of a spy from a neighboring tribe. You will have to decide how many of the events he or she is witnessing the observer should understand, and how that understanding would affect the content and manner of the reporting. You might want to have the events told through the spy's report to his or her king.

Activity 6: Make the story into a play. Decide how many scenes you will need. Sketch out the scenes with three or four steps for each. You will end up with an outline for a brief drama.

Activity 7: Begin as you did in Activity 6, but make the drama into a comedy. Consider what you will need to change and how events might work out. If you like melodrama better than comedy, sketch it out as a melodrama.

Activity 8: Draw the setting or scenery for key points in the work. Be ready to explain the decisions you make about what to show and how to show it.

Activity 9: Recast the story to include some or all female characters. What would be different? Why?

If you were to do all of these activities, you would have an array of works—a kind of portfolio, in effect—that would show something of your abilities to do different things with literature. Each of these activities also results in an act of interpretation. As you read the story and planned your writing or drawing or action, you had to link elements of the original work to ideas you had for extending or retelling or modifying it in some fashion. These are all performances of a kind.

FOR YOUR PORTFOLIO NOTEBOOK

Analyzing a World View

The four poems that follow are all by the same author, Stephen Crane. Without involving anything you might know about the author, consider the view of the world presented by the four poems taken as a group. Read the poems, keep reading records of significant issues, and write an analysis in which you draw some general conclusions about the world view presented by the poems. Your conclusions about the world view will be claims. As data, use specific references to the individual poems. Remember, however, that this isn't four separate assignments. The world view should be reflected in the poems taken as a group.

Your instructor may ask you to present your work in "Reader's Forum," so be ready to explain your conclusions.

The Book of Wisdom
I met a seer.
He held in his hands
The book of wisdom.
"Sir," I addressed him,
5   "Let me read."
"Child—" he began.
"Sir," I said.
"Think not that I am a child,
For already I know much
10 Of that which you hold;
Aye, much."

He smiled.
Then he opened the book
And held it before me.
15 Strange that I should have grown so suddenly blind.

Think as I Think
"Think as I think," said a man,
"Or you are abominably wicked;
You are a toad."
And after I had thought of it,
I said, "I will, then, be a toad."

The Wayfarer
The wayfarer,
Perceiving the pathway to truth,
Was struck with astonishment.
It was thickly grown with weeds.
5   "Ha," he said,
"I see that no one has passed here
In a long time."
Later he saw that each weed
Was a singular knife.
10   "Well," he mumbled at last,
"Doubtless there are other roads."

A Man Said to the Universe
A man said to the universe:
"Sir, I exist!"
"However," replied the universe,
"The fact has not created in me
A sense of obligation."

PERSPECTIVES FOR INTERPRETATION

We have pointed out that writers and books and readers are all situated in contexts, and that these contexts help to determine what meanings are possible. In Chapter 2, we noted that there are many perspectives from which to view a work and that the perspective chosen will bring some issues into the foreground and place others more in the background. For example, it is possible to read "Gretel in Darkness" as a study in the psychology of character or gender and pay little attention to such issues as the life and times of the author, the fairy tale "Hansel and Gretel," the structure and techniques of the poem, and previous interpretations of the poem.

Once again, you cannot stand everywhere when you read a work, and you cannot get everything. Without a particular assignment or agenda, there is no one best thing to do when you read a work. If you will abandon the attempt to get *the* meaning—as there is no one meaning for a work—you will be able to focus on constructing meanings for what you read. You will also be able to concentrate on the various processes we use to construct those meanings. Through such conversations as those you hold in "Reader's Forum" and other group activities, you will also discover the richness of meanings developed when readers take different avenues of interpretation to a work or works.

The guides that follow show processes you can use to explore works from different critical or interpretive perspectives. These questions are the critic's toolbox. There is no rule that says you can use questions from only one perspective, and it is usually more productive to try several approaches. In your experiments with these processes, you should keep track of what works best for you. It is more important to read well than it is to produce a good reading of any one work, so pay attention to what you are learning to do as a reader and interpreter. Like any set of tools, some types of questions work in some situations, some in others. Just as you don't use a screwdriver when you need a hammer, so you don't always ask the same question with each work you read.

Each guide is composed of questions you might think about before, during, and after your reading of a work. You will need outside resources such as reference books to help you to answer some of the questions.

The Writer's Life and Times

In thinking about the author, consider the following:

- What sort of person is/was the author? How old was he or she when the work was written? How does this work fit into the body of work produced by this author?

- Where did the author come from? Does the author's race, culture, or gender tell me anything? Is the work autobiographical to some extent? What important events or relationships helped shape the author's life?

- Was the work written to or about a specific person or persons? About a particular place? In response to a certain event?

- What is/was the author's culture or society like? What important events were taking place? What was the world view? What were the dominant values of the times? Was the writer in sympathy with or in opposition to the mainstream of that culture?

- What other works were produced by other writers at that time? How are they similar to and different from this work?

The Reader

Consider the following questions about yourself as the reader:

- What are the key features of the work that strike you? What words seem important? What images stand out most? What does the work make you think about?
- How does the work make you feel? What mood does it put you in? Can you say why?
- What did you like about the work? Why? What did you not like?
- Does the work remind you of an incident or person in your life?
- How did your views change as you read the work? Did you change your mind about anything? What ideas were challenged or tested by reading this work?
- What is your overall response or reaction to this work? What in you and what in the work connect to make this reaction?

The Work Itself

Note that the questions under this head fall roughly into three subsets: questions about the structure of the work, questions about the characters or speaker, and questions about the idea or lessons or philosophy of the work:

- How could the work be classified as to genre or style? What expectations do you have about such a work?
- What does the title suggest about the people, events, and ideas of the work?
- What is the setting or situation? Who is talking to whom, in what circumstances or surroundings? From what vantage point is the work narrated?
- How is the work organized into chapters or acts or stanzas or parts? What is the content and purpose of each part? What is

the progression of thought from beginning to end (problem-
solution, for example)?

- How is figurative language (metaphor and the like) used to
  make special comparisons, substitutions, exaggerations, ironic
  meanings, contradictions, and paradoxes?

- How is imagery used: descriptions, use of detail, key images
  with value as symbols?

- How is language used: diction (word choice), connotations,
  double meanings or puns, key words, repetitions?

- What patterns do you see in the work: parallels or changes in
  any of the elements above, shifts in tone, changes in pace,
  rhythm, form, or anything else?

- Who are the significant characters of the work? What are they
  like in terms of identity, personality, behavior? What are/were
  important experiences in their lives?

- What motivates each character (or the speaker)? What are their
  goals? What means do they use to try to achieve them? What
  important decisions do they make? How do they act upon these
  decisions?

- What kinds of conflicts are characters involved in? How, and to
  what extent, are these conflicts resolved? How do the
  resolutions affect characters? How do characters change during
  the work?

- How do characters influence and affect each other? How are
  characters' values, attitudes, and actions related to the norms or
  standards of the society within the work?

- What characters can be considered good? In what ways? What
  characters can be considered evil? In what ways?

- What does the work say about people? What people and/or
  actions seem to be approved of? To be condemned? Who and
  what is praised or blamed?

- Are judgments about people or actions made on the basis of
  consequences or results, or on the basis of intentions or
  motives?

- What forces seem to shape or control human events? Do people
  seem to have free will? Does fate control everything? Are
  events and outcomes determined by biological or social forces?

- In what ways is the work about the concepts of good and evil, right and wrong, justice, morality, or ethics? What, if anything, does the work say about how people should act?

Connections to Other Works, People, and Events

When thinking about connections, consider the following:

- What did people think of the work when it was first published?
- What are the dominant or best-known interpretations of the work? What issues are featured in these interpretations?
- How have views of this work changed over time?
- Has this work had any known impact on other writers or on events?
- In what ways do you agree or disagree with the traditional (and other) views of this work?
- How does this work fit into the history of literary art?
- Can you think of another work that this work reminds you of? What is the connection for you? Why do the works seem similar or related?
- Is there a character (or speaker) in the work who reminds you of another character in a different work?
- Is there a scene or event or object or situation that seems familiar or connects with a similar element in another work?
- Does any part of the work remind you of a folk tale, a myth, or similar kind of story, or of a person or event or place in history?
- Are there any names, words, or phrases that come from a familiar source?

FOR YOUR PORTFOLIO NOTEBOOK
Using the Guides

Read one or both of the poems that follow, using one or two of the guides to help you with interpretation (or your instructor may assign specific poems and guides). As you read, jot down answers to some or all of the questions in the guide. When you finish, you will have the beginning of an interpretation from a critical perspective. On the basis of your answers, compose an interpretation from that perspective. You may be presenting your interpretation in "Reader's Forum," so be prepared to explain your answers.

The first poem is a sonnet. The second poem, "Two Dollar Mommy," was written almost four hundred years later. The author is a writer and instructor who lives in New York State.

Sonnet 73
That time of year thou mayst in me behold
When yellow leaves, or none, or few, do hang
Upon those boughs which shake against the cold,
Bare ruined choirs where late the sweet birds sang.
5   In me thou seest the twilight of such day
As after sunset fadeth in the west,
Which by and by black night doth take away,
Death's second self, that seals up all in rest.
In me thou seest the glowing of such fire
10   That on the ashes of his youth doth lie
As the deathbed whereon it must expire,
Consumed with that which it was nourished by.
This thou perceiv'st, which makes thy love more strong,
To love that well which thou must leave ere long.

—William Shakespeare

Two Dollar Mommy
He left money on the ice box
two single dollar bills,
tucked under a doily,
oily and dark with the passage
5   of so many two dollar bills

"Cold cash," he joked,
left to pay
for any little thing
two dollar woman might need today—
10   a newspaper, cigarettes, a quart of milk
for the kids

She once heart pounded stammered asked,
"Maybe you could leave the week's money
all at once. I could make a budget, you know,
15   like in the magazines."

"You'd piss it all away," he said.
His tone implied she would go to bars
or do things with men.

Two dollar woman crossed herself
20   and kissed him good-bye with a heart full
of guilt for her wicked budgetary desires
and the sudden terrorhope that
he would fall into the subway tracks and
they would make a settlement and then
25   she would be free

She descended to the concrete street
to consult with others like herself
who wore housedresses and ankle socks
their husbands feared would inspire lust
30   in janitors and such

After she had talked it out, two dollar mommy
left two dollar daddy and the four penny babies
but returned again in two dollar days

Two dollar daddy punched her happy hello
35   and in the morning left

one dollar.

—Diane Gallo

BUILDING YOUR PORTFOLIO

From now on, this section of the chapter will present a variety of
activities that you can choose from in developing your portfolio. The
activities can be done with almost any work you want or have to
read. If your instructor does not make a specific assignment, select

the activities that will help you to meet your goals, and then match each activity with a literary work. Start by reviewing your goals from Chapter 2.

Correspondence Course

At any point in a work you are reading, pick a character who interests you and write a letter to her or him. Ask a question, offer advice, express an attitude, or do anything else people do in letters. Then write back—from the character's point of view. Given what you have come to know about this character, how might he or she respond to your letter?

Continue the correspondence in one of two ways. Write your own immediate follow-up letter and another response from the character, or continue on in your reading and write another exchange of letters from a later point in the work.

Extending the Action

Novels, poems, essays, and stories start and end somewhere, but most of them don't start at the beginning of time, nor do they end when the world ends. Earlier in this chapter, you saw that *antecedent action* refers to events that we imagine took place before the story begins, and *consequent action* refers to events that might happen after the story closes.

For a work you are reading, plan and then write two to three pages of antecedent action or consequent action (or both) to extend the work. As you are reading, you should keep a reading log or record of important events that you will want to build on or explain in your extension. After you write the extension(s), write a short explanation of the decisions you made to connect the part you wrote with the original piece.

Changes in Meaning, Meaning in Changes

Every work of literature has movement and change. Changes help to develop meanings. What changes is important; equally important is *how* changes occur.

For the work you choose, show how the significant changes in the work relate to meaning. You may wish to refer to any of the following:

- changes in character: values, perceptions, behavior, relationships

- changes in setting: time, place, atmosphere
- changes in narration: tone, attitude, point of view
- changes in other elements of the work

As you read, keep a double-entry reading record of your speculations and conclusions about significant changes and key passages of
the work. You might begin your reading record with your preliminary
reactions to the title and first page (or opening stanza or paragraph) to
see if the work develops as you anticipate. Here are some questions
about change to consider:

- What is the change? From what to what?
- What are the signs that the change is taking place? Does
  everyone (within the work) notice the change?
- What people or events caused the change?
- What were the effects of the change on the main characters? On
  other characters?
- What is your reaction to the change? How do you feel about it?
- How does this change affect your views of the characters, the
  action, or the whole work?

Your Notes

You have probably seen a copy of *Cliff's Notes* or *Monarch Notes* for a
book or play. For this activity, make *Your Notes* for the work you choose
to read. You may wish to include the following items, typical features
of such study aids, or to create features of your own:

- Background of the author, the times, and the work
- Plot summary (by chapter or scene) with critical commentary
  on key points
- Character description and analysis
- Essay questions with suggested responses

Making a Storyboard

A storyboard is a device used to plan productions that include visuals and sound, such as motion pictures, slide shows, music videos,

and television advertisements. A completed storyboard, which looks much like a comic strip, lets you think visually, aurally, kinesthetically, and verbally at the same time. There are places on each frame for pictures, words and other sounds, and directions about movement and duration:

Use this device to plan a movie of a poem. Select one of the poems in this chapter or one of your own choice. Start by reading the poem and marking divisions on the text. How many frames or pictures will you need to convey the sense of the poem? Each frame of the story-board will represent one *shot*, the basic unit of film.

Sketch the visuals that you see for each shot or set of lines. Pay careful attention to camera angle and distance. Think about how long each shot should last, what movement should take place during the shot, and what transitions should occur between shots. You might use a straight cut to transfer immediately from one shot to the next. Or you could fade out and then fade in, or use a dissolve.

Sound deserves attention, too. The sound track will include the lines of the poem, either as dialogue or narration, but can also include music and sound effects.

Kinesthetic Approaches

Characters, speakers, and narrators can be depicted through construc-tions as well as through words. The purpose of a construction is to con-vey character traits and personality through the materials you select and the way you put them together. A mask such as those used by actors in Greek drama to reveal something of a character is one possi-ble construction; an empty picture frame embellished with various arti-facts to convey character nuance is another. Other constructions are possible as well. As you set about making a construction, consider the following points:

- What makes the individual unique? How is he or she different from other people?
- What are the overlapping contexts—physical, psychological, sociological, historical, artistic, and the like—in which the individual must be understood? How is the individual's identity related to the groups and systems and other networks that he or she is a part of?
- How is the individual's identity growing, developing, deteriorating, aging, evolving, and otherwise moving along some path of change?

When you've finished your construction, write a brief explanation of why you did what you did. Use your explanation to present your con-struction in class.

READER'S FORUM

You have seen that contexts are important determiners of meaning. They are also important determiners of learning. The "Reader's Forum" context allows you to learn from a community of readers. As you listen to other readers' presentations, use your "Portfolio Notebook" to jot down works you may want to read, issues you may want to explore, readers you may want to talk with.

Your instructor may assign you a topic to present at "Reader's Forum," or you may choose one yourself from the chapter activities. (The activities are listed in the "Portfolio Progress Report" section that follows.)

PORTFOLIO PROGRESS REPORT

Although they will once again be applied to different activities, here are the same three questions you used for the previous "Progress Report":

1. **Knowledge:** What *do you know* that you didn't know before?
2. **Practice:** What *can you do* that you couldn't do (or do as well) before?
3. **Habits:** What *do you do* that you didn't do (or do as much) before?

For this "Progress Report," review your work with the activities below and then write at least a few paragraphs in your "Portfolio Notebook" to answer each of the three questions.

- your claims about "Inverse"
- your three interpretations of an event
- your practice with ways to mark the text of what you read
- your work with the story of the king's soup (answers to questions and follow-up activities)
- the four Crane poems and your conclusions about the world view they demonstrate

- your work with the interpretation guides (Shakespeare's sonnet and "Two Dollar Mommy")
- your work with the various activities in "Building Your Portfolio"
- your experiences as a speaker and a listener in "Reader's Forum"

MOVING ON

If this chapter is about performances, the next one is about performances with a payoff—essays and other papers on which your grades are usually based. You will see how understanding literary terms and devices can improve your performance on these measures.

4 Using the Language and Devices of Literature

▶▶LOOKING AHEAD

"That's just a figure of speech." That's where this chapter begins, with figurative language in its many forms. We will go on to look at other uses of language and then literary terms organized under the five categories of Burke's pentad, which we described in Chapter 2.

We will show you how to use what you have learned to perform well on literature papers. A key to this is using the claim/warrant/data system of logic. We will even show you how to write bad essays and papers, the usual traps unwary literature students fall into. There will be plenty of practice in essay-writing strategies, including the "Essay Response Plan."

FIGURATIVE LANGUAGE AND WORD CHOICE

One definition of *figurative language* is that it is "language used in special ways." Let's take a little time to examine what that might mean.

The bank teller's window will soon close means "The bank teller's window will soon be moved to a closed position." *This window of opportunity will soon close* does not have anything to do with a real window. It means that a good time period for doing something will soon be over. The first sentence is about a window. Language is being used in a literal sense. The second sentence is not about a window at all. *Window* is used figuratively to represent a time frame. We use figurative language like this so often in our writing and speech that we usually don't recognize that we're using it.

In the terms of I. A. Richards, a figure of speech has two parts, the *vehicle* and the *tenor*. The vehicle is the actual word (or words) used. The tenor is the underlying meaning. In a figure of speech, the vehicle conveys the tenor. In the example above, "window" is the vehicle and the opportunity it stands for is the tenor.

We make ordinary literal comparisons to show that Building A is taller than Building B, that Car C costs more than Car D, that Food E has more calories than Food F. However, when we wish to make unusual comparisons, especially between things not usually associated with each other, we rely on various kinds of figurative language. We take unrelated things and make new connections among and between them.

The purpose for figurative language is to create a new viewpoint or perspective on a topic or idea. We are interested in the vehicle only insofar as it will convey the tenor—the point we have to make about the subject. Of course, there is a shelf life for figurative language. Like some old soldiers, some old metaphors just fade away. They lose their "metaphorness"—their figurativeness—because they become ordinary expressions in the language, taken for granted and unexamined. "Let's cross that bridge when we come to it" makes only the youngest and least experienced of listeners look around for a bridge. Doors and windows of opportunity no longer startle the reader or listener into a new look at the concepts involved. In a way, figurative language, like advertising, creates its own antibodies. Since each figure is a way to create a new meaning, the newness of the meaning is lost when the figure becomes a cliché or overused expression.

In Chapter 1, we analyzed several types of figurative language in terms of the gaps you needed to fill to understand them. Here we will group these types, as well as others, into categories. We will fill the gaps of meaning by analyzing the patterns in each group.

Figurative Comparisons

Comparisons drawing together two unlike things can be stated or implied, brief or extended. In our analysis of figurative comparisons, we will use "A" to represent the main subject or tenor and "B" to represent the vehicle or thing(s) being connected to the main subject. Here are some common types of figurative comparisons.

Metaphor. As we saw in Chapter 1, metaphor can be a general term applied to any connection between two dissimilar things. In its simplest form, however, a metaphor is a figure of speech that says that one thing "is" another: "The road was a ribbon of highway ..." (Alfred Noyes). We might call constructions like these *expressed* metaphors; they say A *is* B.

It is also possible to establish the comparison without directly naming the two things being compared. Look at these lines from Shakespeare's "Sonnet 73":

That time of year thou mayst in me behold
When yellow leaves, or none, or few, do hang
Upon those boughs which shake against the cold, ...

Here the speaker's time of life is suggested to resemble the autumn of the year. This sort of metaphor might be considered to be *implied: A has qualities similar to B.*

In an *extended* metaphor, a single comparison is elaborated in detail and is often the basis for an entire poem or prose passage. An extended metaphor suggests that A is like B in ways 1, 2, and 3. An unhappy relationship might be compared to a war because, in both cases, all of the following may be true:

- something important is at stake
- damage is done to both sides

- innocents are harmed
- fear and pride can be barriers to seeking peace

In a soliloquy in *Henry IV, Part 1*, Shakespeare uses an extended metaphor to have young Prince Hal, an apparent rogue, explain his plans to redeem his reputation. He will, like the sun bursting through the clouds, be all the more appreciated. This is a very visual expression of his plans to change people's perceptions of him:

> I know you all, and will awhile uphold
> The unyoked humor of your idleness.
> Yet herein will I imitate the sun,
> Who doth permit the base contagious clouds
> 5   To smother up his beauty from the world,
> That when he please again to be himself,
> Being wanted he may be more wondered at
> By breaking through the foul and ugly mists
> Of vapors that did seem to strangle him.
>
> —*from* Act 1, Scene 2

Simile. If *like* or *as* is used in a comparison, the figure will be a simile. A simile does what a metaphor does, only it makes an even more direct comparison, as in Christina Rosetti's lines "My heart is like a singing bird/Whose nest is in a water'd shoot." Here, the happy qualities associated with a singing bird are connected to the human heart, the traditional source of emotion. The simile's pattern is A (heart) *is like* B (singing bird).

Note the number of similes in the following poem.

Harlem
What happens to a dream deferred?

Does it dry up
like a raisin in the sun?
Or fester like a sore—
5   and then run?
Does it stink like rotten meat?
Or crust and sugar over—
like a syrupy sweet?

Maybe it just sags
10   like a heavy load.

Or does it explode?
—Langston Hughes

Personification. Personification, as we noted in Chapter 1, is a kind of metaphor attributing human characteristics to objects, animals, or natural forces, as in these lines from Shakespeare's *The Merchant of Venice:* "... In such a night as this,/When the sweet wind did gently kiss the trees ... " In personification, there is always an implied comparison between A, a nonhuman thing (the "kissing" wind), and B, a person.

In these lines from a poem called "Since There's No Help," there are four personifications in a deathbed scene:

Now at the last gasp of Love's latest breath,
When, his pulse failing, Passion speechless lies,
When Faith is kneeling by his bed of death,
And Innocence is closing up his eyes,
Now if thou wouldst, when all have given him over,
From death to life thou mightst him yet recover.

—Michael Drayton

Apostrophe. Apostrophe is a figure of speech in which an absent or dead person, an abstraction, or a nonliving object is directly addressed: "O Death, where is thy sting?" The underlying comparison here—between the item addressed and a person—is similar to that in personification. In this example, A (Death) is like B (a person or being capable of hearing).

Analogy. The comparison often known as a literary analogy sets up a relationship between two dissimilar concepts or ideas. You are familiar with verbal analogies that show that A is to B as C is to D: *shoe* is to *foot* as *hat* is to *head*. In literary analogies, one of the ideas in the comparison is frequently used to clarify the other. Analogies sometimes occur in poetry, but they are also common in literary prose. Here is an example from the essay "Of Studies":

Some books are to be tasted, others to be swallowed, and some few to be chewed and digested; that is, some books are to be read only in parts; others to be read but not curiously [thoroughly], and some few to be read wholly, and with diligence and attention.

—Sir Francis Bacon

Allegory. If the metaphor is extended to encompass an entire work, it might be called an *allegory*. As we saw in Chapter 1, an allegory is a work meant to be read on two levels. The fable of the fox and the grapes, for example, is clearly not about a fox or grapes. Neither does the expression "sour grapes" really say anything about grapes. An allegory usually sets up a one-to-one relationship between elements of the vehicle or story and people or ideas those elements represent. One of the most famous of allegories is a play called *Everyman*. It gives a view of the journey that every man (and woman) will take through life, a journey toward death and final judgment. Characters are named not as people but as personifications, each representing a human characteristic or activity. It is not an accident that the character Good Deeds is the only one who will make the final journey with Everyman.

Substitutions and Representations

Some figurative language involves substituting one thing for another: a thing for a related thing or a part of the thing for the whole thing.

Metonymy. Metonymy involves changing a name for something. In this figure, a term closely associated with a person or thing is substituted for it. For example, in these lines from Shakespeare's *Othello*—" ... he that filches from me my good name/Robs me of that which not enriches him ... "—the word *name* is a substitute for "reputation."

Synecdoche. As simile is a special kind of metaphor, synecdoche is a special kind of metonymy that substitutes a part for the whole, the whole for a part, a substance for a thing made of that substance, or a container for what it usually contains. *All hands on deck* is a command meant to produce entire bodies, not just the hands. *A particular fondness for the bottle* is really attraction to the drink inside. An anonymous poem entitled "Green Willow" begins with the line, "The poor soul sits sighing by a sycamore tree." Here, clearly, *soul* stands for the whole person.

Symbol. We might think of a symbol as both vehicle and tenor—it is itself, and it also represents something else, often an abstraction or idea. In William Golding's *Lord of the Flies*, the conch shell is in fact used as a horn to call the boys to assembly and to show who "has the floor," the right to speak. This is overt and agreed-upon representation, making the conch similar to a judge's gavel. At other levels, though, the conch may symbolize to the reader a number of ideas: the attempt to maintain order, authority, the hope (or the hopelessness) of civilization. When the conch is shattered, a change occurs at all of these levels.

Allusion. In literature, there is a way to suggest an array of associations with just a word or two. This powerful and economical means of suggestion is called *allusion*, a reference to a familiar person, event, or place in history, literature, or myth. Many of the novels of John Steinbeck take their titles from lines in other works: *The Grapes of Wrath, Of Mice and Men, The Moon Is Down, The Winter of Our Discontent. Of Mice and Men*, for instance, comes from a line in a Robert Burns poem that says the best-laid plans of mice and men often don't work out. In "Gretel in Darkness," we recognize Gretel from the fairy tale "Hansel and Gretel."

What happens if there is an allusion and you don't get it? Do you miss the point? Some of it, probably. If you understood that reference in the title *Of Mice and Men*, you might read the novel with more doubtful expectations about the plans made by the main characters. If you knew something of the book of Genesis in the Bible, you would have made more of Frost's line "So Eden sank to grief" in "Nothing Gold Can Stay." But don't spend too much time worrying about missing allusions. We all miss some of them because we have different living and reading backgrounds. Even when we "get" them, we have different associations for what we get.

Changes in Degree

Writers wishing to emphasize a point sometimes exaggerate or understate to catch the attention of the reader or listener. Although exaggeration is much more common, understatement is equally effective.

Hyperbole. Hyperbole is exaggeration for emphasis. Like metaphor, hyperbole also creates its own antibodies: when almost everything is exaggerated, the exaggeration becomes normal and no longer creates emphasis. If you compare the advertising or promotional claims for six or seven products of the same kind, almost all of them will include some extreme claim to be best, fastest, sexiest, safest, or some other superlative.

In literature, hyperbole is used to create an effect rather than to sell a product or political candidate. The effect desired is usually a quality of emotion or a state of mind. A poem about a devastating loss can't just say, "Well, you had to *be* there." The writer's job is to use language to *put* you there, and that language may include hyperbole. Notice how this hyperbole from the essay "Imelda" powerfully conveys a sense of heat:

> The heat of the place was incendiary. So hot that, as we stepped from the bus, our own words did not carry through the air, but hung limply at our lips and chins.
>
> —Richard Seltzer

Litotes. Litotes is the name for understatement, deliberately saying less than what you mean. Understatement is often used for a humorous or ironic effect. In this example from "My Last Duchess," the Duke understates his description of the extreme steps he took with the Duchess:

> ...Oh sir, she smiled, no doubt,
> Whene'er I passed her; but who passed without
> Much the same smile? This grew; I gave commands;
> Then all smiles stopped together....
>
> —Robert Browning

Contradictions, Oppositions, Juxtapositions

In logic, a proposition can be true or false but not both. In geometry, an angle is either a right angle or not a right angle. You must have noticed, however, that in your life some things can be both true and false, both right and not right. Writers have noticed these contradictions, too. You can hate the one you love; you can be too early and too late at the same time. You can use *love* to mean "hate," *perfect* to mean "terrible," and so on.

Irony. As we saw in Chapter 1, there are several forms of irony, but all of them are based on duality or "two-ness." Verbal irony may be considered figurative language because one thing is said but another is meant, as when in Shakespeare's *Julius Caesar* Mark Antony continues to insist that "Brutus is an honorable man." How do you know irony when you see or hear it? There are some clues. In speech, a sarcastic tone gives the clue to the ironic use of language, even if you don't know the context. In print, the context helps you to understand the tone or intent.

Paradox. A paradox is a figure that contains two statements or assertions that, according to logic, cannot both be true. Yet the figure links them in a way that creates a new meaning, one that defies logic but works in the situation. A paradox shows it isn't logical to think that everything will be logical. Let's return to death, a favorite poetic topic. John Donne's poem "Death Be Not Proud" closes with these lines: "One short sleep past, we wake eternally / And death shall be no more: Death, thou shalt die!"

Oxymoron. Like paradox, oxymoron takes two opposing concepts and makes them sit next to each other. The resulting tension or contradiction creates new meaning. *Deafening silence, oppressive solitude, empty joy* are examples. The title of Robert Herrick's "Delight in Disorder" is in itself an unusual opposition. A poem entitled "Thou Blind Man's Mark" begins with a name-calling series that includes several contradictions:

> Thou blind man's mark, thou fool's self-chosen snare,
> Fond fancy's scum, and dregs of scattered thought;
> Band of all evil, cradle of causeless care;
> Thou web of will, whose end is never wrought;
> Desire, desire!
>
> —Sir Philip Sidney

You might think of oxymoron as a shorthand form of paradox. Even a word can be oxymoronic. *Sophomore* comes from two words that mean "wise" and "fool." Unless you are a second-year student, you might not know how one can be wise and foolish at the same time.

Why Don't We Just Say What We Mean?

The issue is not that simple. Just as every painting is not an attempt at photographic representation, neither is every writing an attempt to convey a single meaning in the most direct way. Sometimes suggestion or indirection is required or desired. If you look at the language of advertising, you will find that figurative language abounds. List the model names of twenty or thirty car models and you will probably find ten to twenty figurative uses of words. And the words are carefully chosen. You will not find "Sloth," "Frostbite," "Serf," "Toad," or "Slug" as vehicles to sell vehicles.

The language isn't to blame for all this confusion. We are. We have developed language, just as we have developed every other human tool or extension of ourselves, to be what it is. We have even made up rules and then agreed that they can be broken by everybody (except, perhaps, by students in English classes).

FOR YOUR PORTFOLIO NOTEBOOK
Analyzing Figurative Language

Prepare a written analysis of the figurative language in Langston Hughes's "Harlem" (which appears on pages 110–11). Your analysis should consider such things as the meanings of the figures used, their effectiveness, and their impact in conveying the writer's larger meaning.

FOR YOUR PORTFOLIO NOTEBOOK
Working with a Conceit

Part 1. A *conceit* is a kind of extended metaphor in which the comparison is very elaborate or strained and the connection between vehicle and tenor is maintained at some length. Read the following lines from "A Valediction: Forbidding Mourning," in which a conceit is used to express the unity of lovers who are soon to be parted. When you feel that you understand the conceit, discuss or write answers in your "Portfolio Notebook" for the questions that follow the poem:

Our two souls therefore, which are one,
  Though I must go, endure not yet
A breach, but an expansion,
  Like gold to airy thinness beat.

5   If they are two, they are two so
  As stiff twin compasses are two:
Thy soul, the fixed foot, makes no show
  To move, but doth, if the other do;

And though it in the center sit,
10   Yet when the other far doth roam,
It leans, and hearkens after it,
  And grows erect, as that comes home.

Such wilt thou be to me, who must,
  Like the other foot, obliquely run;
15   Thy firmness makes my circle just,
  And makes me end where I begun.

—John Donne

1. Where does the conceit actually begin in these lines? What two elements are involved in the comparison?

2. What are the steps in the action being described, and how do they connect to the elements being compared?

3. How does the image of a circle being drawn further emphasize the idea of unity?

Part 2. Now try writing a conceit of your own. You can start by mapping points of comparison between the actual subject (tenor) and the thing you compare the subject with (vehicle). Organize these points of comparison in a way that makes sense to you, a way that makes a point about the actual subject *through* your comparison with the other thing. Finally, write the conceit in prose or poetic form.

What follows is a list to get you started thinking about possibilities. The actual subjects are possible topics. The comparative subjects, which do *not* correspond to the topics across from them, are actions or processes that could be used to create the conceit. Feel free to make up your own subject or subjects.

Actual Subjects	Comparative Subjects
a human relationship	planting a garden
telling a lie	playing/watching a specific sport
being born	undertaking a quest
the passage of time	using a tool or device
a changing love	having a nightmare
defeating time	tearing down a house
loss of innocence	chopping wood
a new understanding	an archeological dig

Word Meanings and Choices

We have broadly defined figurative language as language used in special ways—words put together in unusual or unexpected patterns to create new meanings. Even more basic than this, however, are the meanings of the words themselves that a writer uses. Sometimes the very language of the work (or the indirection of it) is the real subject.

Denotation. The denotation of a word is what it is supposed to be used to mean. A basic dictionary will give you denotations. You can look up *automobile* and find out what a car is. However, the meaning will refer to cars in general, and there is no such thing as a car in general. Each car is specific. That's the trouble with denotations. They are about general classes of things, but each of us lives in a particular world.

Connotation. Connotations have to do with what words suggest in addition to what they actually mean. A word like *automobile* is fairly straightforward, whereas words like *limousine* and *jalopy* convey completely different pictures and suggest different types of situations. Writers often choose words based on their connotations to create pictures of characters or places or to convey certain types of messages. Consider the following example from the novel *Breathing Lessons:*

Jesse wore tattered jeans and a black T-shirt with the sleeves ripped off, but it wasn't only his clothes that identified him; it was his distinctive style of running. His gait was free and open, as if he were holding nothing in reserve for the next lap. His legs flew out and his arms made long reaching motions, pulling in handfuls of the air in front of him. Every time Maggie located him, her heart would pinch with love.

—Anne Tyler

Words such as *tattered* and *gait* and *flew out* and *pulling* both describe Jesse's motion and convey the spirit of that motion. What connotations do the verb *pinch* in the final sentence suggest?

FOR YOUR PORTFOLIO NOTEBOOK

Analyzing Connotations

Find a print advertisement or an editorial that uses words rich with connotations. Highlight or underline at least five key words, and then write your associations for each word. Finally, write in your "Portfolio Notebook" about the effect you believe the writer intended by using these words.

BEYOND THE WORDS: ARCHETYPES

Although metaphors seem to have a shelf life—they can get stale pretty quickly—other elements of literature do not fade away. There are certain patterns that are found in literature across cultures and through time: they include character types, settings or objects, and even story lines. These recurring patterns, called *archetypes*, are important in literature, myth, and religion because they tend to evoke similar responses from all peoples and cultures. Here are some common archetypes and some explanations of what they may mean:

Archetypal Characters
- the chosen or ordained one
- the elderly guide or helpful companion

- the trickster or evil one or destroyer
- the giver of life

Archetypal Things and Places

- the mountain (often stands for power or a challenge)
- the garden (often stands for innocence, nurturing, growth)
- the river or other body of water (cleansing, rebirth)
- the sun, moon, and stars (order, deity, control)
- fire (purification, destruction)
- wind (transporter, messenger)
- light (intelligence, understanding, goodness)
- darkness (evil, unknown, mystery)

Archetypal Story Lines

- the quest (for example, Lancelot's search for the Holy Grail)
- the temptation or test or initiation (for example, the labors of Hercules)
- the fall from innocence (Adam and Eve's expulsion from the Garden of Eden)
- the sacrifice (the destruction of Hamlet or Oedipus)

Just as responding to an allusion to Waterloo or Malcolm X or Xanadu can call up a host of associations, so can the recognition of an archetypal story line enrich your reading or viewing of a work. You may recognize the quest pattern in, say, *The Great Gatsby* and decide to do an archetypal reading of the novel. However, don't think of archetypes as "answer keys" to understanding literary works. It's not that simple. A common mistake by literature students is to connect a work to an archetype and then try to beat the work into the exact shape of the archetype. If you sacrifice the integrity of the work in order to "make it fit" a preconceived pattern, you haven't done much of an interpretation. If you want to do an archetypal reading, it is more productive to look for correspondences *and* differences between the work and the archetype. Since archetypes are patterns drawn inductively from readings of works from various cultures and times, there may be no one work that fits the pattern at every point.

Not only will works deviate from archetypal patterns. As a reader, you also have to be careful to be aware through what lens you're interpreting a work and then to examine the lens as carefully as you examine the work. When you see what you think is a quest, what exactly does that mean? A typical, traditional (which means male) quest might have the knight out to rescue the obligatory distressed maiden or damsel. Let's say she's being distressed by a powerful dragon who also guards the treasure when he's not busy distressing someone. The quest is successful when the knight kills the dragon, rescues the maiden and the treasure, and presumably enjoys both. In this conventional version of the triangle, the figures would take on these meanings:

maiden = goal

dragon = barrier

knight = hero

A reader approaching the text from a feminist perspective, however, might have a different interpretation of the story even while recognizing its underlying archetypal pattern. So might a reader who's interested in the similarities and differences among various portrayals of dragons.

FOR YOUR PORTFOLIO NOTEBOOK

Initiations

An archetype that is common in many cultures is the initiation, a rite of passage that takes the initiate from ignorance to knowledge, from immaturity to experience, from childhood to adulthood. Read (or review) some of the narratives listed below and make a chart of similarities and differences in their treatment of initiation.

- "Araby" by James Joyce
- The Grave" by Katherine Anne Porter
- *Their Eyes Were Watching God* by Zora Neale Hurston
- "Seventeen Soldiers" by Hisaye Yamamoto
- "The Man Who Was Almost a Man" by Richard Wright
- "The Rime of the Ancient Mariner" by Samuel Taylor Coleridge

- "Through the Tunnel" by Doris Lessing
- "The Banana Tree" by James Berry
- "The Medicine Bag" by Virginia Driving Hawk Sneve
- "Children of Loneliness" by Anzia Yezierska

LITERARY MAPS THROUGH THE WORDS

Think of a literary work as an unfamiliar map. How do you know what you're looking at? What do these marks on paper represent? You have to fill in many gaps to answer these questions. Suppose a story opens with a description of a young boy walking through a garden. In the garden is a snake. Is the boy a quest hero? Is the snake an archetype or just an animal? Let's look at some levels of abstraction. The chart below shows some ways to think about the snake, a relative of the serpent or dragon. The bottom level is least abstract—just the word and its synonyms. The top level is most abstract—just concepts with no description. Between are other levels of reaction, classification, association, and symbolic use. Perhaps these levels do not make a neat hierarchy, but they do show some different ways of thinking about the snake.

Archetypal Projections:	power, evil, knowledge, unity, temptation
Symbolic Uses:	Garden of Eden, snake goddess, the devil, the eternal circle, Saint George's dragon
Associative Qualities:	hypnotism, death, evil, unknown, poison, deceit, knowledge, power, sexuality
Emotional Reactions/ Connotations:	fear, fascination, revulsion
Image/Physical Features:	long, thin, silent, slithers
Labels/Classifications/ Denotations:	snake, serpent, reptile

So what is the snake? That depends on the rest of the story and on the reader. The snake may be just a living detail of the landscape, or it may be a key feature of the story. The garden may be Eden or just a garden.

And the boy? He may be Adam about to run into Eve, or he may be a boy out for a walk.

There is a story about a discovery of life on the moon. Through his telescope, an excited scientist spotted tiny figures moving across the moon's surface. The figures turned out to be ants in the telescope. The analogy should be clear: As a reader, you have to know what you're looking at as well as what you're looking for. Some guides to works of literature can make it seem as if reading is pretty much a symbol hunt. If you had a key or decoder ring for literary symbols, you could quickly find the meaning in a work. Not so fast. Take *white*, for example. The color is used to represent innocence and purity—except when it is used to represent sterility and lifelessness. And *water*— doesn't that suggest life and cleansing and baptism? Perhaps not when your storm-tossed ship founders and you drown. And is that dog that guards the Gates of Hell "man's best friend"?

There's a common expression that sometimes you "can't see the forest for the trees." Remember that contexts are important determiners on the road to meaning. Always consider any one element in the context of the whole work.

FOR YOUR PORTFOLIO NOTEBOOK
Your Own Ladder of Abstraction

Try your hand at making one of the ladders of abstraction shown above. Copy the categories we have used for the snake, and write in your thoughts at each level about one of these objects: mirror, tree, journey, river, darkness, ladder, circle. Or choose a similar object of your own.

TERMS FOR WRITING ABOUT LITERATURE

Besides being able to understand the language you see used in literature, you also need to be able to use the language *of* literature—that is, the terms commonly employed by people who are critiquing literary works. The chart that follows shows some common literary terms, as well as a few that you might not be as familiar with, organized by the categories of Burke's pentad. This is not the only way to group these terms, and some terms could be placed in more than one category. Again we say there is no one way to look at literature, and so there is no one single way to organize words related to literature. The organization of the chart might be useful because it allows you to think of terms in areas of inquiry, rather than, say, in alphabetical order:

Agent: Who Did It?

speaker	narrator	voice	implied author
persona	narrative mask	point of view	attitude
audience	tone	register	distance
characters	flat character	round character	stereotype
stock character	protagonist	hero *or* heroine	antihero
quest hero	initiation hero	tragic hero	scapegoat

Act: What Was Done?

genre	poetry	drama	fiction
nonfiction	structure	form	lyric
narrative	stanza	plot	exposition
climax	resolution	complications	conflict
subplot	antecedent action	consequent action	counterplot
topic	subject	rising action	falling action
technical climax	dramatic climax		

Scene: When and Where Was It Done?

setting	time setting	space setting	integral setting
description	atmosphere	mood	dramatic situation
physical context	microcosm		

Agency: How Was It Done?

diction	style	conventions	narrative technique

transition	syntax	rhythm	meter
rhyme	sound devices	alliteration	assonance
onomatopoeia	flashback	foreshadowing	suspense
dialogue	soliloquy	aside	microcosm
imagery	metaphor	extended metaphor	simile
analogy	apostrophe	personification	metonymy
synecdoche	symbol	hyperbole	litotes
verbal irony	paradox	oxymoron	connotation
denotation	conceit	archetype	selection and presentation of detail

Purpose: Why Was It Done?

to achieve author's purpose

to develop the themes of the work

to create an effect on the reader

This list is by no means a complete one. Literary handbooks and encyclopedias list thousands of terms associated with literature. We have tried to choose the terms most central to understanding and discussion.

Why do you need to know these terms? *Do* you need to know them? Well, yes, you do need to be able to use some of them when you write or speak formally about literature. One mark of good readers is that they can talk about their work and use appropriate terms. You wouldn't have much confidence in an auto mechanic whose diagnosis of your car trouble was that "the thingie on the whaddya-callit is busted." And just as you'd expect your doctor to know more about anatomy than that the "knee bone's connected to the leg bone," your portfolio readers will expect you to know more about literature than, "I liked it; it had good stuff in it."

But a warning too: attempting to blind your reader in a blizzard of literary terms will be seen for the snow job that it is. Knowledge of terms is only a start. Insightful use of them to explain literature and your abilities with literature is more the point.

Now we go on to explanations and examples.

Agent: Who Did It?

Even in a work that has no identified characters, there is always a presence. Someone must be speaking the words, telling the story. The *speaker* or *narrator* in a poem or story is as important in its own way as characters like Odysseus or Huck Finn. The speaker or narrator speaks directly to the audience, and, except in drama, usually has the most lines. What about your science and history books? Are there speakers in those books? There are, but such textbooks are often written by many people and edited by many others, so a distinctive *voice* may not come through. It may be difficult to picture the person behind the words. (The picture would probably have to be a group photo of writers and editors.) Other works of nonfiction such as essays and articles can have a definite and distinctive voice. You get a sense of who is talking.

This narrative presence, the person you imagine behind the words, is called the *implied author.* If you have read several works by Tim O'Brien or Alice Walker, you can come to feel you know that author. Of course, you really don't. You know that the author is not the *persona* or *narrative mask* whose particular personality colors the telling of the story. You know that the author has chosen a deliberate *point of view*—first person ("I"), second person ("you"), or third person ("he" or "she" or "they," privy to the thoughts of one or all characters)—from which to tell the story.

The voice of the speaker or narrator also conveys an *attitude* to the *audience.* This attitude is partly a function of *tone,* or the feelings expressed toward the subject, and partly one of *register*, the level of formality of the language. The voice can be confidential and informal or abrupt and very formal. The voice helps to determine the *distance* or degree of involvement between speaker and audience and between speaker and subject. An audience can be ignored or invited into the narrator's secrets, and a subject can be celebrated or trashed, depending on the author's purpose.

Most works you read include *characters.* You find out about characters through what they say and do, through others' responses to them, and through direct description. Like narrators, characters come in a variety of shapes and sizes. A *flat character,* one not fully developed, may be needed for some action but not be central to the story. In *Julius Caesar,* we need Decius to lure Caesar to his death at the Senate, but we do not find out why Decius wants to do this. A *round character* will be more fully developed, and we will come to know motivations and other elements of personality. Cassius and Brutus tell us their thoughts and reasons for decisions.

There are some *stereotypes* that we encounter often in literature. If you know stereotypes, you can fill in the blanks with recognizable types:

the poor but honest _____

the dizzy or (ditzy) _____

the evil _____

the smooth-talking _____

the _____ with a heart of gold

Stock characters are both similar to and different from stereotypes. Although stock characters are recognizable and predictable, they tend to show up in specialized genres. The witty servant, the bragging fool, and the absent-minded professor belong mostly to comedy. The evil fairy belongs to fairy tales, the sly trickster to myths and fables.

Some characters are more important than others. The *protagonist* is the main character, the *hero* who is involved in and resolves (or is resolved by) the conflict. The word *hero* means "main character," not necessarily "good guy" or even "guy." An *antihero* is a main character who is not especially brave or honest or wise but still gets the most attention in the work. The more modern the work, the less likely is the hero to have all the traditional heroic virtues.

There are some familiar types of traditional heroes. The *quest hero* is at the center of a dangerous adventure to save the city or country or planet. An *initiation hero* undergoes some arduous trial to join the ranks of adulthood or some other elite group. A *sacrificial hero* is so named because the salvation of a group requires the sacrifice of this character. The *tragic hero* is a figure who, partly by fault, partly by circumstance, must die to expunge the evil from the community. The *scapegoat* generally must die also. Before death, the sins of the community are heaped upon the scapegoat, who may not have asked for such an honor.

Then there are other characters. An *antagonist* is the main character's chief opposition. Lex Luthor, for example, is Superman's antagonist in many episodes. A character used as a *foil* is used in comparison and contrast to better develop the main character.

Act: What Was Done?

The first "what" to consider is *genre*. What type of work are we dealing with? One way to classify by genre is to divide by four: *poetry, drama, fiction,* and *nonfiction*. Each has its own *form* or *structure*.

Poetry has dozens of forms, but can generally be classified into two broad types: *narrative* and *lyric*. The flow of ideas is often from problem or tension to solution or resolution. Forms are usually based on *stanza* structure (for example, quatrain, sonnet) and line structure (iambic pentameter, alexandrine).

Fiction (novels and short stories, for the most part) has a similar flow from problem to solution, but fiction's *plot*, or sequence of events, is usually developed by stages:

exposition: opening of story, introduction of setting and characters

conflict: the internal or external problem or tension

climax: turning point at which outcome of the conflict is determined

resolution: tying up of loose ends and closing of story

Longer works usually include *complications* (more players or more twists and turns), a *subplot* (a smaller story spun off from the main story), or a *counterplot* (a secondary plot that contrasts the main plot's action). These help to keep plots realistically complex. Although not strictly part of the plot, the *antecedent action* of a story is the events the reader can conclude must have happened before the story opens. We might use a name such as *consequent action* to refer to the events the reader imagines would happen after the close of a story. Even at "The End," not everything ends.

In nonfiction, the "what" is often called the *subject* or *topic* of the work. Main ideas and details in nonfiction are generally developed with opinions, reasons, proofs, cases, illustrations, examples, reports, facts, observations, and the like. Biographies, articles, essays, and letters are common forms of nonfiction. Most textbooks are nonfiction.

Drama's *rising action* leads up to the *technical climax*, the turning point or point which determines the outcome, perhaps inevitably. The *falling action* takes place from the climax to the end of the play. Through the play, there may be several *dramatic climaxes*, high points of suspense and energy.

Scene: When and Where Was It Done?

Everything happens somewhere, even if the somewhere isn't very well defined. That somewhere is the *setting*. The *time setting* can be as general as the twentieth century or as specific as two minutes before midnight on July 3, 1776. The *space setting* is equally important. It can be as general as "on Earth" or as specific as in an attic over a shop on a certain street in Amsterdam.

The setting is a key feature in some works. In *Lord of the Flies*, the island might be called an *integral setting*—that is, the story could only take place here. In other works, the setting is sketchy, providing only a vague background for the action. The amount of *description* of the setting is a clue to its relative importance to the work. The setting of *Lord of the Flies* is also a *microcosm*, a small world that localizes the action but can also be compared with the larger world outside the work.

A setting helps to create the *atmosphere* or emotional background of the work. The atmosphere or *mood* can be light and funny in a romantic comedy but black and foreboding in a Gothic novel. "It was a dark and stormy night" has become a joke about a cliched setting.

In poetry, elements of the setting are involved in the *dramatic situation*—who is talking to whom in what *physical situation* or context. In Matthew Arnold's "Dover Beach," the listener is invited to come to the window and look out. In many of Shakespeare's sonnets, the speaker appears to be addressing someone, but we are not sure who it is or where it is happening.

Agency: How Was It Done?

One aspect of this category is the language or figurative language used, which we have discussed in detail earlier in this chapter. Another important but not so obvious factor is the *selection and presentation of detail*. What does the writer decide to tell us? In what order? In what way? *Diction*, or word choice, is an important feature of the "how" of literature. In "Mirror," if you substitute *horrible monster* or *scary creature* for *terrible fish*, you change the poem's effect.

Diction involves *imagery*, words chosen to evoke in the reader mental pictures, sounds, and other sensory responses. Often imagery is intermixed with metaphor and other figurative constructions. In poetry in particular, various *sound devices*, such as *alliteration* (repetition of initial consonant sounds), *assonance* (repetition of vowel sounds, as in Poe's line "While in the wild wood I did lie"), and *onomatopoeia* can create certain effects within text, as do the writer's choice to use *rhyme* and a regular *rhythm* or *meter*.

Other aspects of the writer's *style* include choices about the *conventions* of language, the usual and accepted ways of doing things. It is conventional in fiction, let's say, to write in sentences and paragraphs. Yet some writers have produced works consisting of chunks of one or two sentences. Others have written "sentences" that are two- or three-page rambles. Still others have challenged conventions of *syntax*, or rules for basic word order and grammatical structure. *Narrative techniques* have become less conventional also. Modern writings may shift point of view with no *transition* or announcement to that effect.

A basic story line may be enhanced by such features as *flashback*, returning to reveal an earlier event, and *foreshadowing*, suggesting what is to come later, usually with the purpose of creating *suspense*. It is possible to "flashforward" also, but this can turn out to be awkward and contrived.

Drama, like most fiction, relies on *dialogue*, words spoken by characters. Other conventions of drama include the *soliloquy*, in which a character alone on the stage reveals thoughts to the audience, and the *aside*, in which a character on the stage makes a confidential remark that the other characters pretend not to hear.

Purpose: Why Was It Done?

There are three traditional answers to this question, all of them implied by the triangle of writer, work, and audience you saw in Chapter 2: to achieve the author's purpose, to develop the themes or ideas or meanings of the work, and to create an effect on the reader(s).

Do these three answers cover everything? Hardly. They are really aspects of a rhetorical approach to literature, an approach that has governed most literature instruction for decades, if not centuries. The answers suggest this analogy: The writer, with some intent, puts a message (the meaning) in a bottle of a certain shape and size (the work) and floats it out to an interested party (the reader). If the reader finds and opens the bottle, the meaning is clear, and an effect on the reader has been achieved.

Reader-response theorists and deconstruction theorists would beg to differ with this neat little picture. They do not see meaning as a football thrown by a writer and caught by a reader. The whole issue of gaps filled by an active reader (see Chapter 1) suggests that readers decide on meanings and that theme is somewhere out there in space between the reader and the work. The literature bumper sticker might read *Meaning Happens*. Perhaps the most interesting aspect about literature nowadays is the number of ways even to think about what literature is. If earlier arguments among critics concerned which are the right answers, more recent arguments are about which are the right questions.

In Chapter 1, you saw some ideas about the nature and purposes of literature. We can't tell you what to think, only what some have thought.

FOR YOUR PORTFOLIO NOTEBOOK

Using the Pentad for Interpretation

Use one of the five areas of the pentad to write claims about one of the literary works included in this book (or one of your own choosing). Remember that a claim should include data, a reference to the text, or other evidence. If the warrant is obvious, you do not need to state it. Use as many sentences as you need to complete the claim and try to relate your point about the term to a point about the whole work. Here is an example of a claim about "Two Dollar Mommy" built around the term *tone* from the Agent or "Who Did It?" area:

> There are three speakers in "Two Dollar Mommy": the husband, the wife, and the narrator, who clearly sides with the wife. The narrator's tone makes it clear that Two Dollar Daddy's suspicions are unfounded.

TECHNIQUES FOR WRITING ABOUT LITERATURE

In Chapter 3, you learned about creating claims and warrants and about some of the perspectives you can use in analyzing. In this chapter, you have learned about, or reviewed, literary terms and terminology. Let us see how some of this information can be brought to bear when you are asked to put what you know into writing. We will focus here on specific writing assignments, or essay questions, posed to you by instructors. These assignments, if they suit your larger purposes, can easily become elements of your portfolio. Further, when you have an assignment to write on something of your own choosing, you will have an approach to follow. If you determine early in the process not only the topic but also the critical perspective(s) you will use, your paper of analysis or interpretation will come more smoothly and efficiently than if you just start reading and writing with no plan.

Reviewing a Work

Imagine that your class has finished reading Jean Rhys's *Wide Sargasso Sea*, and now an instructor has an assignment for you involving one or more interpretive questions about the work. The assignment is either given to you in advance or sprung upon you as an in-class writing assignment. In either case, how do you get ready?

The best way to prepare is by anticipating the areas of questions and doing your thinking ahead of time. Making a study guide of the work as you read it (see Chapter 2) will cause you to pay attention to important elements of the work—the elements from which questions are usually taken—and will give you brief notes from which to study. Questions on two or more works are likely to ask for comparisons, so preparing study guides for the works will allow you to make your own comparisons ahead of time.

The pentad is another helpful device. Most essay questions are going to ask you to relate one of the other four pentad categories to the "Why?" category. In the ancient world, all roads led to Rome. In the literary test world, most roads still lead to *theme*. So you can expect to find questions with terms like *the author's purpose*, or *the themes of the work*, or *the effect on the reader*. Even if no one of these is directly stated or asked for in the question, you should probably travel one of these roads anyway. *Meaning* is pretty much what literature questions are about, whether they ask you to guess the "right" meaning or to develop your own views. Whatever the question, you are unlikely to go wrong by relating your answer to a view of the whole work.

Writing about Theory and Criticism

An assignment frequently posed by instructors is to define or illustrate a formalist—or deconstructionist or feminist—approach to what you are studying. One way to get at this sort of knowledge is to use these questions as a guide for determining how critics from the particular school in question view a work:

- *What is the question they ask when they read and discuss a literary work?* Some critics ask questions that are subjective, that is, about themselves as they read the book. Others tend to be more objective and seek to describe the book as if it were a bug or a landscape outside of themselves. The questions might include, "What is it? What does it mean? Is it any good? What is it like? What category can I put it in?"

- *What do they focus on when they look at a piece of literature?* Some focus on the work in isolation from its background and history; others focus on the circumstances surrounding the book. Some focus more on what the book is about; others more on how the book is written. Within these broad sets of focus, there may be particular details that one group of critics will concentrate on.

- *What are their beliefs or attitudes?* Some critics are quite explicit about their beliefs as to what makes a good book or piece of literature. Some are also explicit about their beliefs about society or the human character or religion or some other set of ideas.

Once you have identified characteristics of a particular critical approach, you can go ahead and discuss the piece of literature from that viewpoint.

Some Responses: The Bad and the Good

There are some well-tried ways to write *bad* responses to essay questions. We will consider two of them in terms of claim, warrant, and data. Let's say the question is this: "Show how the supernatural elements in Macbeth contribute to the meanings of the play."

Bad Answer Number One is a lengthy discussion of themes and meanings that hovers in the fog and philosophical air but never gets at anything specific in the play. This answer is all claim and no data or warrant. Bad Answer Number Two is all data: quotes from the play, references to the witches, Banquo's ghost, the dagger, the apparitions, even the recipe for the witches' brew—everything but a claim about the contribution of all this to the meanings of the play. The quote fest is no better than the claim fest.

Of course there are other ways to compose bad answers. You might ignore the question entirely and write about some other, more interesting topic. You might be unable even to figure out what the question is asking you to do. You might paraphrase the entire work. You might write an interpretation log, dragging the reader through every agonizing step of your reading and thinking. You might go through a poem, for example, and tell what every line means or does and never talk about the whole work. You might sprinkle claims about like confetti with no attempt to connect them, leaving the reader to clean the sidewalk. And, of course, you might wander off into an exposition about psychology, philosophy, mythology, cultural history, biography, or something else.

A good answer, by contrast, has a balance of the three features:

claims: interpretive statements from you

data: quotes or specific references to the work in question

warrants: justifications for connecting the claims to the data.

Try to keep this balance by planning before writing and then keeping track while writing. Making a brief outline before you write will help you to establish important claims and data before you start making sentences. Five minutes of outlining can save you fifteen minutes of wandering while you're developing your answer.

You can generally establish the warrant for your whole paper by using a perspective on literature that is recognized by the reader/evaluator and is appropriate to the task at hand. Since the question about *Macbeth* is pretty much a formalist question (relate one element to the whole work), use the formalist perspective to develop your answer. If the question is a historical-cultural one (for example, "Show how the conditions of society at the time contributed to, and then were affected by, the publication of *Uncle Tom's Cabin*"), the formalist view is still legitimate, but not as useful or appropriate for this task. Use a historical-cultural approach instead.

Another element of your study plan should be to familiarize yourself with the guides to perspectives in Chapter 3 and relate those to the kind of response required. If your class has spent much of its discussion time on the social context of a work (*The Jungle*, let's say), then be ready to use the guide that focuses on connections. If your course of study of *Beloved* has centered on the writer's views, then be ready for a question from that perspective.

An Essay Response Plan

The most important reading you do with an essay assignment is the reading of the question or task. If you don't answer the question, it probably won't matter how well you do whatever else you do. The more complicated the question, the easier it is to misread it and miss the point, or at least some of it. So your first problem is to define the task. Let's use a typical essay question that could be applied to virtually any prose selection: "Show how the passage's diction, tone, and organization shape the reader's responses to the action and the central characters." We will get ready to answer this with a four-step plan:

1. **COUNT:** How many elements must you write about?
   Sample response: Five elements: diction, tone, organization, reader's responses to action, and reader's responses to characters.

2. **RELATE:** How are the elements related? Try using one of these to see the connections between and among parts:

   ... through the use of ...
   ... for the purpose of ...
   ... affects the reader by ...
   ... develops meanings by ...

   Also determine what is the main claim of the paper, the most important issue or issues to write about.
   Sample response: Reader's responses to action and character are shaped by the other three, so reader's responses are the key issues.

3. **FRAME:** Frame your response by expressing the main claim of your answer in a sentence or two. This will be your working thesis to guide you through the task. It will also establish the perspective from which you should interpret the work.
   Sample response: Although readers may be shocked by the violence of the action in this passage, they must admire
   _____ (give characters' names) for their refusal to meet violence with more violence.

4. **OUTLINE:** Jot down the supporting claims and data you might use to develop your answer. Finish with at least a tentative conclusion you might make about author's purpose, development of meanings, or effect on the reader—whichever is most appropriate for the question.

Sample response:

Main claim: Although readers may be shocked by the violence of the action in this passage, they must admire _____ (give characters' names) for their refusal to meet violence with more violence.

Claim about diction: contrast between words (examples from text) describing assailants and words (examples from text) describing central characters.

Claim about tone: narrator's tone is approving and sympathetic toward central characters (example from text)

Claim about organization: first three paragraphs are short and violent; last paragraph is longer and more thoughtful

Conclusion: Build on the ideas you have established and return to the shaping of the reader's responses.

After some practice, this process takes only five to ten minutes. Even if you have time for only one draft of your writing, you will have time for *two drafts of your thinking.* You might even make the conclusion to your outline the introduction to your answer. You will need to write your way to a complete answer to the question, but at least your outline will give you a map to follow.

This outlining technique also allows you to craft your first sentence carefully. Since you know where you're going with the paper, you won't need to write two paragraphs of general stuff to get warmed up and home in on the question. The first paragraph of your answer is important, so get off to a good start. A sentence that combines a text reference (data) to a claim shows an evaluator that you know what you're doing.

As you are writing, keep checking for claims, data, and warrants. A good answer to a writing assignment has a balance of the three features. If you have quoted two sentences or lines, *stop!* You're probably headed for plot summary or a collage of quotes with no claims. If you have written two paragraphs with no data, go back and make some connection between your claims and the text you're supposed to be writing about.

Pay just as much attention to the final sentences. An especially strong or weak ending leaves a final impression on your reader. One way to end strongly is by connecting the "So what?" of the work and topic to something else:

- other works by the same author
- other works with comparable subject, narrators, characters, settings, symbolism, and so on
- other works in the same form or genre
- other works in the time period or for the same audience
- other related issues or works from the same critical perspective

FOR YOUR PORTFOLIO NOTEBOOK

Write Using an Essay Response Plan

Read "The Man by the Fountain." Then make an essay response plan as you prepare to complete one of the following assignments:

- Write an essay in which you compare the different images related to the fountain and their effect upon your understanding of the story. Your essay will be judged on the quality of your answer to the question as well as on its organization, style, and use of language.
- Write an essay in which you show the techniques the author uses to develop the characters' changing perceptions of each other and themselves.

The Man by the Fountain

As always, John Deweck sat by the fountain.

The spring sun loomed up out of the seething foam. The children honoured the memories of heroic admirals. Their galleons and cutters tacked to and fro across the wide pond. Nursemaids and grandmothers glanced anxiously at frocks and trousers. Over the wide world the fountain sang, thrusting a quivering plume of water at the scudding clouds. Liquid pattered noisily into bowls of marble.

John Deweck sat on his usual bench, speaking to no one. There were a few rules he stubbornly clung to. People spoke so much ill of each other. He no longer listened to their chatter. He had eyes now only for students and soldiers, for young girls and children. Young people fascinated his old carcass. He knew a great deal and had forgotten even more. He craved for youth and approached death's kingdom with reluctant steps.

One by one the frequenters of the fountain left the park. It was time for lunch. John smiled without quite knowing why. Now that he was alone, it seemed to him that he was the head park keeper. It was Thursday. The day on which his wife always used to serve him veal-steak with a delicious sour sauce and potatoes as round as marbles. She had been able to work miracles with a potato. Since her death he had fallen into irregular eating habits. Three slices of bread and jam in the morning. At midday, often not even a bite. Round about five, some lumpy porridge with rusks and some fruit. Usually a sour apple. Sour apples, he believed kept the mental juices clean and preserved understanding.

He sat now alone with the violence of the fountain.

Perhaps some little boy would turn up? He longed for a serious conversation. Eyes that were still keen swept the avenue that led to the outskirts of the town. Far off in the distance, as in a dream, the little boy came into view. The youngster came tearing up to him, flopped down on the bench and gazed spellbound at the rippling surface of the pond and at the dragons letting the water flow over their green breasts.

"Hello, young man," said John Deweck solemnly.

The child stared at him but said nothing.

"Isn't it your dinner-time?"

"I'm not hungry." said the boy. "I eat once a day. Raw buffalo-meat, as I roam the prairie on my bronco."

"Well, now," said John Deweck, "Well now. . . who might you be then?"

The boy looked up at him full of pride.

"I am the last of the Mohicans. I lost my friend—the paleface. He was caught in an ambush. But I scented danger. Now I wander alone through the wood and valley. . . ."

"Where are your feathers?" asked old John sternly.

The child gazed at him with lively interest. Tiny flames flickered in the golden eyes. He flushed with excitement.

"I don't wear feathers in enemy country," he said in a whisper. "But still, I'm on the warpath. I've no war paint on but I've dug up the hatchet. I am the last of my tribe. Are you my friend or foe?"

"What a thing to ask! My name is John. I have always been the foe of the buffaloes and the friend of the Indians. I made a blood-pact with Winnetou. Now I am too old for the hunt. Against whom have you dug up the hatchet?"

"Against the tribe of grown-ups," answered the boy. "They threaten my hunting grounds and my freedom. They don't understand a thing. How can an Indian live in stuffy school-buildings?"

"Of course he can't," said John. "Though a paleface myself, I'm all for freedom, too. But still, I think school is necessary . . ."

The youngster threw him a piercing look.

"Perhaps you're a spy," he said thoughtfully. "The enemy is cunning."

John Deweck gave a high-pitched laugh.

"Nonsense. Take a look around. We're quite alone here. No, I'm not a member of the tribe of grown-ups."

"How strange. So old, yet still a good Indian."

The old man gave a loud sniff. He held his hand out to the young brave.

"Peace," he said, "and many scalps."

"I'll tell you my adventure," said the boy, "provided you can keep a secret."

"Even if I was bound to the torture-post I wouldn't breathe a word."

"This morning I had to hunt for buffalo. As you know, the time has come. Besides, I'm looking for a squaw for my new wigwam. I was creeping out of the kitchen when Dad caught me by the hair. He walloped me for not being ready for school. I didn't make a sound. Only cunning could save me. Meekly I let myself be led to Hook Nose."

"Who is Hook Nose?"

"The school chief," replied the boy. "He's not strong but he's terribly cunning. He laughed like a wild horse and spoke of giving me lines. At ten o'clock, during break, I sneaked out at the gate. I ran as fast as I could. . . I don't want to go home again. My homeland is the prairie. Tonight I'm looking for a boat and tomorrow I'll be sailing across the seas."

John Deweck looked at the fountain. Impetuously as life itself it leapt up towards the light of the boundless sky. Cherubs spattered with water, blew on their conches as if to warn of impending danger.

A wrinkle creased the aged forehead.

"It's not going to be an easy plan," sighed John Deweck.

"I *must* get a boat," said the boy stubbornly. "You have got to help me."

Heavy clouds drifted towards the spring sun. The birds were silent in the pruned trees.

"First come and eat in my wigwam," faltered John Deweck.

"I'm not hungry."

"You can't refuse bread and salt . . ."

The boy thought this over.

"Your mouth speaks the truth," he said. "I must set out on my long journey free from hunger. But I shan't eat meat."

"Bread and salt, O warrior . . ."

The boy trotted at the old man's side, looking neither left nor right. He thought of the wild scents of the prairie. He had met an old buffalo-hunter who gave him invaluable tips.

They stepped into the police station. The door closed behind them with a bang. The boy looked about him and understood.

He sat down on a bench and freely volunteered information to a fat man with a ruddy complexion. His head sank on his chest. He did not even glance at John Deweck.

The car arrived shortly afterwards. The father stepped out and thanked the old man. The boy took his place in the car. Suddenly, he turned to the buffalo-hunter.

"You belong to the tribe of grown-ups," he said. "You have betrayed my confidence. I will pay for it at the torture post. I despise you."

He spat on the ground.

"What did he say?" asked the father.
"That you ought to make him happy," said John Deweck.
Father and son vanished in a cloud of dust.
"The youth of today," grunted the inspector.
Slowly the old man paced through the streets of the little town.
He was never seen again at the fountain.

—George Hebbelinck
(Translated by
Gilbert de
Landsheere)

BUILDING YOUR PORTFOLIO

As in Chapter 3, the activities in this section can be done with almost any work you want or have to read. If your instructor does not make a specific assignment, select the activities that will help you to meet your goals, and then match each activity with a literary work.

1. Review the section on figurative language and explore a new poem by noting the figurative language and discussing its effect on the reader. You may use "Mirror" or "Gretel in Darkness" or a poem of your own choosing.

2. Write your own significant figures. Write a poem, an article, or a short piece of fiction and try to include seven figures of speech in your writing. Be careful not to end up with a shopping list. The figures should be integrated and related to the purpose of the writing.

3. Fulfill any or all of these assignments by using the essay response plan:

   In literature, we meet individuals who have strengths of character. In changing contexts, however, strengths can become weaknesses. Choose a work of literature in which this turnabout takes place. Identify the individual and the strength of character. Show how, because of a change in contexts or circumstances, that strength turned into a weakness and comment on the significance of this reversal to the audience's response to the work.

Show how the author's use of diction, imagery, and figurative language develops the meanings of the poem. (Try this with "Mirror" or "Gretel in Darkness.")

In some works, the setting is little more than a place for the action to happen. In others, the setting is an integral part of the work—perhaps the action could not or would not happen somewhere else. Choose such a work and explain the importance of the setting both to the events of the work and to the accomplishment of the author's purpose.

4. Invent a character and embroil him or her in a conflict of great significance to the community. Then plot out three ways for the story to be resolved:

   - as a quest story
   - as an initiation story
   - as a scapegoat or sacrificial hero story

As an alternative, read or view *One Flew Over the Cuckoo's Nest*. Decide which story archetype best fits what you read or see. Write a summary of the story in terms of that archetype.

5. Read the prologue of Joseph Campbell's *The Hero with a Thousand Faces* and write a more detailed example of the monomyth he describes in "The Hero and the God" section. You will be adding detail to these three stages:

   - the separation or departure
   - trials and victories of initiation
   - return and reintegration with society

Find a book or movie whose story line parallels, at least partly, the pattern and write an archetypal interpretation of the work. Or make up your own story line with characters for a book or movie based on the pattern. Plot out the specific events of the story to parallel Campbell's outline.

6. Do a rough analysis of a work of your choice using the framework of the pentad. Use the appropriate terms from each section to comment on the text. When you have finished applying terms, decide which area or areas of the pentad make the best point of entry to the work and prepare an interpretation focusing on that area or areas.

7. Go into business for yourself and write *Your Notes* for a literary work of your choice. These guides typically include historical-biographical background, a plot summary, character analysis, interpretations, and essay or discussion questions and suggested answers. You could do this "straight," using literary terms and uncovering archetypes sparingly but appropriately, but it might be more fun to do a takeoff or parody on the form.

READER'S FORUM

Your instructor may assign you a topic to present at "Reader's Forum," or you may choose one yourself from the chapter activities.

PORTFOLIO PROGRESS REPORT

Here are the same three questions you used for the previous "Progress Report":

1. **Knowledge:** What *do you know* that you didn't know before?
2. **Practice:** What *can you do* that you couldn't do (or do as well) before?
3. **Habits:** What *do you do* that you didn't do (or do as much) before?

For this "Progress Report," review your work with the activities below and then write at least a few paragraphs in your "Portfolio Notebook" to answer each of the three questions:

- your analysis of the figurative language in "Harlem" and "A Valediction: Forbidding Mourning"
- writing a conceit

- your work with analyzing connotations
- your analysis of the initiation archetype in one or more works
- your ladder of abstraction
- your interpretation of a literary work organized by the pentad
- your essay response plan and actual response to "The Man by the Fountain"
- "Building Your Portfolio" activities

MOVING ON

Chapter 4 was about solo performances, but Chapter 5 asks you to join the orchestra and perform in a group. There are more than one hundred parts available.

5 Dress Rehearsal: A Portfolio of Portfolios

▶▶▶LOOKING AHEAD

This chapter has two important features that make it different from most other chapters. First, all activities in the chapter are geared toward group presentation within your class, and you will have to make decisions about what to prepare and then how to present your work. There are several portfolio projects and more than one hundred activities for you to choose from: the round table, the canon and the coffee shop, the hypertext, and more.

Second, the "Portfolio Progress Report" for this chapter will be a cumulative summary of how you have grown so far in the way of knowledge, practice, and habits. You will do a self-assessment, much like the one you did in Chapter 2, and have a chance to take stock of your work and redefine your goals. Both group presentations and self-assessment have been options in every chapter, but here they make up the entire chapter. Your work here can serve as a dress rehearsal for your final portfolio performance.

BUILDING YOUR PORTFOLIO

Do you remember connecting the dots to make a chipmunk or a boat or a house? Connecting the dots is like painting by numbers—someone else has decided what the finished product should look like, and your part in completing the project involves following directions, not making decisions.

Creating a portfolio is different. To begin with, you have to select the dots. Then you have to arrange them. Then you have to decide how many to connect and in what ways—all this as a literature student. Later, when you're no longer taking courses, you will have even more decisions to make. As an independent reader, you will have to decide if there will even be dots: Will you read at all?

We mean this chapter to serve as a stepping stone to your presentation portfolio. You will have an individual part in a group performance, and your part will affect the whole. At the end of the road, when you present your portfolio, you will be the one that performs all of the parts.

Here is an overview of the options for group portfolio presentations. Any or all of them could be worth videotaping for review and assessment:

- an array of activities for "Law Like Love"
- a round table of critical perspectives on "The Yellow Wallpaper" or *Their Eyes Were Watching God*
- an array of activities related to *Macbeth*
- a role play by characters or authors of various times and cultures
- a list of generic activities to do with any poem
- a pairing: *The Things They Carried* and *Song of Solomon*
- a hypertext on *Mansfield Park*
- an option to consider the above projects to be a menu of choices and to connect the dots your own way to create another class portfolio project.

"Law Like Love"

In this option, the first few activities will be more or less dictated to you; then you will branch out on your own. You will be dealing with a poem called "Law Like Love." Begin by writing your reactions to the title:

- Write about each word separately. What do you associate with each? What does each make you think of?
- Write about the words taken together. What is the effect of the combination? Which word do you think will be most important? Why?
- Write about your expectations for poetry. What do you expect to find *because this is a poem?*

Now do your first reading of the poem. Keep a double-entry reading log of your impressions, hypotheses, questions, wonderings, and other responses. As you read, try to answer these questions in your log:

- What seems to be the most important word in the poem? Why?
- What is the clearest picture or most visible image? Can you sketch it? What feelings does it bring forth?
- What are your reactions to the speakers in the poem? How many are there? Which do you agree with? Disagree with?
- Look back at your responses to the title. How does your first reading compare with your expectations?

Law Like Love
Law, say the gardeners, is the sun,
Law is the one
All gardeners obey
Tomorrow, yesterday, today.

5   Law is the wisdom of the old
The impotent grandfathers shrilly scold;
The grandchildren put out a treble tongue,
Law is the senses of the young.

Law, says the priest with a priestly look,
10   Expounding to an unpriestly people,
Law is the words in my priestly book,
Law is my pulpit and my steeple.

Law says the judge as he looks down his nose,
Speaking clearly and most severely,
15   Law is as I've told you before,

Law is as you know I suppose,
Law is but let me explain it once more,
Law is The Law.

Yet law-abiding scholars write;
20   Law is neither wrong nor right,
Law is only crimes
Punished by places and by times,
Law is the clothes men wear
Anytime, anywhere,
25   Law is Good-morning and Good-night.

Others say, Law is our Fate;
Others say, Law is our State;
Others say, others say
Law is no more
30   Law has gone away.

And always the loud angry crowd
Very angry and very loud
Law is We,
And always the soft idiot softly Me.

35   If we, dear, know we know no more
Than they about the law,
If I no more than you
Know what we should and should not do
Except that all agree
40   Gladly or miserably
That the law is
And that all know this,
If therefore thinking it absurd
To identify Law with some other word,
45   Unlike so many men
I cannot say Law is again,
No more than they can we suppress
The universal wish to guess
Or slip out of our own position
50   Into an unconcerned condition.
Although I can at least confine
Your vanity and mine

> To stating timidly
> A timid similarity,
> 55 We shall boast anyway:
> Like love I say.
>
> Like love we don't know where or why
> Like love we can't compel or fly
> Like love we often weep
> 60 Like love we seldom keep.
>
> —W. H. Auden

Now select one of the following activities to complete to contribute to your class portfolio performance for the poem.

1. Note the number of times and the specific places where *law* and *love* are used in the poem. Use a book of quotations to help you find five quotes about law and about love that are relevant to your reading of this poem. Arrange the quotes in some way to convey your thinking. You might make a poster, a transparency, a 35mm slide, a computer graphic, or something else.

2. Write your own comparison "_____ Like _____" and then develop it in a poem. Choose a concept or idea or emotion that is hard to define directly and say something new about it. Compare it to another concept, object, or person that is similar, at least in your mind. Establish four or five points of similarity, as Auden does. Think about rhythm and rhyme. Do you want your comparison to have regular rhythm, meter, or rhyme?

3. A dialogue is a conversation. But there are different kinds of conversations. An *eristic* dialogue is an argument—each side tries to win by making a stronger or more powerful case than the other side. Debates and courtroom trials are eristic by nature. Some less formal conversations turn out this way too. A *heuristic* dialogue is quite different, more an exploratory discussion. The object is not to win but to learn, to understand something better by talking to someone with differing views.

   Choose two speakers from the poem and write a dialogue between them to show how they might discuss the concept of law. Decide early in the writing how the dialogue will end—with one winner or with two learners. Possible speakers:

- a gardener
- a grandparent (the old)
- a grandchild (the young)
- a member of the clergy
- a judge
- a scholar
- a crowd
- an "idiot"
- the "I" of the poem

You might use a line from the poem as a starting point for the dialogue. For presentation to the class, two of you can take the parts and play out the dialogue.

4. In line 35, the speaker addresses another person: "If we, dear...."
   Let's say this person has been present and listening during the entire poem. Who might the listener be? What is this person's history with the speaker? What might he or she be thinking about while listening to the speaker's words? What might the person's response be after the speaker has finished?

   Imagine yourself as this listener and have someone read the poem aloud to you. As you listen, jot down your reactions and ideas. Then write one of the following:

   - a series of fragmentary thoughts as the listener listens
   - the listener's response after the speaker has finished

   You and your reader might turn the poem and your work on it into an oral presentation.

5. Poems come from people, and people live in human contexts: times, places, societies, families, friends, and associates. Use library and on-line resources to compile a biographical sketch of W. H. Auden. You can go beyond simple data of when and where he lived to do some speculating about more interesting ideas: How did he live? Why did he write? What else did he write? What events in his life seem most important to you? How was he regarded by important others in his time? At what point in his life was this poem written?

When you have finished, go back and read the poem again, taking notes once more about your reactions. How has your new knowledge about the author's life and times added to your views of this work? Be ready to explain how your research findings led to your new views of the poem.

6. Read the poem as a formalist interpreter would, looking only at the poem and its structure. The poem has sixty lines and a number of stanzas, but how many *parts* does it really have? What is the *structural logic* of the poem? Explore this question by dividing the poem into two groups of lines, then three groups, and then four groups, or any other number you like. Each version will give a different reading of the poem. For each version, write a label or heading for each line group and an explanation of how the parts fit together. Choose the version that makes the most sense to you and explain the reasons for your choice.

7. Cast the poem as an oral reading and tape record a dramatic reading of the work. First, decide how many voices or parts you need. For each part, build a character (you may even want to use makeup and costumes and act this as a scene). Mark the passages of text for tone, emphasis, pauses, and the other considerations of oral interpretation. Conduct the reading (or enactment) for the class.

Round Table of Critical Perspectives

In Chapter 3, you saw four guides to reading from critical perspectives. Select a work to read together. (We suggest "The Yellow Wallpaper" by Charlotte Perkins Gilman or *Their Eyes Were Watching God* by Zora Neale Hurston.) Working as individuals or in teams, prepare written interpretations of the work from all four perspectives. Then hold a round table to see what issues become more or less important from each perspective. Since the guides are just that—guides, and not the final words on any type of interpretation—seek out further readings in critical theory, psychology, sociology, and other disciplines to support your interpretations. For example, you may want to compare and contrast readings from various theories of psychology. Freud, Maslow, Jung, Erikson, and Skinner would certainly have different ideas about what makes people (or characters) tick.

In the round table presentation, each critical perspective should be outlined in a brief overview to get some issues on the floor, and then the panel should continue the discussion. The goal should be not so much seeking closure as developing rich and multilayered interpretations.

"Something Wicked This Way Comes"

The activities that follow are based on Shakespeare's *Macbeth*. Most can be done by individuals or by small groups.

1. Retell the story as a modern detective story. Cast Macduff as a detective from a crime series in fiction or other media.

2. Write Lady Macbeth's suicide note. Allow her to reflect on her motives, actions, and feelings.

3. Be a casting director and cast the play with people from your school community. Be sure to explain your choices and to tell what aspects of personality or character must come through for each part.

4. Decide what visuals you would include with the text if this play were to be illustrated. Draw a series of illustrations and match them with lines of text.

5. Write an investigative report of Macbeth's cover-up. Use Woodward and Bernstein's *All the President's Men* as a source to help you see what approach to take and which characters in the play to "interview" for information.

6. Determine how you would play the role of a character so you can audition for the part. To prepare, follow one character through the whole play and keep a reading log of his or her motivations, actions, and responses to other characters, as well as your thoughts about how to play the part.

7. Be Scotland's busy obituary writer and write notices for all named characters who die during the play. Or use the style of *Spoon River Anthology* and have each character do his or her own.

8. Assume the Weird Sisters get together one last time after the action of the play. Write their dialogue to show if they think they caused or merely predicted the events of the play.

9. Research the concept of the divine right of kings and explain what it might have to do with this play.

10. Hold a talk show interview with one of the characters at a specific point in the play. Take the role of a particular interviewer or host.

11. Write Macbeth's diary, in blank verse or rhymed couplets. Focus on five to ten key moments of the play when you think he would be inclined to write.

12. Hold a congressional hearing or a grand jury investigation of Macbeth and the murder of Duncan and Banquo. Call the first session right after the banquet at which Banquo was to be guest of honor.

13. Join "Kingnet," the on-line network of kings. Write the E-mail and on-line conversations between Macbeth and the other kings (specify which ones) he turns to for advice in times of trouble. Some kings you might include are Midas, Oedipus, Henry V, and Solomon.

14. Explore the connections among four contexts of the play:

    • the original story of Macbeth on which the play is based
    • the setting within the world of the play
    • the Elizabethan setting in which the play was performed
    • the time and place in which you are reading the play

15. Write, enact, and film a sixty-second video preview for the film version of *Macbeth*. Decide whether you want to include the most important moments, the most violent or dramatic ones, or both.

16. Make a scene map of the play that includes, scene by scene, the characters, setting, and a brief summary of the action.

17. Read three or four critical articles on the nature of tragedy or, more specifically, on *Macbeth* and present a comparison of the issues and views discussed by the various writers.

18. Use any two guides from Chapter 3 and do interpretations of the play from two perspectives.

19. Design the sets and costumes for a scene or two of the play.

20. Audiotape "The Greatest Hits of *Macbeth*," twelve oral readings of the best lines from the play. Make each "hit" at least a minute in length, including an introduction that gives the context of each.

The Literary Canon and the Coffee Shop

There have always been hangouts—coffee shops, restaurants and bars, and private homes—where the literati would congregate to talk shop. A new one just opened, and any literary figure with an opinion is welcome. The topic under discussion is the literary canon—the body of works that should be read by a person who wishes to be well-read or cultured or educated. Questions include the following:

- What should students read in literature courses—what kinds of works, what specific works?
- What authors, genres, and cultures should be represented?
- What justification is there for these works, these types?
- What results should be expected?
- Who should decide?

You can play the role of any character or author you have read who could conceivably have an opinion on the topic. To prepare, you need to get into character, to build a role, just as you would for a role in a play. You need to know what motivates the character, what ideas the character holds dear, his or her speech manner and mannerisms, even some key words and phrases favored by the character.

To conduct the role play, you need one person to play the proprietor, who is a peace keeper, moderator of sorts, and director of questions when things get slow. You can involve as many literary figures as you like, but larger crowds can get unwieldy. A workable number seems to be six to eight. The rest of the class, besides being an audience, can track the flow of the discussion with some sort of listening log.

You can start things off by having two characters read aloud the following dialogue. If no two figures fit these roles, have two audience members start the ball rolling by reading the lines:

Speaker 1: Wiser heads than yours have determined the curricula and courses of study for thousands of years. It is the role of the educated to decide what the uneducated need to do to become educated. You can't just throw the baby into the library and say, "Read things until you are educated."

Speaker 2: Only a fool would pretend to know what someone else should read. People in power are always making lists of things that others need to do. How can some stuffed shirt from two hundred years ago decide what I need to do now? His ideas are as dead as he is.

Speaker 1: Then you would have the lunatics running the asylum? Every student at every level would decide what is good for her or him? What works to read? What to do with what is read? Whether to read at all? Educational institutions wouldn't need instructors, just bigger libraries?

Speaker 2: Yes. There is no list of books that one must read to be educated—not now, not ever. Literature reading lists are just attempts to preserve the status quo. The people in authority make them for the people who would like to gain authority. Literacy and literature are both political.

Speaker 1: There are some works so important to the development of our culture that a person who hasn't read them is simply ignorant. One cannot be a citizen without some knowledge of the cultural and literary heritage she or he is a part of.

Speaker 2: I can't imagine any works that are so important in and of themselves—that will give me anything of value that I can't get from reading what I choose to read.

And so on.

Eighteen Things to Do with a Poem

This next group of activities was derived from a rough blueprint for an entire portfolio. The purpose was not so much to cover all the literary bases as to establish many possible routes into a work. Perhaps the list will help you if you wish to develop your own class activity as an option for this chapter's performance. The categories in the list can easily be jumping-off points for your own ideas.

To begin, select a piece of literature to work with. Any of these activities (or a selection of them) can be done with a poem in this book or with any other poem. With some slight modification, they can be done with a work of any type. Work on your activity either alone or in a small group but keep your focus on the *whole piece*.

1. **Reading:** Conduct research on the author, period, or genre.

2. **Writing:** Transform the poem to prose or drama or write a sequel or response.

3. **Speaking/listening:** Prepare an oral interpretation or respond to one.

4. **Literary use of language:** Explain the figurative language (or one figure) in relation to the whole poem.

5. **Informational use of language:** Report on the reading or interpretive strategies you used to get meaning from the poem.

6. **Social use of language:** Discuss interpretations, responses, connections to your own life.

7. **Critical or evaluative use of language:** Research and define the "best" critical perspectives on the poem.

8. **Group work:** Share responses to build an array of interpretations.

9. **Linguistic response:** Comment on tone, tune, mood, style.

10. **Logical/mathematical response:** Explain rhythm, pace, rhyme, other sound devices.

11. **Musical response:** Create music to fit the poem and prepare an explanation of your intent.

12. **Bodily/kinesthetic response:** Dance, enact, mime, sign, choreograph, or otherwise perform the poem. Combine your performance with a written explanation of your interpretation.

13. **Visual/spatial response:** Design a book cover to capture the essence of your written interpretation of the work.

14. **Range:** Compare the poem with other works with respect to style, themes, topics, effects.

15. **Flexibility:** Adapt the poem for written/spoken presentation to a younger audience.

16. **Connectedness:** Connect issues in the poem (for example, *change*) to your own life experiences, other characters and other works you've dealt with, other disciplines.

17. **Conventions:** Recompose the work into a sonnet, cinquain, or other poetic form.

18. **Independence:** Design and explain your own reading method or protocol for interpreting: What did you need to do to understand this work?

A Pairing: *The Things They Carried* and *Song of Solomon*

Here is a range of possible activities designed by Noreen Benton that you can complete as a response to two novels, *The Things They Carried* by Tim O'Brien and *Song of Solomon* by Toni Morrison. The difference between this and other projects in this chapter is that all of the activities stem from a central, essential question.

Read or review the two novels. Then complete four to six of the following activities from the perspective of the central question. Conclude the project with a summary that synthesizes your work with the activities.

> **Central Question:** What happens when we examine the narratives of our own lives in juxtaposition with the lives of those in the literary works we are engaged in reading? (Why are the other peoples' stories important for our own lives?)

1. O'Brien states in his novel, "But this too is true: stories can save us." Discuss how this is true for any of the characters in these two novels. Then discuss how it might be true in your life.

2. Evaluate O'Brien and Morrison as writers and storytellers. Do these books matter today? What relevance/significance do they have for you? For the rest of us?

3. Choose ten great/important lines from each novel and discuss why you selected them.

4. O'Brien says *The Things They Carried* is a work of fiction. Yet there are many things in these pages that point to the possibility of its being nonfiction. Read his autobiographical work, *If I Die in a Combat Zone...*, and analyze how much of the novel has a basis in reality.

5. Both of these novels are filled with incredibly memorable characters. Choose a character from each work and discuss why this person will stay with you for a long time to come. What aspects of each character's life/personality can you identify with?

6. The naming of people in *Song of Solomon* is a very significant act. Discuss its importance in relation to the story; then move away from the book and interview acquaintances about the extent to which names have shaped their lives.

7. Many different paths were taken by characters in these two novels. Discuss some of the decisions made and their consequences. Then talk about decisions you have made in your own life that have made a difference.

8. Both of these novels are set in tumultuous settings—the Vietnam War and the civil rights movement of the 1960s. There is much to research regarding these events and this era. Choose an aspect that interests you and, together with others who have chosen this area, teach the class what you consider to be some essential things about these times. What bearing did decisions made then have on contemporary life and values?

9. Form one panel to represent a Vietnam-era draft board and one consisting of conscientious objectors and war protesters. Stage a mock debate about the whole war situation. Try to get inside the motivations of the characters in whichever side of the debate you find yourself on.

10. Both Morrison and O'Brien write about what they know well—the African American experience and the Vietnam War. Write a piece about something that you know well and has particular significance for you. Compare your event with Morrison's or O'Brien's.

11. Interview a Vietnam veteran or someone who was an adult during the civil rights movement in this country. Find out as much as you can about the person's attitudes before, during, and after an important event. Look for ways you can identify with the person. Write up the results.

12. Read other novels set during the civil rights era or the Vietnam War. Discuss these as well as the genre of "historical fiction" and its import for you and other students.

13. Both of these authors deal with aspects of love in a variety of ways. Discuss the meaning of love for several characters in these books. Relate your findings to your own insights about this human condition.

14. *Song of Solomon* is as much about the women characters as it is about the two main male characters, Milkman and Guitar. Choose one of the women to write about. Trace her changes and motivations, her goodness, and her weakness throughout this novel. Then write about a woman in your life. What is it that makes her unique/significant? What would she want you to include in her story?

15. The parent/child relationship is profoundly drawn by Morrison in *Song of Solomon*. Choose a parent/child relationship from this novel and discuss what it is about family that matters so much. Extend the discussion to poems, songs, plays, and films about this topic that have had an effect on you.

16. Discuss the theme of survival in these books and in your own life.

17. Write twenty opening lines of your own life story. Try to emulate the style of O'Brien or Morrison.

18. These novels contain some very startling/downright rude awakenings (coming of age moments) in them. Talk about these in the texts and then talk about some of your own "awakenings."

19. Choose a character from either novel and place him or her in the other's life. For example, have Rat Kiley or Kiowa meet Guitar and Milkman. Or have Guitar go to Vietnam. Write about what happens and what you learn from it.

20. Write a series of letters from Vietnam (as a character in O'Brien's book) to a character in *Song of Solomon*. Try to communicate personal insights about what is going on.

21. Send one of these novels to a friend along with a letter explaining why you think he or she should read it.

22. There is only enough money to buy one of these two novels for a course called "Saving Ourselves through Stories." Which one would you argue should be purchased? Present your case convincingly.

A Hypertext on *Mansfield Park*

In this activity, you will work with a group to create an electronic portfolio called a *hypertext*. Each member of the group will keep his or her part of the portfolio work in a separate file; then the separate files will be combined into one huge work.

The advantage of a hypertext is that it is a multidirectional text, one that the reader or user can enter and move through in any one of a number of different ways—no two readings are alike. The hypertext consists of a number of text or artifact "spaces" (the term used to describe each separate text section) created and arranged into a network by the various writers. The goal is to have the portfolio represent the writers' work both collectively and individually. Viewers may rearrange the artifacts, make different connections, and comment on one or more of the artifacts or the ensemble. Ultimately the text can be scanned onto a disk to be manipulated, copied, and reviewed by any number of people through copied disks, a local network, or possibly even a World-Wide Web home page.

To create your hypertext, choose a work of some complexity, such as a long novel or a play, that has many different things that could be said about it and a number of different approaches to it. You might take a computer program for creating hypertext like *Storyspace* and make a format that looks like this:

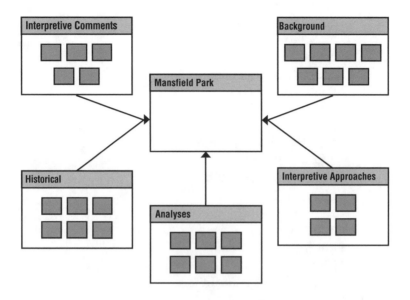

The following format was developed for a class project on Jane Austen's novel *Mansfield Park*. The time of this novel is around the beginning of the French Revolution; the location is an English country house whose owner makes his money running slave-worked sugar plantations in the Caribbean. Neither the revolution nor slavery is directly mentioned in the work, but there are veiled allusions.

Each space in the hypertext is given below with its space number to identify the group to which it belonged, but only the information about the first space is filled in. Some of the omitted information was text, some was pictures, and some consisted of articles found on the Internet and World-Wide Web.

2.1 Mansfield Park
Mansfield Park was written by Jane Austen and published in 1814. There are a number of different ways it can be viewed and studied. Take a tour around the spaces. Some of them have questions or comments; some are to be filled in. Feel free to add a space or make a link.
2.2 Background
    2.2.1 Literary Sources
    2.2.2 Geography
    2.2.3 Social Structure

2.2.3.1 Women
2.2.3.2 Servants
2.2.3.3 Family economics
2.2.3.4 Aristocracy
2.2.3.5 Changes in family
2.2.4 Politics of the Time
2.2.4.1 Current ideas
2.2.4.2 French Revolution
2.2.4.3 American Revolution
2.2.4.4 William Pitt
2.2.5 English Country House
2.2.5.1 House design
2.2.5.2 Daily life
2.2.5.3 Servants
2.2.6 Role of the Navy
2.2.7 Clergy
2.3 History of the Book and Author
2.3.1 First Reviews
2.3.2 Film Reception
2.3.3 Publication History
2.3.4 Publishers and Printer
2.3.5 Film Versions
2.3.6 Jane Austen's Life
2.4 Interpretive Approaches
2.4.1 Psychological View
2.4.2 Feminist View
2.4.3 Cultural Interpretation
2.4.4 Political Interpretation
2.5 Analyses
2.5.1 Allusions
2.5.2 Tone/Voice
2.5.3 Structure
2.5.4 Characters
2.5.5 Style
2.5.6 Setting
2.6 Interpretive Comments

Not all of the material in a hypertext like this needs to be original work. When appropriate, certain kinds of material—background articles, maps, graphics—can be downloaded or scanned in, together with information about the source. Material dealing with the text itself will most likely be written by group members. The last set of spaces in the *Mansfield Park* hypertext included various critical responses written by students as they worked on the project.

One advantage of a project like this is that others can read what has been written and comment on it. They are able to draw *links*— lines of connection between two spaces—from what they have read to their own comments and also from one topic to another. With *Mansfield Park,* for instance, links could be drawn between particular points in the text and the reader's understanding of them, between different pieces of background information and their relevance to the text, and among the different kinds of critical approaches. A person reading the hypertext might create his or her own links or follow someone else's or go through all of the topics in a hierarchical order as in the outline above. The number of different ways of connecting spaces is nearly infinite.

When the hypertext seems completed, each participant can put his or her part of the work into a personal portfolio. To demonstrate work with linking, a person could print a graphic of the relevant section of the hypertext and include that as well as the writing that he or she had done.

Your Way

The only direction for this option is that you make up your own directions. As an individual or working in a group, create an array of activities for a work, author, genre, issue, or other point of focus— and then complete the activities for a later performance.

READER'S FORUM

This "Reader's Forum" is a group rehearsal or practice for what will later on be a one-person show: your portfolio presentation. Your instructor will probably want to schedule these performances so as to showcase the activity.

Your instructor may assign you a topic to present at "Reader's Forum," or you may choose one yourself from the chapter activities.

PORTFOLIO PROGRESS REPORT

This "Progress Report," as promised, has a larger purpose than to review your activities within this chapter. Instead, you will be looking at the progress you have made as a literature reader and interpreter and seeing how to make your portfolio reflect these changes.

A Cumulative Self-Assessment

In Chapter 2, you did a preliminary self-assessment of yourself as a reader and language user. Now you should reflect on what has changed and on how you have grown as you have worked your way through this book. You may want to review pages 62–67 of Chapter 2 for self-assessment directions, and you will certainly want to review your "Preliminary Self-Assessment" to see what has changed. Here is the beginning of one student's self-assessment, based on the first of the four language purposes:

> *Language Purpose*: reading for information and understanding
> *Typical Example:* I like seeing where a work and author came from, and also what impact the work had on readers of the time, so I will typically do some background reading in these areas.

Range

least————————————————————XX——————————most
1   2   3   4   5   6   7   8   9   10   11   12
(Exploring critical perspectives has got me reading psychology, sociology, and history and culture.)

Flexibility

least————————————————————XX————————most
1   2   3   4   5   6   7   8   9   10   11   12
(In "Reader's Forum" and other activities, I have learned to present to a small group or to an entire class.)

FOR YOUR PORTFOLIO NOTEBOOK

Cumulative Self-Assessment

Here are the four language purposes that you will be assessing yourself on:

- reading for information and understanding
- reading for literary and aesthetic response
- reading for critical analysis and evaluation
- reading for social interaction

Here are the five criteria you will use to assess each purpose:

- range
- flexibility
- connections
- conventions
- independence

For each rating for each language purpose, give a typical example from the activities you have completed in this course. Rate your usual performance on each scale and give an explanation of each rating in a sentence or two, as in the example above. The result will be a total of twenty ratings, five each for the four language purposes.

Redefining Your Goals

You wrote four goals a while back—does it seem a long time ago? In this chapter, you have completed another self-assessment and also played your part in some performance activity, a kind of portfolio in itself.

Now you should review your goals for two purposes: first, to see what you have accomplished and what remains to be done, and second, to redefine those original goals and bring them into sharper focus. Whenever we as instructors come up with a plan for a lesson or book or course of study, we have to get into it a little to see what's right and what's not so right about that plan. Our experience in trying to achieve our original goals tells us how we might want to modify those goals. For example, this book has gone through about seven stages of redefining. The contents outline we began with—our goals, in a way—has been changed again and again. We have said things like the following, and more:

- "We should do more of this."
- "We haven't really got room for that."
- "Do we really want to get into that?"
- "This part of Chapter 1 has to go in another chapter, maybe Chapter 6, and we don't need a separate chapter for that other stuff."

We have had the advantage of working together as writers and getting responses from editors, reviewers, instructors, and students. You can also have the benefit of collaboration by working with your instructor and with other students. But do your own thinking first.

FOR YOUR PORTFOLIO NOTEBOOK

Goal Reevaluation

Read through the four goals you set at the beginning of your portfolio work. Reflect on your work in this chapter's performance and in activities from other chapters. Then answer these questions about each goal:

1. To what degree have you accomplished this goal? How do you know? What evidence do you have in the areas of knowledge, practice, and habits?

2. What is left for you to accomplish for this goal? What do you need to read? What do you need to do with what you read? What kinds of evidence do you need to produce?

3. Read your answers to questions 1 and 2. With this in mind, how do you want to redefine this goal? Do you want to extend it or to limit it? In light of what you have done, what do you now want to do?

Use your answers to write an addition or extension for each goal, and add these to your goal statements.

MOVING ON

You just finished a cumulative self-assessment and a redefinition of your goals. Now you will move on to see the connectedness of things, ranging from connections within a single work to connections across literary and cultural contexts.

6 Making Connections

▶▶▶LOOKING AHEAD

Cross-cultural, interdisciplinary, Pan American, trans-Atlantic, sequential, cyclical, Internet, constellation—all words that refer to patterns and connections. This chapter shows you the importance of seeing patterns and connections, though of a slightly different sort. Here's what one instructor said about making connections:

> The student who can begin early in life to think of things as connected, even if he revises his view with every succeeding year, has begun the life of learning.
>
> —Mark Van Doren

As we have said before, more is usually better—more reading, more kinds of works, more ways to read, more ways to respond, more readers to read with. The same is true with understanding literary relationships. This chapter is about making connections in a number of ways:

- within a work
- between a work and your own life experiences, your own writing and expression
- between and among readers
- between and among works
- between and among cultural and literary contexts

Throughout the chapter, and particularly in "Building Your Portfolio," you will get a chance to put what you have learned about connections into practice.

THE CONTEXT OF CONNECTIONS

Some of the things we try to make connections with are concrete and complete; some are more fluid. Let's say you find a conversation already in progress. You could join it, agree or disagree with what you hear, extend the conversation by asking and answering questions, or just sit and listen. Or you could walk away. You have choices. You can be in or around this conversation with varying degrees of connectedness.

Or say you come upon a river. You could get in, immerse yourself, and drift along with the current. You could actively swim downstream, adding your energies to the current. You could resist the current and swim—or try to swim—upstream and against it. You could cut back and forth and do all three: at different times joining, drifting with, and resisting the current. You could taste the water—maybe try to drink it all. You might stay out of the water but study the river, noting its path and rate of descent, the volume and rate of its flow, the makeup of the river bed, and its beginning and end. You could go float in a glass-bottomed boat and see what you could see of denizens and other details of the river. You could examine aerial photos of the river and see how it connects and relates to other water and land forms. You might study not the river but its effects: erosion, deposits, weather, and the like. You could do a geological dig to determine the history of the river.

Each of these activities would connect you to the river in a particular way but might also make other kinds of connections impossible. Again, there are choices to be made. Let's borrow a term from economics—*opportunity cost*. If you spend your money—or analyze the river or interpret a book—in one way, you can't do it in other ways. That one choice comes at the expense of other choices you might have made.

Look at the backside of a cliché: If you can't see the forest for the trees, then you can't see a tree for the forest either. When you read, you can't get it all. In fact, there is no *all*. You can't be everywhere at once or everyone at once or do everything at once. So don't try. Be aware of your reading purpose to begin with and then plan accordingly. It's also helpful to be aware of what you might be missing, the opportunity cost of reading what you choose to read in the ways you choose to read.

LITERARY CONNECTIONS

The guides to critical perspectives (see Chapter 3) provide some overviews for making connections. The connections we will be dealing with in this section are bridges between and among literary works themselves.

Connections within a Work

The title and first pages of a book often suggest much of what is to come. If you are keeping a reading log, you should certainly spend some time writing about the title and the opening scene. Later, reviewing your responses and speculations will tell you what to reread. The circular nature of many works may not be apparent because we typically read from the first page to the last, but that is not the only way to read. Reviewing first and last stanzas, pages, chapters, or scenes will probably show you something new about the work.

You can design a reading log, and your reading agenda, to read for changes in character, for scenes of violence, for stylistic devices, for figurative language, for key words, for anything you want to read for. You can use an aspect of the pentad or of the study guide as an area of focus for your reading.

These devices are flexible enough to let you follow a new insight or interest that comes up while you are reading. Early in the novel *A Separate Peace*, an important event occurs at a tree. Early in the novel *Their Eyes Were Watching God*, a different but equally important event happens at a tree. When you notice such an event and want to explore its significance to the rest of the book, you can reset your reading agenda to follow the use of the tree and trees in general in the work. Later, you might branch out to compare the two books or to discover the mythological and symbolic significance of various kinds of trees.

Here is what one student wrote in her response journal about some of the tree imagery in *Their Eyes Were Watching God:*

p. 10 "Janie had spent most of the day beneath a blossoming pear tree in the back-yard."

Then she kisses Johnny. Is this the Tree of Knowledge of Good and Evil? Buddha's tree of enlightenment?

p. 18 "So Ah wrapped Leafy up in moss and fixed her good in a tree. . . ."

So Janie's mother was left in a a tree for protection? Are the tree spirits operating here?

p. 26 "The noon sun filtered through the leaves of the fine oak tree where she sat and made lacy patterns on the ground."

Last time under a tree preceded a change: she kissed Johnny and then had to marry Logan. Is she ready for another change? Do the trees signal growth or change?

Connections between a Work and Your Experiences

The response guide ("The Reader") in Chapter 3 asks you to look at the work and to look at yourself to see what connections lead to meanings. In a way, such an approach is similar to tests based on projective techniques in psychology. In the most famous of these, the Rorschach or inkblot test, the idea is simple: when a person tells what the inkblot calls to mind, he or she is telling more about himself or herself than about the inkblot. In another projective "test," called the Thematic Apperception Test, a person is shown a series of drawings of people in various undefined situations. For each drawing, the person orally constructs a story to explain what is pictured. Transcriptions of the narratives are analyzed for the frequency of occurrence of certain themes. While one person's narratives may be filled with constructive relationships and achievement motivation, another's, based on the same drawings, may be ridden with strife, unhappiness, and failure. All reading is projective in the sense that you, as a reader, have to make meaning of the symbols on the paper. You have to *bring* meaning-making contexts to the work you read.

Age is one important factor in determining our meaning-making contexts. For example, teenagers who read or view *Romeo and Juliet* tend to ignore the feud (in fact, to ignore most of the adult characters) and focus on the love story of the title characters. Older readers and viewers, who can identify with the parents and officials, tend to see less of the love story and more of other issues in the play.

The musical *West Side Story*, a modern version of the Romeo and Juliet story, situates the lovers as members of warring communities and gangs: Puerto Rican and anglo. Consider how these different contexts might influence your viewing of the play:

- whether you were seventeen or fifty-five years old
- whether you were Puerto Rican or anglo (or something else)
- whether you lived in an urban or rural area
- whether you were a gang member or a law enforcement official

FOR YOUR PORTFOLIO NOTEBOOK

Your Own Contexts

Try this activity to see what kinds of contexts you bring to a work. Read part of a work—probably about one-third or one-half will do. You need to get to a point where there are real conflicts but no clear resolutions. Stop reading and project three different endings for the work. These are not *predictions* of what will happen; rather, they are *projections* of what could (or should) happen. Write a paragraph or so for each ending to tell what happens and include key events or turning points along the way. Then, for each ending, explain why the ending makes sense in one of these ways:

- *logically:* because it follows the "rules" of cause and effect (for example, a wise investment is made and pays off)
- *psychologically:* because the outcome can be traced to a strong trait of character or a powerful motive (a desire for revenge)
- *morally:* because it feels right, your sense of justice is served; this is what *should* happen (good is rewarded, evil is punished)

- *archetypally:* because it fits a pattern of events common in literature or myth (an initiation, for example)
- *symbolically:* because it builds on the symbolic value of a significant object or representation from the early part of the work (a tree, a music box, a letter)
- *your way:* because (explain your criterion)

As you continue reading, compare what actually happens with your projections. The object is not to guess what the author is thinking but to discover how you think while you read and what kinds of contexts you bring to a particular reading situation.

Connections between and among Readers

The activities in "Reader's Forum" and in Chapter 5 have allowed you to make connections with other readers in your class. Other ways to make connections (beyond ordinary conversations) include dialogue journals and readarounds.

As we discussed in Chapter 2, a dialogue journal is a reading journal that is meant to be shared with another reader. Frequently dialogue journals are correspondences between people reading the same work; however, they can also be between people reading two entirely different things. In that case, the journals work as comparisons between the two works as well as comments on the original works. Here is an example. The first comments are by someone reading Camus's novel *The Stranger*, while the second comments are from someone reading "Life, Friends, Is Boring," a poem by John Berryman.

Quote from text	First reader's comments	The partner's comments about the first reader's comments
"I suppose one gets used to anything after a while"	"Gets used to anything"? Is that the best we can expect from life? Why doesn't Meursault *want* anything or even react strongly to	The speaker in my poem reacts, all right, but he has the same reaction to everything: "That's boring." Maybe your Meursault figured

anything? He's so emo-   something out: don't
tionless. Why isn't he   expect too much and
bored to death?   you won't be let down.

The partner can ask questions, speculate, draw conclusions, or make any of the kinds of responses you make in your column. It should be interesting for you to see how someone reacts to your responses, especially in light of what he or she is reading. When you are finished with the work, the journal should be a good conversation piece. If you want to make things more complicated, you can set up the journal in four columns, leaving you with room to write back to your partner's comments.

A readaround needs three or more people. Each person in the group brings a response journal, reading log, or other piece of work. The works are passed to the left, and each person reads the work of another, giving responses and suggestions either right on the work or on separate paper. After a predetermined time (say, five to eight minutes), the works are passed to the left again and the process is repeated. By the end of the session, you will have an array of reactions to the work you brought to the group. You will also have a number of views from other readers. Some of these will help to inform your understanding and interpretation. The readaround should give you some new ideas to pursue.

As with the dialogue journal, the readaround can be done with people all reading the same work or reading different works. This process works much in the same way as a writing group or workshop.

FOR YOUR PORTFOLIO NOTEBOOK

Do Your Own Readaround

Choose a literary work and a group to work with and conduct a readaround. Try this one while you are all reading the same work. As you read, give written responses and take your own notes on ideas you want to pursue.

Connections between and among Works

In earlier chapters, you saw how to use claim, warrant, and data to make assertions and interpretations about your reading. Here we will look at the same logic as it can be used to make connections between works. We will call the device the *comparative claim*. Its purpose is to make a connection between two works by showing how they are similar and yet, even within that similarity, still different in some important way. It is too simple merely to say things are alike or not alike.

This device is pretty versatile. You can talk about characters, symbols, settings, diction, purposes, or anything else worth including in a literary discussion. You can write comparative claims from any of the critical perspectives. Using this device in your thinking and writing will help you to make a point about a significant issue and then back it up with evidence from the texts.

You start by defining a similarity. Imagine that you have just read D. H. Lawrence's story "The Rocking-Horse Winner" and "Storm Warnings," a poem by Adrienne Rich. Of them you can say, "Both works are about loss of love." But don't stop thinking there. Go on to find a significant difference within that similarity: "In the poem, the speaker is struggling to 'master' the 'disaster' of the loss of love but not striving to regain love. In the short story, the young boy loses even himself in the quest to restore lost love."

Another reader can argue with this interpretation but can also see where the idea is coming from. Let's try another comparison from an archetypal perspective. We will use the same short story but compare it with the story about the king and his soup (Chapter 3):

> Both narratives contain archetypal patterns relating to the quest for knowledge. The boy-hero of the quest seeks to know the unknowable in order to win love. The means of the quest are successful but not the ends. He dies after winning luck but failing to win love. The king in the soup story also becomes obsessed with the unknowable—in this case, with forbidden knowledge—and destroys himself and his entire community as a result.

Once again, there are other ways to read these two pieces, but the claim makes *this* reading clear. This device works well as a discovery writing when you are having trouble finding a point of focus for a paper or other presentation. Try writing comparative claims from different perspectives until you write something that really works for you. You will probably come up with the kernel of a paper. Even if you are working mainly with one piece, it is effective to find a contrast or counterpoint. In a paper on a single work, the comparative claim may be a grace note that enhances your performance.

The steps to follow in writing comparative claims, then, are these:

- identify an area of focus: narration, purpose, archetype, and so on
- establish an important similarity
- within that similarity, establish a significant difference
- say "So what?"—why is this worth talking about?

That fourth step seems obvious, but *it is the one most often left out of papers and literary discussions.* Remember that this device's purpose is not just to make a comparison but to use a comparison to assert meaning.

Another way to make connections is, of course, to use pairings, as in the portfolio activity in Chapter 5 that worked with *The Things They Carried* and *Song of Solomon*. Instructors and textbook writers make such pairings because they see some worthwhile harmonies and discords between the works. But you can go into the pairing business for yourself. You can pick two works to pair and go ahead and read them, making connections as you go. You don't have to stop at two. In Chapter 3, we asked you to make connections among four poems by Stephen Crane. There is no limit.

FOR YOUR PORTFOLIO NOTEBOOK

Write Comparative Claims

Read the following two poems. Then, in your "Portfolio Notebook," write at least three comparative claims about the two works. Your instructor may have you present your claims to the class or to a work group.

Death
O death, rock me asleep,
Bring me to quiet rest,
Let me pass my weary guiltless ghost
Out of my careful breast.

5   Toll on, thou passing bell;
Bring out my doleful knell;
Let thy sound my death tell.
Death doth draw nigh;
There is no remedy.

10   My pains who can express?
Alas, they are so strong;
My dolour will not suffer strength
My life for to prolong.
Toll on, thou passing bell;
15   Bring out my doleful knell;
Let thy sound my death tell.
Death doth draw nigh;
There is no remedy.

Alone in prison strong
20   I wait my destiny.
Woe worth this cruel hap that I
Should taste this misery!
Toll on, thou passing bell;
Bring out my doleful knell;
25   Let thy sound my death tell.
Death doth draw nigh;
There is no remedy.

Farewell, my pleasures past,
Welcome, my present pain!
30   I feel my torments so increase
That life cannot remain.
Cease now, thou passing bell;
Rung is my doleful knell;
For the sound my death doth tell.
35   Death doth draw nigh;
There is no remedy.

—Anonymous

Death, Be Not Proud
Death, be not proud, though some have called thee
Mighty and dreadful, for thou art not so,
For those whom thou think'st thou dost overthrow
Die not, poor Death, not yet canst thou kill me.
5   From rest and sleep, which but they picture be,
Much pleasure, then from thee much more must flow;
And soonest our best men with thee do go—
Rest of their bones and souls' delivery!
Thou'rt slave to fate, chance, kings and desperate men,
10   And dost with poison, war, and sickness dwell,
And poppy or charms can make us sleep as well,
And better than thy stroke; why swell'st thou then?
One short sleep past, we wake eternally,
And death shall be no more: Death, thou shalt die!

—John Donne

Connections to Previously Read Selections

Clearly another kind of connection that you make when you read a story or a poem is the one between what you are reading and other selections you have read. Some critics refer to this by the fancy term *intertextuality*, but it is a common habit of memory both for readers and for writers. After all, we don't usually read a book with a completely blank head. Most writers have also read various stories, poems, and plays; and echoes of these may very well come into their heads either intentionally or unintentionally. This leads to the idea that any text is part of a web of texts. The idea is not new, but there is a long-standing debate as to whether the web is in the text, the mind of the writer, or the mind of the reader. One may argue that all three are probably true.

In *The Road to Xanadu*, John Livingstone Lowes undertook one of the most extensive studies of intertextuality ever engaged in. Anyone truly wanting to study intertextuality should deal with this study, which explored every book that Samuel Taylor Coleridge might have read and how it impacts on "The Rime of the Ancient Mariner" and "Kubla Khan." Lowes found that he could trace images and metaphors to a number of books of travels, religion, poetry, and fiction. How Coleridge put these pieces together to form two first-rate poems shows the hand of a master.

Another critic, Harold Bloom, has talked and written a great deal about influence. He argues that most writers are aware of the writers that came before them, and they strive to touch base with those authors but not be intimidated by them. Writers like Shakespeare have been enormously influential, and any person who writes a sonnet is aware of the people like Shakespeare, Milton, Wordsworth, and Keats who wrote sonnets before them. The influence of one generation upon another and one writer upon another is what creates the idea of a "school" of writers, like the realists, the Beat poets, the Nuyoricans, and the like. The fact of influence is one reason why literature is studied historically.

For you as a reader, it may be enough to see what connection you think you see between a particular work and other works you might have read. Some of these connections are linked to archetypes, where a figure in one story reminds us of figures in other stories and therefore to a whole set of associations. But sometimes the story is transparently related to these other stories.

Here is a little test of connections for you. Read the following passage, based on a famous story that has been disguised in a modern form. Which of the characters listed below do you think the passage is based on? Write the letter that corresponds to your choice.

As she walked through the strange part of town, she was a little nervous. Then an older man, nice-looking but a little tough, stopped her. "Where are you going, little girl?" he asked. "To take these books to my aunt on South Street," answered the little girl. But she would not let him go with her; her mother had told her to watch out for strange men.

a. Cinderella   **c.** Sleeping Beauty
b. Goldilocks   **d.** Little Red Ridinghood

The passage is like the story of Little Red Ridinghood, so you would choose (d) Little Red Ridinghood.

FOR YOUR PORTFOLIO NOTEBOOK

More Connections

Read the following examples and then try to figure out which character the passage is based on.

1. Old Petersen had had a good life, a good farm—the richest in the country, a happy family, a nice tidy income. Even so, he wasn't proud, just thankful. Then the locusts came and ate his wheat, someone poisoned his wells, and, to cap it off, his children died of diphtheria. What happened, Petersen wondered, what had he done? It was enough to make a man lose his faith.

   a. Job   c. Barabbas
   b. Exodus   d. The Fall of Man

2. Orville came into the room and told his mother, "Now that I've finished high school, I'm going on to learn everything about everything; science, history, music—everything. I don't care how I get this knowledge; just so I get it. Then I'll know everything. I'll have the power I want."

   a. Faust   c. Job
   b. Hamlet   d. Macbeth

3. Charlie whistled as he thought about it. Everything had gone right for him after he'd had to leave Readville, on the other side of the divide, just because he'd been warned by the gypsy that he was going to have trouble. He'd come into Melrose and just happened to stop the gang that had been terrorizing the town. So they made him sheriff. He'd married the mayor's widow, a lovely woman, even if she was older. "Yes," he thought, "I guess that old gypsy was wrong. I've sure found happiness, not trouble."

   a. Joseph   c. Jason
   b. Oedipus   d. Saul

4. Ernie walked into the dance not sure what was going to happen. His crowd had fought with the group that was giving the party, but he was in a mood; his girl had just left him. He was spoiling for

something. He looked across the room, which was smoky and dark. He saw her and knew this was it. He walked over. "Hi. Who are you?" She looked up, and he could see the light in her eyes was like his. "I'm Linda."

a. Venus and Adonis
b. Romeo and Juliet
c. Tristan and Isolde
d. Pyramus and Thisbe

5. He hadn't been sure before, but now he was. His little brother, Sid, was the one who was going to be the success; he was going to get everything. It wasn't that Sid was better or brighter or anything, just luckier. And this made Sam mad, so he wanted to kill his little brother. And one day he did.

a. Cain and Abel
b. Moses and Aaron
c. Caesar and Brutus
d. Damon and Pythias

6. Sean didn't know what to do. His father had died mysteriously—was it cancer? Now his mother was about to marry Uncle Ed. It was so sudden. Sean was suspicious. But he needed proof.

a. Julius Caesar
b. Macbeth
c. Hamlet
d. King Lear

7. Elaine had been waiting—how long was it? Eddy had been gone twenty years—first in Vietnam and then touring through the South Pacific. Each time he'd been about to come home something came up. Meanwhile, lots of guys had been trying to get her to declare herself a widow and marry them. She'd tried every trick to stall them. She'd heard Eddy was on his way home.

a. The Aeneid
b. The Odyssey
c. The Ring Cycle
d. The Upanishads

8. Ollie was worried. He'd been put in charge of the whole community, but he didn't know what to expect. Then he learned that if he gave up his reading glasses he could see into people's minds, but he could never read again. He thought and thought. "This would be good for my people, even though it's a sacrifice."

a. Vishnu
b. Buddha
c. Zeus
d. Odin

9. The planet was doomed. Nick knew it, but he also knew others didn't care. So he decided to try to save as many people and animals as he could and colonize the next galaxy. Everyone laughed but he went ahead.

a. Arthur
b. Oedipus
c. Abraham
d. Noah

10. Rose was a master calculator. She could figure out a balance sheet in less than an hour given the raw numbers. The company thought she was indispensable. Then the new director brought in a computer expert. He challenged Rose to see who could do the books faster and more accurately. It was a close race but she won—at what cost?
a. Pocahontas
b. Annie Oakley
c. John Henry
d. Paul Bunyan

BETWEEN AND AMONG CULTURAL AND LITERARY CONTEXTS

For some people, *multicultural* is a term of praise; for others, it is a red flag. As far as literature is concerned, it is simply a principle that there is a vast collection of stories, poems, plays, and other documents written by or about the millions of people in the United States and the rest of the world, including those who have often been forgotten in the official histories and anthologies. The world is a global village, and the literature we read reflects—or should reflect—that fact.

Often in literature classes you do "internal analysis," which isolates author and work from its surroundings. But you can also do "external analysis," which sees author and work as having close connections with those surroundings.

Some of the artists whom we study in an American literature course descend from the peoples who were here before the European discoveries of the area we call America—the people whom we call Native Americans. Others are those who came as immigrants but not as conquerors: those who came as slaves; those who built the railroads or toiled in the factories. They came from Europe and its surrounding islands, from Africa, from Central Asia and the Indian subcontinent, from China and Japan and other parts of the Pacific Rim, from the Caribbean and Central America. They came under cramped conditions, many of them forced to come by people in their homeland who were only too happy to drive them out. Once they got here, they worked long hours in conditions that we would think tortuous. Many who worked twelve-hour days were young children.

Each group produced the literature and art that help to define its culture within our society and thus help to define our society as a whole. Much of the literature treats major human and social rituals—birth, child rearing, maturation, marriage, old age, and death—frequently within the context of the major defining events of a group's history. For blacks in the Americas, one defining event is the diaspora, or dispersal, from Africa. For African Americans of the United States, it may be more particularly slavery and emancipation. For early European settlers, it may have been the American Revolution and the division between Yankee and Loyalist; for others, it may have been the brutality of a civil war that divided North from South. For later arriving groups, it may have been the entry into this country through Ellis Island or some tragedy in their homelands. For some Jewish Americans, it may be the pogroms or the Holocaust. For some Arab Americans, it may be the loss of Palestine or the imperialism of people like T. E. Lawrence. For some Irish Americans, it may have been the famine of 1848. For some Latinos, it may be Catholicism's supplanting of the Aztec or Mayan religions; for others, it may be the fact of dictatorship under Trujillo or the Somozas. For Chinese Americans, it may be the railroads and the brothels of San Francisco. For the Lakota, it may be the Battle of Wounded Knee. For Japanese Americans, it may be the internment camps. Nearly all of these defining events are times of tribulation and survival. It is from them as well as from rituals and ceremonies that the values of a culture emerge.

That literature is an expression of and a lens into various cultures is, according to many people, one of the main things that gives it value. We like to think that literature "expresses us," is "part of our heritage," or explains us to the world. We like this even in small ways, in the kinds of inside jokes that we tell but don't want outsiders to tell about us.

Multiculturalism is simply acknowledging that literature is written by people and that it is important to look at the works and the writers and who they are and where they stand on various issues. So from this perspective, when you read a poem or a story, you also read the author. The process of reading is a process of getting to know something about who wrote the piece, of making connections between you and the author through the text. You start that process by going through the writer's words. Sometimes you can find out information about him or her from other sources. Then you use that information together with your reading of the text to help you bridge the gap. But you must be willing to see that the work was written by a real person who had a life and worries and concerns and comes from a particular culture and lived at a particular time. That person is writing about his or her world.

We can read John Milton's poetry as the work of an Englishman, a defeated and disgraced Protestant radical, and a blind person. All these connections help us to see a work like *Samson Agonistes* more clearly. Similarly, if we see Gwendolyn Brooks as American, African American, woman, urbanite, Midwesterner, civil rights activist in the 1960s both in the South and in Chicago, these facets of the poet help us read such strong descriptions of racial intolerance and its consequences as in her poem "The Ballad of Rudolph Reed."

When we read, we also need to understand *Samson Agonistes* as a drama and "The Ballad of Rudolph Reed" as a poetic object. But by being aware of cultural aspects, we are not only reading the writer but making connections to a cultural context and understanding ourselves as culturally situated readers.

FOR YOUR PORTFOLIO NOTEBOOK

Seeing Cultural Connections

Part 1. Read the following poem by Ron Welburn. Use a response journal format to respond to it.

Once to Run
Run.
Run, Indian, run.
Run while you can.
Here comes the white man.
    (from a song by Buddy Red Bow)

Run, Red, run,
'Cause he's got a gun
And he's aimin' it at your head.
    (Paraphrase of a late '50s pop song)

Forced to run, dispersed, pursued,
hunted like rabbits and rounded up
like the free ponies of the canyons,

we ran through layers of masks
5   settling about us the way mist
makes the tree trunks hard to see.
We ran into copper and silver, into cash registers;
we ran into automobiles that took away our names;
we disappeared into TV, finding ourselves
10   lost on another continent.

We ran in and out of dreams
slipping around on liquor and vomit
and forgetting, hating the morning.
We ran holes into our moccasins
15   and thorns shredded skirts and breechclout.
We lived with whatever men and women
sheltered and loved us, offering the
marks of Africa and Europe, and pressed on,
leaving them to say: "You may live with them
20   a lifetime and never have or know them."

We ran daily and yearly,
we ran in and out of watering holes
burning our throats and yellowing our eyes.
We ran our progeny and hounded them
25   with our inconsistencies.
My brother over there lost color
the way one does with a skin turn;
he ran until the bloodhounds ran with him
at his command;
30   he ran as hair sprouted along his legs
and weighed down his chest.

My sister over there ran as through fire.
Her hair crinkled and she no more walked
on her toes.
35   She ran until the impact of heat
flared her nostrils and flattened her nose;
she ran until she began to sway
side to side in her stride,
running with her shoulders.

40   Wolves snapped at her thinned calves,
      tearing buckskin.
      She ran and ran into and beyond
      the slave whip and the cotton fields
      and moved stealthily down Chicago streets
45   to shuffle dance in a storefront sanctified church.

      I ran with them,
      I ran as if every horse
      from family memories
      carried a pale rider.
50   I ran, my flesh tongued by bullets
      shot through the bodies of every Apache
      killed in *Rin Tin Tin* and every
      Skin along the Mohawk.
      I ran, wolved and bulleted,
55   until I could no longer see my dreams
      and could only guess at visions.
      I ran hotly pursued into a grazing cul-de-sac
      where I looked like so many
      who'd found refuge before me.

60   We who had no land owned arms full of sorrows.
      We who had no nation stood confused with new prophets.
      We who sought mates among the enemy ground
      our teeth and said, It is good.
      We who married overseas chased our dreams
65   the way coyote chases his tail.

      We who attended Hampton and Howard found "the good life."
      We who worked jazz and TV passed on into the lights.
      We have run and will run no more.
          Ours is the steady return.

Part 2. Now read this excerpt from an article that Welburn recently wrote. When you have finished, review and react to the notes in your dialogue journal. Note the changes or deeper understandings you have come to as a result of reading the article.

from **SEEING AND LISTENING: A POET'S LITERACIES**
by Ron Welburn

My father enjoyed telling a story about burying money with the blood of a bull or a vicious animal that I found fascinating yet certainly implausible. Years ago, a person buried a stash of money or valuables that way. And when anyone or a group of men went to dig up this cache, the odor of the bull's blood would become over-powering. Sometimes men quit. If you intended to continue you weren't supposed to say anything or complain before getting the money out of the ground else you would lose it all. One time this happened. A group of men were digging and the deeper they dug the stronger the scent of the bull's blood became. Finally, they struck the box and the smell got more powerful. Then, one of the men got aggravated and said aloud, "Get that damned bull outta here!" The money then divided within the ground and could be heard jingling as it moved off in many directions. It was never recovered. So the story goes.

My father's mother never believed this story. But it's a good tale and I enjoy it. I like the fact that it's weird and unbelievable and that it involves money, something we tend to be avaricious about that can bring us no good in the long run. This was one of the many stories I heard when I was growing up as a child in my hometown of Berwyn, Pennsylvania and in Philadelphia where I did most of my schooling. The stories that particularly fascinated me were these set in Chester county from Devon through Berwyn to West Chester on down to Kennett Square, Avondale and West Grove. . . . I loved these tales of the ghostly and the inexplicable; I loved them because my families enjoyed them as part factual and part lies. They were as real to me as any young reader hearing Washington Irving's *Legend of Sleepy Hollow.* In fact, there used to be a headless horseman who rode around on Devon Hill. Or so the story goes. And there would be automobile accidents in Radnor as people tried avoiding a woman trying to cross Lancaster Pike in her nightgown at Martha Brown's Woods.

This was part of the orality I inherited from my family. How and why I became a writer and poet in light of this I cannot explain. What I understand of literacy and my own experience stems from these local legends, and I prefer also to believe stems from my appreciation of the narrative styles of those who told me. My father's manner was dry and matter-of-fact but he appreciated humor and liked to tease. His mother's recitations were concentrated and musical and as reverent as another of her son's, my uncle Charlie's, was irreverent. My mother's family has a style based in wonder of fact and supposition. I learned a lot from my mother about the ghostly stuff and about their grandmother who was born a slave in Delaware, and who with her son kept the family together after his wife, a Cherokee woman, died. One of my uncles tells stories with this tone of wonder while another could hold us spellbound by emphasizing the kind of details that begged plausibility. As much as I read and was encouraged to read as a youngster, they were special as my first real storytellers. Their stories instructed me in style and technique and theme. I appreciated their individuality of style. They helped develop my ears. I developed writing skills by another means. I did quite well with four years of high school Latin. In ninth grade my classmates paid me a nickel per translation assignment. I was reading ahead, because I wanted to keep up with a buddy who went to another school. Those years of reading and translating the periodic sentences and extended clauses of Caesar's Gallic wars, Cicero's orations, and Vergil's *Aeneid* affected my syntax irrevocably; but it seemed to put me on an inside track for reading Faulkner. In these days of talking about cultural literacy I believe the combination of what I listened to and what I read enriches me constantly, because I remember, and because I never felt my Chester county legacy of tales was any less significant to my identity than Cicero's brilliant expose of Cataline. And so my favorite poets and writers blend the learned with the ironies of traditional storytelling: Borges, Faulkner, Garcia Marquez, Momaday, Ellison, Fitzgerald, Wallace Stevens, U'Tamsi, Morrison, Nin just as a few in no particular order.

I am a Pennsylvanian, descended from the original inhabitants of the Delmarva Peninsula, the Chesapeake region, and the Great Smokies. And I'm descended from peoples brought forcibly here from Africa. This combination of Native and

African, at one time in my life the African-American holding
emphasis, this rural-small town birth and urban upbringing,
have all affected my listening and seeing profoundly as a
writer and poet. I don't know if my poems and stories or their
personae *sound* Pennsylvanian. Wallace Stevens is eastern
Pennsylvania's best-known poet and I've come rather late to
appreciate his work; yet let me be bold to say that we enjoy
apparently the colors and birds and the sky, and we know
something of love and disappointment that we express in special ways. Like Stevens, I love music; I doubt that we sound the
same, however. When I heard a tape of Stevens speaking, or
reading his poems, although I realize that one's reading voice
may differ from one's casual speech, I listened and didn't hear
the kinds of patterns I grew up with.

...My Cherokee grandmother died when my mother was
five so much of her speech came from her eighty-year-old
grandmother, the ex-slave from Delaware. My father's mother
was a Lenape or Nanticoke or Piscataway mixed with a tribal
group that had hid out in the mountains of upstate Pennsylvania. I've come to understand a certain standoffishness the family had; part of their ease about things lies in knowing who
they were, just enough not to want to be bothered with nonsense. They were independent and proud but not arrogant.
That's another long legacy. It's their stories that mean so much
for now. I can't separate their content from the inflections of
the way they were told in that pure rural southern Pennsylvania speech where parts of words are swallowed, where *e*'s
sound like *i*'s and a fire was *a fahr*. With these mannerisms, I listened to the stories of people being sealed up in walls of old
houses, of my great-grandmother struggling with her horse to
drive past a scene of roadside death, or an old woman who fed
the bodies of the dead to the crows. It was my inheritance, and
at age twenty-three I made a conscious decision to be a writer.
It was the best way I knew to preserve some of that legacy and
extend it.

My grandmother taught me how to listen just by pointing
out what she was listening to; and from my father I guess I
learned the importance of trying to see what I was looking at.
My mother introduced me to subtlety. How my responses and

perceptions are the result of my Indian ancestry or Black ancestry, I don't fully know. A love of sky and the land, of birds; a
belief in this Turtle continent as a mother land and not some
place else. And yet a favorable response to field hollers and
blues, and to jazz and jazz orchestrations. So many Native
Americans in the eastern United States have lived in the
African-American world and constitute a unique color line,
responding to all sorts of seemingly contradictory symbols and
feelings but holding on to something that is Native. This might
be in the preference for a certain type of shoe or an innate ability to put certain kinds of things together and insure survival
in hard times. I've learned to see many sides of an emotion and
an issue, even when I disagree. I appreciate and see relationships and shapes, ideas and designs, peripheries and vor-
tices—my first published poetry collection was entitled
Peripheries (1972). It seems that I can understand the edge of
things because that's where I have been: looking in; almost
good enough; watching; measuring; and absorbing; listening. I
find great poetry in a flock of birds rising to the air and changing shape; and there is something of absolute poetry in certain
recorded jazz solos like John Coltrane's on "Autumn Sere-
nade" sung by Johnny Hartman, and George Adams for
"Flowers For A Lady" on *Mingus Moves*.

My alma mater, Lincoln University in Pennsylvania, invited me about ten years ago to participate in a Langston Hughes festival. I spent the nights at the home of emeritus
psychology professor Henry Cornwell and his wife, Sophie, a
librarian and Spanish teacher. The day of the festival as the
professor and I set out eastward across the track field that once
was a plain field, two red-tailed hawks flew above, intersecting our path, performing as it seemed, some kind of playful yet
celebrative ritual. I stopped and watched them swoop and
glide and soar and speed up in the air drafts heading north
over the rolling hills that characterize Chester county. They
were not eagles but they reminded me of Scott Momaday's
description of two eagles in *House Made of Dawn*. They made
spirals and arabesques and I saw their presence and flight as
special and just as holy as Momaday's eagles. I felt blessed and
was glad to be alive that day. Those red-tails may have been

there to celebrate the award I did not then realize I would receive that evening. But at that moment they confirmed for me the beauty and freedom of the imagination and reaffirmed my connection to the land, that I was a part of this very old land. I saw their flight as wonderfully mysterious as birth and love and dying. I have never written about that morning until now; obviously, I will never forget it. Poets and writers tend to see with the heart. The hawks and I were in the same place for a reason. I suppose I attach significance to these kinds of things, and I can't separate it from academic questions about cultural literacy. Irony intrigues me as does paradox. I have an idea about cycles and circles. My poems and stories are attempts to articulate my emotions and perceptions, and I employ concrete or abstract and elliptical diction as the occasion demands. Seeing and listening interact and sometimes trade functions. There's so much noise in our world that the subtle is hard to find; but I'm still able to hear a leaf fall.

BUILDING YOUR PORTFOLIO

As usual, you may choose any one or several of these portfolio activities, depending on your own needs and interest.

Connections within a Work

1. Understanding patterns is one way to see connections within a work. We have patterns of words, structures, images, events, and symbols; their arrangement can be linear, chronological, spatial, parallel, clustered, intersected, and more. Just as you might respond to an individual word in a word-association game, you respond to patterns as well.

   Any pattern you could make in two or three dimensions you can establish in a work. You might discover a pattern of repeated words, sentences, or line structures. You might see an image or description (light contrasted with darkness, perhaps) repeated at significant moments. You might notice the presence of a significant object or symbol whenever an important event happens. Perhaps every moment of tension is followed by an anticlimax. Perhaps everything—characters, events, settings—comes in threes. In *Macbeth*, there is an interplay between the dualities of inside and outside, positive and negative, personal and social, moral and political, appearances and reality. If you interpreted the work from this perspective, you would be looking for the whole to be more than the sum of its parts.

Use the guide that follows to look for patterns and resonances within a work you are reading (or have to read). Make notes on each of the following; then choose one or more dominant patterns to focus on and write an analysis based on them:

- What patterns do you see: words, structures, images, events, symbols, anything else?
- What is the arrangement of each pattern: linear, clustered, something else?
- How are the patterns related to each other? Can you make a map or chart or drawing of them?
- So what? How does this look at the connections among the connections of dots inform your reading and understanding of the work?

2. Every work of literature has movement and change. The action changes. The level of tension changes. Characters change. Circumstances and surroundings change. Point of view, authorial voice, tone, diction, imagery, rhythm, and everything else on the list of terms and concepts can change. Even the rate of change can change. And, of course, the reader's views of anything and everything can change.

What changes is important; equally important are *how* and *why* changes occur. To understand the significance of change in a work, note when changes take place and why they are happening: what causes them, how we are aware of them, and what they mean inside and beyond the world of the work.

Keep a reading log to track important kinds of change related to a main character in a work you are reading. The following are possible character changes. Don't try to deal with all of them, but select a few worth following:

- a character's self-perception
- a character's perception of other characters
- a character's perception of important places (home), objects (a talisman), or past or anticipated events (childhood, death)
- a character's perception of time—the past, the future, the passage of time, one's place in time, escape from time
- a character's goals or values
- a character's speech and behavior (word choice, methods of dealing with conflict)
- other characters' perceptions of this character
- the reader's perception of this character

When you are finished, you will have the basis for a paper or talk.

Connections between a Work and Your Experiences

3. Reader-response theorists see reading as an interaction between the norms and values of a text and the norms and values of a reader. Use the guide that follows to help you articulate the nature and results of your confrontation with a work. Answer these questions as you read:

- What are the key features of the text that strike you? What responses, reactions, feelings, associations, or speculations arise?
- What issues in the work are placed in the background? In the foreground? What values are stated or implied in the text? How do these compare with your own views? How do they challenge your personal views? Do you re-see or change your views as a result of the reading?
- How do your views of the work and subject change as you read? What meanings are you formulating? When and how do they change as you proceed? From what to what?
- What kinds of gaps do you have to fill in? What contexts of knowledge and experience are you required to apply? How do you infer, hypothesize, make guesses, or otherwise make connections?

- How do you look forward and back, decide on things, change your decisions, form expectations, react when they aren't fulfilled, question, ponder, reject or accept, and reach new understandings?
- What has happened to you as a result of reading? What personal views have been reversed, modified, challenged, or confirmed by this reading? What are you now—after reading—that you weren't before reading?

Connections between and among Readers

4. Review your notes from a dialogue journal you have been keeping or from the readaround you did earlier. Then write a paper showing how your view of a literary work changed because of the insights others gave you. You might want to organize this paper into two general parts: "What I thought then" and "What I think now."

Connections between and among Works

5. This activity involves various possible pairings. You could do some traditional pairs, such as *My Fair Lady* and *Pygmalion* or *West Side Story* and *Romeo and Juliet*, but we suggest you try others that are less obvious. In each case, you will have to decide how to handle the works as well as supply the "So what?" Here are some interpretive possibilities:

- use one work as a lens through which to read the other (for example, look at "Mirror" through "Sonnet 73")
- explain one work through the other (use "Hansel and Gretel" to explain "Gretel in Darkness")
- start a correspondence between characters or speakers from the two works (Grendl and Mordred on E-mail)
- switch characters and contexts and tell what might happen (put Ahab or Odysseus in *Going after Cacciato*—or any other modern quest story)
- retell one story as a character from another might tell it (let Two Dollar Mommy retell "To His Coy Mistress")

Now here are some suggested pairings:

- "Life, Friends, Is Boring" (John Berryman) and *The Stranger* (Albert Camus)

- *The Great Gatsby* (F. Scott Fitzgerald) and "Siren Song" (Margaret Atwood).

- *Jane Eyre* (Charlotte Bronte) and *Wide Sargasso Sea* (Jean Rhys)

- *The Bluest Eye* (Toni Morrison) and "The Blue Bouquet" (Octavio Paz)

- "Law Like Love" (W. H. Auden) and "The Book of the Grotesque" (introduction to Sherwood Anderson's *Winesburg, Ohio*).

6. Select two or more works (from those listed above or your own choices) and write five comparative claims about them, one claim from each area of the pentad. Organize the claims as a hypertext and ask a classmate to work with it and tell you how he or she reads it.

7. Select one of the critical perspectives from Chapter 3 and write comparative claims for each part of it for two literary works. Decide which work to feature overall and use the comparisons to highlight that work in an interpretive paper.

8. Make your own mini-anthology composed of fifteen or twenty works you consider important. Make a contents outline of titles that shows how you want the anthology organized (see Chapter 2 on ways to organize). Write a foreword that explains your principles of selection and introduces the book.

9. A *chrestomathy* is a selection of passages brought together to help one to learn a language. A primer in French or Spanish is such a work— read this stuff and you will learn the language. In this case, the language we're interested in is the particular language of the literature classroom. Compile a group of texts that, when read (and viewed or heard), would allow the learner to experience how you and your classmates experience the literary language of your classroom. Just as one could set the flavor of Renaissance language by reading and hearing Renaissance works, one can also get the flavor of your literary language. Your chrestomathy could include literary texts, papers and responses, pictures, tapes, and anything else you think will be instructive. Include a brief introduction that defines the language you are setting out to teach and explains the selections you include.

Connections between and among Cultural and Literary Contexts

10. Plan and conduct your own multicultural study by selecting groups of works from a number of different cultures. Use one of the guides to perspectives in Chapter 3 to organize your approach. The historical-cultural perspective is an obvious one but may not be the most interesting. For a performance, you might try the format of the "Coffee Shop" portfolio activity explained in Chapter 5.

READER'S FORUM

The focus of this chapter is making connections, so your instructor may want to organize "Reader's Forum" activities around the categories of connectedness. If you schedule your own activity, be sure to explain what kind or kinds of connectedness your presentation relates to.

Your instructor may assign you a topic, or you may choose one yourself from the chapter activities.

PORTFOLIO PROGRESS REPORT

At the end of Chapter 5, you completed a midpoint assessment and a revision of your goals. Now here are the "Progress Report" questions for you to answer about your work in making connections:

1. **Knowledge:** What *do you know* that you didn't know before?
2. **Practice:** What *can you do* that you couldn't do (or do as well) before?
3. **Habits:** What *do you do* that you didn't do (or do as much) before?

For this "Progress Report," review your work with the activities below and then write at least a few paragraphs in your "Portfolio Notebook" to answer each of the three questions:

- the response guide in which you projected three endings to a story
- the results of your readaround

- your comparative claims about "Death" and "Death, Be Not Proud"
- the stories patterned after famous stories
- your comparative analyses of Ron Welburn's writings
- the various activities you responded to in "Building Your Portfolio"
- your experiences as a reader and speaker in "Reader's Forum"

MOVING ON

You saw how to make connections within a work, as well as across works and readers and cultural contexts. In the next chapter, you will move on from connections to evaluations: how to make useful and valid judgments about the quality of what you read.

7 Evaluating and Judging Literature

▶▶▶**LOOKING AHEAD**

To this point in your education, most of your work has been judged by others. Now it is your turn to do some judging. In this chapter, you will see distinctions among interpreting, criticizing, and reviewing. You will learn the basis for making judgments about literature, as well as some means of justifying those judgments.

You will have an opportunity to develop and practice your own criteria for evaluation. You might even try to save "Little Libbie," if you are so moved. At the end of the chapter, you will be able to sketch a portrait of yourself as a reader.

SUBJECT TO INTERPRETATION

Much of what we have been writing about so far in this book deals with how people interpret what they read. Interpreting is making meaning out of the poem and the text, crossing the gaps and breaks in the text as we describe it. But interpreting is not all that people do with what they read or see. A good part of a critic's time is spent judging or evaluating what has been read—that is, deciding and then explaining what is good or bad about it.

Some people say that the main job of a critic is this analysis and judging; interpretation is something else. "After all, you don't interpret a pie at a county fair," as one critic put it. Other people believe that interpretation is the main task; the critic must accept the potential greatness of all works of literature. "The critic's job is not to praise or blame but to understand," another critic has said. Praising or blaming—that is, making judgments—is the job of the reviewer, the person who decides on behalf of a reading public what, of all that is published, is worth paying attention to.

Criticism in the sense of judging or evaluating is really comparison. You are comparing the new book or poem or film to ones you already know and trying to decide where it fits in your scale of one to ten. Sometimes you are comparing the new book to a set of criteria, rules, and models for a good book that you have derived from your previous reading. After you have read a number of books, you develop a mental picture of what sort of book you think is good. Then you rate the new one by trying to fit it into the blueprint. (By the way, this is precisely the same process that teachers use when they judge your papers or your portfolio.)

Whether it is the job of the critic or that of the reviewer, evaluating literary works is something people do and something you may be called upon to do and defend in one or more of your courses. How do you make these decisions? How do you support them? What about the classics? How do you write reviews? And what place do reviews have in the portfolio?

BASES FOR JUDGING LITERATURE

When people judge what they read, they usually base their judgment on one or more criteria that involve such things as the appeal of the work, the value of what it says, and the effectiveness of its language and style. Critics and reviewers of literature use similar criteria. They look, for example, at what the writer says and at how he or she says it. They can treat the *what* in terms of emotional impact or intellectual content. They can treat the *how* in terms of form, tradition, and intention. Here are some of the questions that critics, and you, can ask in evaluating a work.

Is the Emotional Impact Successful?

This question involves whether the work succeeded in arousing an emotion in you, and secondly whether that was the emotion you think the author wanted you to have. These two questions are not quite the same. Take a look at the following poem:

Little Libbie
While eating dinner, this dear little child
Was choked on a piece of beef.
Doctors came, tried their skill awhile,
But none could give relief. . . .
5   Her friends and schoolmates will not forget
Little Libbie that is no more;
She is waiting on the shining step,
To welcome home friends once more.

—Julia Moore

This poem, by Julia Moore, known as "The Sweet Singer of Michigan," and also parodied in *Huckleberry Finn*, was written as an elegy and published in the local newspaper. We believe that Julia Moore intended us to feel sad and sorry for little Libbie's parents and family. But most people who read the poem cannot help laughing at the literal depiction of the child's death and at the clumping rhythm of the piece. The emotion aroused is not the emotion intended.

Often writers, particularly in longer works, will want their readers to feel a number of emotions. A novel or a play about a serious subject will often have a break with humor so that the tension can be released. In *Macbeth*, Shakespeare presents the murder scene and then follows it immediately with a brief scene of the drunken porter opening the gate for those who will discover the murder. This is one of the most famous examples of "comic relief" in literature, since we will have worked up a great deal of tension watching Macbeth and Lady Macbeth plot, execute, and then discuss the bloodiness of the murder. First a knock is heard, stopping the action and the intense emotion; then the scene shifts to the soliloquy of the drunken porter. It lasts only about two minutes; then the murder is discovered and the horror comes back. There are no comic moments in the play after that. Shakespeare has successfully roused our emotions and then broken the tension.

The same device is used in horror films and in suspense novels. Sustaining an intense emotion for a long period of time is difficult, and it can make the reader uncomfortable. More commonly, an intense emotion will be briefly held. A lyric poem may hold an emotion like sorrow or ecstatic love for the period of a page or two, but a longer poem or a novel will have peaks of emotion interspersed with periods of calm. The success of an emotional piece, then, usually lies in its capacity to have you both feel the emotion and remember with pleasure that you felt it.

Is the Content Believable?

One of the main criteria concerning the content of a work of literature is that it is believable. Some critics only accept as good those works that could really happen in this world. They do not accept literature with talking animals or spaceships or the like. If a novel is historical, all characters must speak and act the way they would have in the period under discussion. Such critics will often find fault with a work because nobody in it ever has to go to the bathroom.

If you adopt this criterion, you may be limiting yourself. After all, there are two kinds of belief: belief *that* and belief *in*. Let us take the example of a fairy tale like some of those of Hans Christian Andersen. The first sentences announce that the story may not be literally true:

- "There once was a prince, and he wanted a princess, but then she must be a *real* princess. . . . "
- "In a village there once lived two men of the selfsame name. . . . "
- "Far out at sea, the water is as blue as the bluest cornflower, as clear as the clearest crystal, but it is very deep, too deep for any cable to fathom, and if many steeples were piled on the top of one another, they would

not reach from the bed of the sea to the surface of the water. It is down there that the mermen live."

We know that probably such a prince did not exist, that there may not have been two men with exactly the same name, and that there is no place where the mermen live, but we are willing to enter into the world of the story. As we read, we engage in what the critic Samuel Taylor Coleridge called "the willing suspension of disbelief that constitutes poetic faith." We are ready to believe in the characters of the story for the time we are reading it or watching it. During that time, there may be a princess who can feel a pea underneath a large number of mattresses; two men, Big Claus and Little Claus; or a world of mermen and the Little Mermaid.

We enter into the world of the story or play. But sometimes the writer can do something that makes us fall out of that state of faith. Suddenly we do not believe. In a historical work, one of the characters may suddenly say something that doesn't fit, such as when Odysseus says in a film version of *The Odyssey,* "So long, Cyclops!" At times, the writer may do this on purpose to remind us that it is only a story, but that is a deliberate stepping back from the work.

When we judge a work for its credibility, then, we usually judge whether or not we are successfully led into the world of the work, not whether the events could actually have happened.

FOR YOUR PORTFOLIO NOTEBOOK

Classify a Play

Look at the first few lines of the following play. What can you tell about the world of the play? Is it a realistic play? Is it going to be humorous or serious? Which part—title, cast, setting, or opening dialogue—gives you the clearest clues as to what is going to happen?

Out at Sea
Characters
    Fat Castaway
    Medium Castaway
    Thin Castaway
    Postman
    Butler

The action takes place in a single act and with a single set, which represents a raft out at sea. Three shipwrecked men, in smart black suits and white shirts, with their ties correctly tied and white handkerchiefs sticking out of the top pockets of their coats, are each sitting on a chair. There is also a large trunk on the raft.

FAT: I am hungry.
MEDIUM: I could do with some food.
THIN: Are the provisions entirely exhausted?
FAT: The provisions are entirely exhausted. There is not the tiniest morsel.

—Slawomir Mrozek

Is the Content Imaginative?

When we judge a work to be imaginative or unimaginative, we go beyond whether we can actually believe in the work. We step back and say whether or not the writer created a world that is interesting and enjoyable to inhabit. Most authors write stories, poems, or plays that might begin with the phrase, "What if . . . ?" What if a man murdered his father and married his mother without realizing it (*Oedipus Rex*)? What if a woman fell passionately in love with the willful and passionate adopted childhood friend of her youth even though she was married to the staid neighbor's son (*Wuthering Heights*)?

The idea behind these two stories, the "what if," is an interesting one, and we wonder what would be the consequences if we accept the question. Often, however, we look at the question posed by the idea of the book and respond "So what?" to the "What if?" We don't find the idea particularly imaginative and interesting. This can often happen with books or stories that are based on very commonplace events, such as a story about a first romance. Whether you are evaluating the content and saying that it is trite and unoriginal or evaluating the way the writer handles the genre (see below, pages 212–13) may sometimes be a tough call. Probably you are doing both.

Is the Content Important?

It is one thing to say that the content is imaginative and interesting; it is another to decide whether it is trivial or important. Some contemporary writers may bring up an important issue of the time, such as AIDS, the environment, or atomic destruction. Other writers will deliberately stay away from these sorts of issues and deal with more timeless subjects, such as the loss of a parent. We can say that both sorts of issues are important ones that people have to deal with. Is one more important than the other?

Critics often distinguish between the subject and the theme. Shakespeare wrote a play about a young prince who suspects that his uncle murdered his father. He sets out to establish whether his suspicion is true and gets involved in a series of intrigues that lead to the death of a whole number of people. You might say that a court intrigue is not a particularly serious subject even though the story involves a number of deaths. It's about as serious as an episode of *Murder, She Wrote*. But at the same time you can argue that Shakespeare is dealing with issues of appearance and reality, of the psychology of revenge, of action as opposed to thought, of the importance of family relationships. By these criteria, *Hamlet* is not just a mystery drama but a full-scale tragedy.

Some people have read Coleridge's *Rime of the Ancient Mariner* as a poem about the killing of wildlife. As a poem about shooting albatrosses, it spends a lot of words on a subject that may not deserve such attention. But a good number of other people would say that the poem only uses the incident of the shooting of the albatross as the springboard for a meditation on guilt and on the power of the imagination to redeem people from a selfish worldliness. Then the poem is seen as much more serious.

Judging whether a work is serious or not is a risky business. Many critics have gotten into arguments about whether one topic is more serious than another. That's a rather fruitless argument. More important may be whether you think the writer has treated a serious topic seriously or not. At this point in history, writing a comedy about people in concentration camps would seem to be inappropriate. It is just as inappropriate to write poems that begin as these do:

> Spade! With which Wilkinson has tilled his lands
>> —Wordsworth, "To the Spade of a Friend"

> Inoculation, heavenly maid descend!
>> —Anonymous, quoted by S. T. Coleridge

> How brave a prospect is a bright backside!
>> —Henry Vaughan

These are three lines quoted in the volume *The Stuffed Owl: An Anthology of Bad Verse*, compiled by D. B. Wyndham Lewis and Charles Lee. One of their criteria for inclusion is a mismatch of emotion and seriousness. It may be possible to write a serious poem about a spade or inoculation, but these are not topics with which we usually associate serious literature.

A mismatch of the seriousness of the topic and the seriousness of the work may work in a satire or allegory. John Donne wrote a satirical love poem about a flea; Robert Burns wrote a satire about a louse. Franz Kafka wrote a story about a man who turns into a cockroach. This work, *Metamorphosis,* may start out to seem silly, but it turns into a psychological masterpiece according to many critics, who see the transformation as being mental rather than physical.

FOR YOUR PORTFOLIO NOTEBOOK
Make Your Own Judgments

Compare "Little Libbie" with these two poems on the death of children. How would you rank the three poems on the handling of content? What are the criteria underlying your choice? Write your ideas in your "Portfolio Notebook" and be ready to discuss them in class.

Upon a Child That Died
Here she lies a pretty bud,
Lately made of flesh and blood:
Who as soon fell fast asleep
As her little eyes did peep,
Give her strewings, but not stir
The earth that lightly covers her.
                        —Robert Herrick

katrina
Katrina, now you are suspended between earth and sky.
Tubes feed you glucose intravenously. Naked you lie
In your special room in Ward Fifteen. Is your life
Opening again or closing finally? We do not know, but fear
5   The telephone call from a nurse whose distant sympathy

Will be the measure of our helplessness. Your twin brother's
Two-month-old vigour hurts us, remembering
Thin straws of sunlight on your bowed legs kicking
In defiance of your sickness, your body's wasting.
10 Against the black velvet of death threatening
Your life shines like a jewel, each relapse a flash of light
The more endearing. Your mother grieves already, so do I.
Miracles do not tempt us. We are getting in early,
Although we know there is no conditioning process which
  can counter
15 The karate-blow when it comes,
No way we can arrange the date-pad to conceal
The page torn-off, crumpled, thrown away.
Katrina, I had in mind a prayer, but only this came,
And you are still naked between earth and sky.
20 Transfusion-wounds in your heels, your dummy taped in
  your mouth.

—Bruce Dawe

Is the Writer Sincere?

Judging the sincerity of the writer is also tricky. The writers we listed above who wrote about spades and inoculation were probably quite sincere in their appreciation of what they were writing about. But there are other cases where a writer is writing a story about a serious event, and we suspect that he or she is just capitalizing on the market. This is often the case with fiction or "true fiction" pieces about recent murder cases or scandalous divorces. Many of the made-for-television films are written to capitalize on sensational stories in the news.

Famous writers in the past have also based their works on current events, and even great writers often wrote about topics in order to please a patron. When Shakespeare wrote *Macbeth*, he did so at a time when James VI of Scotland was coming to the throne of England as James I, and some have said that he included the witches' prophecy of the long line of kings descended from Banquo just to establish the legitimacy of James. Perhaps such was the case, but we can no longer establish whether Shakespeare was sincere or not. At any rate, it is hard to judge the play good or bad based on this one accusation.

Is the Content Morally Appropriate?

Related to sincerity may be the issue of morality. Often we judge a work by whether it deals with a moral issue from a perspective with which we agree. We probably would not call a poem good if it attempted to celebrate the virtues of cannibalism. But there are a number of works dealing with topics about which opinion has changed. Many eighteenth- and nineteenth-century writers spoke condescendingly about people different from them. Bret Harte wrote about "the heathen Chinee," Edgar Allan Poe appears to disparage women, Edgar Lee Masters's "The Congo" refers to the savagery of Africans. Clearly, these works deal in what we now know as demeaning stereotypes.

Does that mean the works are no longer good? This has become a political question rather than one of literary judgment. Some works, like Shakespeare's *The Merchant of Venice* and Mark Twain's *Huckleberry Finn*, have been banned in certain places because they appear to advocate anti-Semitism and anti-black beliefs. But critics have also defended both works on the grounds that the writers take up the issues of prejudice but do not necessarily advocate being prejudiced. In other cases, people know that certain writers were prejudiced or that they held political ideas with which we no longer agree. A number of major twentieth-century writers were communists, even Stalinists. A number held strong religious beliefs, and some, like Salman Rushdie and H. L. Mencken, criticized religious groups. Many readers may disagree violently with these positions. Does that mean the various pieces they have written are bad?

There has been a great deal written in the past few years about this issue. Some argue that we should reject those works that do not fully support our contemporary moral values. Others argue that since moral values change, it is wrong to use such a criterion to deny value to a particular work. Another aspect of the issue is whether the work should be separated from the author. Some critics argue that the particular morals of an author are irrelevant if the work does not take up a morally offensive position; others tend to discount the work because of the position or behavior of the author. Several famous writers have been in prison as criminals or have been in mental institutions. Should those facts color the judgment of the quality of their work?

A third aspect of this criterion is not whether the morality expressed in the work is "correct" or not, but whether the writer has raised the moral issue at all. Critics have praised Mark Twain because he raised the issue of slavery in *Huckleberry Finn* and raised it as a moral issue rather than simply a political one. Critics have made the same claim about Shakespeare. This is different from the works of writers who glorified the "old South" and the idea of the "happy slaves" and seemed to be unconcerned with the moral question.

Is the Work Well Written?

The questions about how well the work is written are as complicated as the questions about the content of the work. A well-written work, according to various critics, is one that

- uses or doesn't use interesting and novel words
- has vivid or familiar imagery
- uses metaphors or is absolutely literal
- has or avoids a strict rhythm and rhyme (if it's a poem)
- has a clear beginning, middle, and end or can be seen as never starting or ending
- has sharp characterization or uses familiar stock characters
- has no loose ends or leaves something to your imagination
- has a single or multiple point of view

There are many more variations on these criteria. One of the major features of stylistic preferences and criteria is that the fashions in style in literature have changed about as much as fashions in clothes or furniture.

There have been times when people have favored writing that was filled with ornate language and metaphor, and a writer like Edgar Allan Poe was clearly admired. At other times, critics have praised writers like Ernest Hemingway with his almost flat language and limited use of metaphor. The variations in style today are such that one will find terse and ornate writers, poets who use rhyme and traditional forms, and poets who use free verse and a seeming lack of form. Critics will praise one or the other style, and in fact the same critic can praise both.

The one stylistic criterion to which most critics adhere is that of consistency. If a writer chooses a particular style, critics want the writer to stay with it throughout the book or the poem. A particular style sets the reader up to expect that certain things will happen; a story told from one point of view should stay with that point of view unless there is some clear signal that a switch is coming. A poem that begins as a ballad should probably end as a ballad. To break out of a style is to jar a reader. Breaking out works only in certain kinds of selections that ask the reader to play along with the game of interrupting the stylistic flow.

Is the Work Effectively Written?

If it is difficult to come up with a firm objective criterion for style, it may be easier to come up with one for effectiveness. An effective piece of writing is one that does its job well. This means that the critic is thinking of the rhetorical effect of the piece of literature. If the work is a psychological thriller, the effect presumably is to make the reader's skin crawl. Whatever the writer does to strengthen that effect is to be praised as contributing to it; whatever detracts from that effect may be held against it.

The praise for the porter scene in *Macbeth* is praise for rhetorical effectiveness as well for emotional effectiveness. In fact, the two are often closely tied, but when we make the judgment of rhetorical effectiveness, we are looking at *how* Shakespeare did it, focusing on the timing of the scene, its relatively brief length, and on the fact that the scene's tone shifts from humor to horror. Another example of rhetorical effectiveness can be found in this short poem:

A Poison Tree
I was angry with my friend:
I told my wrath, my wrath did end.
I was angry with my foe:
I told it not, my wrath did grow.

5   And I water'd it in fears.
Night and Morning with my tears;
And I sunned it with smiles,
And with soft deceitful wiles.

And it grew both day and night,
10   Till it bore an apple bright;
And my foe beheld it shine,
And he knew that it was mine.

And into my garden stole
When the night had veil'd the pole:
15   In the morning glad I see
My foe outstretch'd beneath the tree.

—William Blake

Many critics have praised the way in which Blake sets up the contrast
between openness and hypocrisy. The open approach gets two lines;
the hypocritical one gets fourteen. It takes a long time to work revenge,
and we do it by nursing a grudge. The use of the series of *Ands* at the
beginning of several lines adds to the mounting succession of nasti-
ness. Then there is the break before the last two lines and no *and*; the
result simply follows as a logical consequence of what has gone on
before. The poem is simple and direct, and its effect is one of relentless
logic and just plain meanness. Form and meaning work together well.

FOR YOUR PORTFOLIO NOTEBOOK

Your Own Judgments Again

Look at the following poem. Aside from being written in stanzas, how
is it divided and how does the division affect your judgment of the
quality of the poem? Do you think the structure makes the poem work
or works against it? Write some notes on your ideas.

To Make a Play

To make a play
is to make people,
to make people do
what you say;

to make real people
do and say
what you make;
to make people make
what you say real;
to make real

people come to see
what you do.
They see what *they*
do, and they

may go away undone.
You can make
people, or you
can unmake. You
can do or you
can undo. People

people make up
and do what you

make up. What you
make makes people
come and see
what people do

and say, and then
go away and do
what they see—
and see what

they do. Real
people do and say,
and you see and
make up people;

you make up make up
and make people;

people come to
see—to see
themselves real,
and they go away

and do what you
say—as if they
were made up
and wore make-up.

To make a play
is to make
people; to make
people make

themselves; to
make people
make themselves
new. So real.

—May Swenson

Does the Work Use the Genre Well?

Often a critic will say of a film, "It's a horror film, but it's a good one."
The critic implies that he or she doesn't really think that horror films
are as great as some other kind of film, but this one is a good example
of its kind.

Earlier in this book we discussed genre, or the form of a work of literature. A particular genre develops a kind of blueprint for a work.
Many horror films have some scenes in which ordinary people are suddenly confronted with whatever the horror may be. Often the scene
involves people at home cooking or watching television, and then outside the window is ... THE HORROR. This becomes a convention of
the genre, a part of the blueprint for horror films to use.

The same sort of convention is associated with different genres of
prose and poetry as well. The ballad, for example, "should" tell a story

of romance and treachery—a love tale, for example, where someone dies, or the tale of a hero or attractive villain (Robin Hood or Jesse James). It is supposed to use repetition and a particular meter and rhyme scheme. In Elizabethan times, a stage tragedy was "supposed" to be written in five acts and in rhymed or unrhymed verse.

Various critics have tried to write the "rules" for a particular genre—"the perfect short story," for example, or the ideal sonnet or one-act play. In some genres, there is a formula that publishers have established. In the past, you have probably read some series books or romances. Many of these have a formula so that each book will be like the others in some respects. Some of the more famous series, like Nancy Drew, were written by "factories" of writers who had the genre's formula and could turn out a new book quickly and easily. It wasn't a question of doing the genre well but of making each work seem like the others.

Computer programs are now available for writing certain kinds of formula books, and people have tried to program other genres as well. The results have generally not been successful. The rules or conventions for most genres are not so strict that one can program a template. Nonetheless, most critics have in their heads a model of "a good short story," which may or may not be exact. When they read a new short story, they consciously or unconsciously hold it up to the model and judge whether the new one fits or not. If it doesn't fit, it may be judged as a poor example.

Does the Work Use Tradition Well?

For some kinds of critics, tradition is as important as the genre. These critics also have a model in their heads, but it is a model of "how things have usually been done." Traditions help to form our notions of the genre, of course, but there are other kinds of traditions that tend to work across genres. Critics will talk about the "epic tradition," the "Romantic tradition," the "realist tradition," or the "feminist tradition." This defines not only a way of writing or a form but an attitude and perhaps even a selection of content.

In the history of film, for example, there emerged a tradition around the Western. It was in part based on fiction like Owen Wistar's *The Virginian* with its famous line, "When you say that, smile!" Later writers like Zane Grey and Louis L'Amour also contributed to the tradition. It became popular in film through such characters as Tom Mix, Hopalong Cassidy, and the Lone Ranger. The Western developed a whole set of clichés such as the white horse and white hat, the mustached villain, the corrupt sheriff, and the chase. As one critic has argued, these clichés quickly become archetypes, so that we take one look at a character in a Western and a whole set of associations and images follow from it. The Western tradition itself is an evolution of earlier romantic traditions of the ideal hero and perfect villain and the war between absolute good and absolute evil.

Once a tradition like this is established, a new work that calls itself a Western or is set in the same type of locale will be judged according to the tradition and particularly to the "classics" of the tradition (in this case, works like *Shane, Stagecoach,* and *High Noon*). The work may try to go along with the tradition or use it to break with it or play against it in some way.

Traditions, some critics have argued, are important to literature and a strong influence on writers. A writer may see himself or herself as part of a tradition or as breaking with it or changing it in some way. Because of the breaks that writers make with a previous tradition, they are often part of the evolution of that tradition, one of the forces that keep it a strong influence on future writers.

Is the Work Original?

This judgment, of course, is the flip side of the previous two. Many critics like the new as opposed to the traditional. They see as one of the strong points of a novelist like Isabel Allende or Jane Smiley the fact that they have done something that other writers may not have tried. They are unique or individual in their writing style rather than simply a copy of a genre or a tradition.

Critics have singled out the works of Shakespeare on this criterion. They claim that he took a set of traditions for the sonnet and for the play and made them into something new. There were other revenge tragedies before *Hamlet,* but in that play Shakespeare did something new with the characters, made them more complex, made the revenge more complicated, added a new dimension to the genre. At the end of the seventeenth century, Shakespeare was condemned for having violated the conventions of tragedy. His works were seen as not following the "rules" that some critics thought had been established for the good play. But other critics like Alexander Pope and Samuel Johnson praised Shakespeare for being an original poet, one who did not abide by the rules but created new ones.

Other writers whom we now admire were seen as doing something "new" in their time. Fyodor Dostoevsky, Jane Austen, Langston Hughes, and others have all been praised for bringing something new and original to writing. Being original is often a virtue; but being too original, of course, can mean simply that you are unread. When critics use the criterion of originality, they can use it either to praise or damn the author.

Does the Work Fulfill the Writer's Intention?

Finally, there is the judgment about whether a work successfully did what the author wanted to do. This is like a rhetorical judgment, but rather than argue back from the effect on the reader, it argues forward from the stated (or unstated) intention of the writer.

Like the other criteria, this has been a controversial one. Some critics have argued that the intentions of the writer don't particularly matter. A work like Walt Whitman's *Song of Myself* has been seen as representing the poet's attempt to write the Great American Poem. To some extent this is possibly true; what writer doesn't want to be seen as great? But is that the driving force behind Whitman's type of rhythm and imagery? Similarly, Harriet Beecher Stowe has been praised for writing a novel that advanced the cause of emancipation. That was possibly part of her intention, but she probably had other intentions when she wrote *Uncle Tom's Cabin*. As the movie producer Samuel Goldwyn once said to his writers, "If you want to send a message, try Western Union."

The problem with judging a work by its intention is that it is first difficult to decide what the intention was and then to say whether or not the writer met it.

FOR YOUR PORTFOLIO NOTEBOOK

Save Little Libbie

Look again at "Little Libbie":

> While eating dinner, this dear little child
> Was choked on a piece of beef.
> Doctors came, tried their skill awhile,
> But none could give relief. . . .

5 Her friends and schoolmates will not forget
   Little Libbie that is no more;
   She is waiting on the shining step,
   To welcome home friends once more.

                                    —Julia Moore

Given all the criteria we have discussed, is there any way you could make the case that this is a good poem? What criterion would you choose, and how would you make the argument? Write your ideas in your "Portfolio Notebook."

FOR YOUR PORTFOLIO NOTEBOOK

Judge the Reviews

Here are a number of reviews that have appeared over time (collected in *Rotten Reviews: A Literary Companion*, edited by Bill Henderson, which we recommend for a marvelous collection of reviewers' insults). Look at each to identify what criteria or criterion the reviewer has chosen and decide how the reviewer might go about supporting it. You may continue the review for a paragraph or so.

1. Mark Twain in 1897 on *The Deerslayer* by James Fenimore Cooper:

   In one place in *Deerslayer* and in the restricted space of two-thirds of a page, Cooper has scored 114 offenses against literary art out of a possible 115. It breaks the record.

2. Yvor Winters in 1932 on *The Bridge* by Hart Crane:

   A form of hysteria.... One thing he has demonstrated, the impossibility of getting anywhere with the Whitmanian inspiration. No writer of comparable ability has struggled with it before and it seems highly unlikely that any writer of comparable genius will struggle with it again.

3. John Burroughs in 1897 on *A Tale of Two Cities* by Charles Dickens:

Last winter I forced myself through his *Tale of Two Cities*. It was a sheer dead pull from start to finish. It all seemed so insincere, such a transparent make-believe, a mere piece of acting.

4. *The Springfield Republican* in 1884 on *The Adventures of Huckleberry Finn* by Mark Twain:

A gross trifling with every fine feeling.... Mr. Clemens has no reliable sense of propriety.

5. *The New York Herald Tribune* in 1951 on *Catcher in the Rye* by J. D. Salinger:

Recent war novels have accustomed us all to ugly words and images, but from the mouths of the very young and protected they sound peculiarly offensive ... the ear refuses to believe.

6. Voltaire in 1768 on *Hamlet* by William Shakespeare:

It is a vulgar and barbarous drama, which would not be tolerated by the vilest populace of France, or Italy ... one would imagine this piece to be the work of a drunken savage.

7. *The New York Times* in 1961 on *Catch-22* by Joseph Heller:

... it gasps for want of craft and sensibility.... The book is an emotional hodgepodge; no mood is sustained long enough to register for more than a chapter.

8. *The Saturday Review of Literature* in 1925 on *The Great Gatsby* by F. Scott Fitzgerald:

Mr. F. Scott Fitzgerald deserves a good shaking.... *The Great Gatsby* is an absurd story, whether considered as romance, melodrama, or plain record of New York high life.

9. Thomas Bailey Aldrich in 1892 on Emily Dickinson:

An eccentric, dreamy, half-educated recluse in an out-of-the-way New England village—or anywhere else—cannot with impunity set at defiance the laws of gravity and grammar.... Oblivion lingers in the immediate neighborhood.

10. Arthur Cleveland Coxe in 1850 on *The Scarlet Letter* by Nathaniel Hawthorne:

Why has our author selected such a theme? ... the nauseous amour of a Puritan pastor, with a frail creature of his charge, whose mind is represented as far more debauched than her body? Is it in short, because a running undertide of filth has become a requisite to a romance, as death in the fifth act of a tragedy? Is the French era actually begun in our literature?

Justifying Your Judgments

As we hope you have gathered in reading through the last sections, there are two main points about judging or evaluating pieces of literature. The first is selecting your criterion or set of criteria. The second is putting the evidence together to support it.

Selecting the criterion means not only choosing whether you are going to make your judgment on, for example, the seriousness of the content. You will also have to decide which position about seriousness you are going to take. Are you all for deadly seriousness in a particular work, or do you think that literature should also have some fun and that this work is a bit too serious for its own good? The same choice applies to all of the criteria we have set forth in the previous section. A lot of critics and philosophers have made the distinction between "It is good" and "I like it": the first is objective, while the second is subjective. But with judgments about literature, the two merge.

We take what we like and then seek to find a more objective way of establishing that other people who share our criteria will also come up with the same liking.

What this means in practice is that you should follow the same principles of argument and persuasion that we have described in earlier chapters. As in other kinds of critical writing, so it is in evaluation. You have to state your claim (whether you think the work is an eagle or a turkey), set forth the warrants (which of the many criteria you are using and what your take on those criteria is), and then find the data in the text (and in other texts) to support the claim. It's that simple.

The only problem is getting others to agree with you. They have to accept your criterion, at least for the purpose of the review, and they have to agree that the work in question succeeds or fails by that criterion.

This means that your support must include a clear definition of the criterion that possibly explains why you have chosen that particular one or why you think it is an important criterion. Here you may need to explain that the criterion is important enough to count as the main criterion by which to judge the work. Then you will need to find the specific qualities of the book or poem that meet or fail to meet the criterion, and you will need to give examples to support the point. Here, there is always a problem as to whether your example is so small a portion of the book that it is not worth mentioning or so major a part of it that the whole book depends on it.

FOR YOUR PORTFOLIO NOTEBOOK

Write a Review

Write a review of one of the poems or prose pieces you read in another chapter of this book. Select a criterion or two on which to evaluate the work; then make your claim and assemble the data to support it.

DESCRIBING AND DEFINING LITERARY CANONS

One of the much discussed topics about literature these days concerns what is called the *canon.* If there is to be a value to literature and its study, a part of that value should lie in the presumed worth of particular texts, of a canon. Establishing a canon is taking the principles and criteria for evaluating literature and saying this particular set of principles helps us decide what we will read or what we will study. We can have a canon of well-written books, of books that are somehow significant, books that represent a particular cultural tradition, or some combination of these.

Some people argue that a canon is made up of classics, but determining a classic is not always easy. Some people say that a classic is a work that has stood the test of time. At the same time, there may be a change in fashion. When we were students and dinosaurs roamed the planet, the classic novels for high-school students were by Thomas Hardy, George Eliot, and Walter Scott. When we began teaching, the "classic" adolescent novel was *Mr. and Mrs. Bo Jo Jones*. It is no longer in print as far as we know. A classic is a book or a writer who won't go away. People keep trying to dump the writer or the book, but the work persists despite all the changes in fashion. Many would argue that a writer like Shakespeare is a good example of this kind of classic. He is hard to dismiss and has been ever since he began writing.

It may be hard to come up with a canon of books or authors that stands up for all people for a long time. A canon says to the people of a particular society or group in society that some common experiences are critical to the very idea of being a member of that group: "What, you have never read X? Well, you really have to read it right now!" For a course or literature department, a canon makes the claim that the curriculum is not based on "any old book" but on those books that refuse to be overlooked, that insist on our coming to terms with them. Instructors assert a canon in citing the Gettysburg Address or *The Wizard of Oz* or *Malcolm X* and in saying that people should not waste their time on *Sweet Valley High*. You assert a canon when you decide which books, films, or CDs you will buy or which you will select from a list.

We are not arguing for a particular canon or attacking the traditional canon of dead white European males. We are saying, with the critic Harold Bloom, that given the large number of things that are available and the short amount of time you have to read, you need to establish some ground rules for what you will read. Doing this will help explain your habits as a reader and justify them to other people. You may be a sci-fi freak. That's great. What are the principles by which you select which sci-fi books to read? Who are the authors that you keep going back to? How did you come by these titles and authors? The important point is that each reader, as well as many groups of readers, decide that some books should be read, rather than settling for any book. The crux lies in the principles by which the decision is made.

How do you establish those principles? Can you examine the various books that you have read and thought worthwhile and draw up some principles by which you would include other books in your list of worthwhile books? That is the way you make a canon.

FOR YOUR PORTFOLIO NOTEBOOK

Review Literary Canons

Go to some database and find a list of the best-sellers of twenty (or forty or eighty) years ago. Are any of the books still in print? Look at the reviews of those books and see if you can determine what criteria were operating then. Or look through the bookshelves of some older person you know. Interview the person about the books that he or she thinks of as classic and that everyone should read. Can the two of you reach a definition of the person's taste? How does it compare with yours? Write up your results and ideas in your "Portfolio Notebook."

BUILDING YOUR PORTFOLIO

There is clearly a place for reviews in a well-rounded portfolio, as well as a place for asserting your private literary canon. The following activities provide options in both of these areas:

1. What are your criteria for a good novel? Can you identify a set of general principles by which you make your ratings and choices? Write out your criteria and then check the reading you have done in this class against them. Do your choices correspond to your criteria? Now compare your ideas with those of a classmate or friend. On what principles do you agree? What are the major areas of disagreement?

2. You are the reviewer for a local newspaper. Select a new book from the "recent titles" selection of your local bookstore or library and write both a two-hundred-word capsule review and a one-thousand-word feature review. What did you have to include in the short one to make sense? How hard was it to do?

3. One of the favorite exercises of instructors, quizmasters on television, and admissions directors is to have you select the ten books that you would take to a desert island. Aside from *How to Build a Seaworthy Raft* and *The Art of Sailing a Small Craft*, what would your choices be? Look over these choices and see if you can discover some principles lying behind your choice. Is this your canon? What might you add to it by way of types of book or individual titles? Can you do the same for films or videos?

4. One of the things you will probably put in your portfolio is some sort of portrait of you the reader. Looking over the criteria and the exercises you have performed, write a draft of your self-portrait as a reader. How does your canon affect that portrait? How does what you say about yourself here compare with the autobiography you did in Chapter 1?

5. Here's a way to use your judgment about literature in a different way. Choose a short work you find especially good—it meets your criteria for a good work. Then work backward and write a bad earlier draft of the work. Make five or six changes that would make the work less good. Try making one change to show each of your evaluation criteria. For example, if *economy of language* is one of your criteria, take a succinct expression from the work and make it wordy and diluted in your earlier bad draft.

   When you have finished, you will have illustrated your evaluation criteria in reverse, sort of an "after and before" picture.

READER'S FORUM

Since all of the activities in this chapter are matters of judgment and opinion, you should expect to have to defend your views. Be sure you can explain why, how, and on what basis you hold the views you present about readers, works, and canons.

Your instructor may assign you a topic to present at "Reader's Forum," or you may choose one yourself from the chapter activities.

PORTFOLIO PROGRESS REPORT

Here are the same three questions you used for the previous "Progress Report":

1. **Knowledge:** What *do you know* that you didn't know before?
2. **Practice:** What *can you do* that you couldn't do (or do as well) before?
3. **Habits:** What *do you do* that you didn't do (or do as much) before?

For this "Progress Report," review your work with the activities below and then write at least a few paragraphs in your "Portfolio Notebook" to answer each of the three questions:

- evaluating the opening of a play
- comparing three poems on the death of a child
- judging works by various criteria
- saving "Little Libbie"
- identifying reviewers' criteria
- examining changing canons
- working with various activities in "Building Your Portfolio"
- presenting in "Reader's Forum"

 MOVING ON

In this chapter, you were the judge; in the next chapter, you will be judged. You will see how some of the criteria and logic used to judge literature can also be applied to portfolios and presentations. And then, of course, you will present your portfolio.

8 Putting It All Together

>>>**LOOKING AHEAD**

In war movies, some grim-faced sergeant always seems to say "This is it" just before everyone has to jump out of the airplane or assault the beach or storm the machine guns. Well, this is it—but *it* should be more fun and quite a lot safer.

We will review some possibilities: what a portfolio could show about you, some levels of audience, ways to put the portfolio together, kinds of reviews and presentations and evaluations. Then you will present your portfolio. There are a number of steps you will have to take to put it all together: assess, review, assemble, present, and wait. In this chapter, we will help you through those steps, looking over your shoulder a bit.

In the final project of the chapter, you will complete a summative self-assessment to measure your growth and assess what you have accomplished for each goal. The last part of this process is a final reflection, looking back over your work from start to finish.

STEP 1: REVIEW YOUR WORKING PORTFOLIO

Somewhere, somehow you have created a working portfolio. It is filled with stuff—papers you have written, reading logs and reading notes, tapes of performances, pictures, photos, programs of plays, files on computer disks, perhaps drawings you have made or dust jackets you have designed. Maybe it is arranged chronologically or in some other kind of order; maybe there is no order at all. The first thing you have to do is get it all out and go through it. Look it over. Take an inventory of what's there. Then begin to figure out what you might do with it.

Consider Your Goals

One way to gauge the value or perhaps the role of each piece is to look at it in terms of the goals you set for yourself at the beginning of the course. Read each goal again, along with the redefinitions you wrote in Chapter 5. Consider also your work on projects and your "Portfolio Progress Reports." Then answer the questions that follow. Think in terms of range, flexibility, connectedness, conventions, and independence.

- What sort of a reader of literature have you become?
- What sort of a writer and talker about literature have you become?
- What do you now know about literature and the material in this course?
- What do you think you can now do with the particular texts or the particular kinds of ideas that the course has been about?
- What habits of reading, discussion, or writing have you developed?

One way to use these questions is to assemble your responses into a checklist, following the model in Table 8.1.

To fill in this table, you can begin with what you think now about yourself and list the kinds of changes you sense have occurred since you began the course. Or you can begin with the various pieces in your working portfolio—the evidence or artifacts. Look at each piece.

TABLE 8.1 Matching Goals and Evidence

Points about Myself	Evidence/Artifacts
About me as a reader: • • •	
About me as a writer/critic: • • •	
About my knowledge of course material: • • •	
About my habits as a reader and student: • • •	
Other important things I have learned: • • •	

What does it tell you about you? What do you think it would demonstrate to others about you? The same piece can, of course, serve more than one function:

- A series of entries in a reader's log can tell a person something about what sort of reader you are and also what habits of reading you have developed.

- A paper can say something about you as a critic of literature as well as about your knowledge of literary theory or cultures.

- A taped discussion can say something of how well you can organize your ideas and also how well you work with others.

- A program of a play you worked on, together with a review, can demonstrate your commitment to literature and the theater as well as your leadership capacity.

Consider Your Audience

As you look through the materials in your working portfolio to see where they might go and what they might show, give some thought to your audience. Every work has a number of contexts, and so does your portfolio. To whom are you planning to show your portfolio? Where are they going to see it—in a classroom, an office or study, an auditorium, or some other public place? Under what circumstances are they going to look at it: As judges who will give you a grade or decide whether you are to be admitted or accepted somewhere? As a jury that might give you an award? As visitors to a museum or recital hall? Here are some points to consider:

- Is it for your instructor and your classmates? If so, what do you want them to realize about you? How do you want them to judge you—in terms of what they have seen of you during the year? Or is there another side to you that they should be aware of?

- Is it for other students and instructors? If so, what do they already know of you? How should you use that knowledge to shape your portfolio? Do you want that general impression to be solidified or changed?

- Is it for admission to another course or program or for a job? In this case, the audience consists of strangers, people who probably are looking at you in relation to a lot of other people whom they also do not know. What materials should they see to make a strong first impression?

- Is it for a larger community than the academic one? If so, how is it defined? How much do you know about it? What do you want to tell it?

- What is the payoff with each level of audience?

Consider Your Purpose

Think also about the purpose of your portfolio as you review your materials. What do you want the portfolio to show about you?

- *It could show your growth and learning over time.* In that case, you will want to include early and late works that you have done, particularly early and late works of the same type. For instance, if you want to show your development as a critic, you might select an early composition about a poem you have read and a later one. What does the difference say about you as a critical reader and as a writer about literature?

- *It could show your absolute accomplishment in a particular form.* You might have really developed strength as a person who can relate literary works to their historical backgrounds. To show this strength, you would probably need two examples of the sort of research and relating you can do. These examples might be papers you have written for your literature course and possibly for another course where you were able to do the same sort of work.

- *It could show your versatility and flexibility.* You might have become a person who can express critical statements in a number of forms (writing, acting, and art, for example). Or you might have become able to write criticism, imitate the style of authors you have studied, and translate their works into cartoon form. Your portfolio might then stress this sort of variety with examples in each of these forms.

- *It could show your ability to make connections.* You might have learned how to relate what you read to other subjects you are studying, to other courses in literature you have taken, and to current events and issues. To demonstrate this in your portfolio, you will need to add material from other courses or done in different contexts besides your literature course.

- *It could show your ability to work alone and with others.* You might have been involved in collaborative projects and performances as well as have taken initiative in developing a topic of your own interest. You might have worked with others as a team player and as a leader. What in your portfolio can show this sort of variety?

- *It could express your personality as a reader and writer.* This is a tricky approach to take. You want to be individual, probably, and you want to stand out in a group. But you want to make sure that the personality you express is an attractive one. Maybe you are a great creative genius who can express wonderful insights about literature spontaneously but who hates the discipline of grammar, spelling, and neatness. Will expressing yourself spontaneously have the effect you want? Have you proved that you can be disciplined when you choose to be but have decided to show off your creative disorder as well? That you might be able to pull off. But you might simply be seen as a sloppy person who doesn't care about his or her work.

Your portfolio is like a paper you write. It has a subject—you. It has a point of view—the take on yourself that you are going to adopt. It has an audience—the people who are the primary viewers of the portfolio. It has a purpose—whether you are going to express yourself, inform the audience, or persuade the audience to make a decision about you and your work.

You should first decide on point of view, audience, and purpose. Think also about the evaluation criteria that might be used to judge your work. Then you are in a good position to work on the final assembly of your portfolio.

PORTFOLIO ACTIVITY

Begin the Selection

Evaluate your working portfolio. Determine how the pieces in it reflect the goals you have set for yourself. Then consider what the audience and purpose for your final portfolio will be. Make some fairly final choices as to what materials you will keep.

STEP 2: ASSEMBLE THE PIECES

You have all the pieces of your portfolio. Some are scattered around you on a work surface; others are neatly contained on a disk or in the hard drive of your computer. You have defined the audience for the portfolio, established a purpose and perspective, and made an initial selection of materials. Now you need to put everything together and assemble the whole. There are two aspects of this assembly, both of which you should attend to: the conceptual order and the logistical order.

Conceptually, the portfolio is a summary of you. It contains a number of pieces that people will look at in order. Usually the order is the one you choose, but people can shift things around and choose their own way of looking at the material unless you compel them to follow your plan. You probably can't force them to choose your order, but you can persuade them.

Logistically, there is an effective way to deal with the parts of the portfolio. If the portfolio is all on a disk or cassette, your audience may be forced by the technology to follow a certain order unless there is a mechanism for skipping around. If the portfolio is a combination of materials (papers, videos, illustrations, and the like), it may make sense for people to use one technology at a time rather than skip around. If the portfolio is all on paper, you have the option of binding it or leaving it loose-leaf or in a box.

Selecting a Conceptual Order

As you saw in Chapter 2, a collection of writings might be organized in a variety of ways. Here we will review some of those ways, as well as add a few others that might work for you. Each of them has its strengths and its limitations, of course, and we cannot say which is right for you in the situation you are in. Here are some of the ones that have been successful.

Chronological. One of the most common orders, it traces your progress through the course or through the period that your portfolio is representing. It is the sort of order that tells your audience: Here is where I was then and here is where I am now.

Generic. This is an order that follows your progress through different genres of literature. It can show that you can read and respond to a variety of different types of genres. The generic order may be particularly useful if you are studying literature that is presented through a variety of media such as book and film.

Historical. This is an order that would show how you can deal with works of literature from different periods in history. It is useful if you want to show your versatility in understanding a variety of different styles and uses of language.

Thematic. This is an order that shows how you treat different literary themes and ideas. It may show how you can make connections among the themes or draw different themes into one large concept.

Critical Stance. This is an order that might be used if you have tried a variety of different critical approaches. You might want to show your strength with each one.

Medium. If you have worked in a number of different media, you might wish to highlight the fact by demonstrating first your writing, for example, and then your cinematography, your acting, and your musicianship.

Goals. If your four goals are still clearly defined and able to be demonstrated, your portfolio could show your growth and achievement for each of them.

Practice to Performance. As you developed your strength in different media or forms of work, you might show how you changed and improved as you went from initial conceptions to final products. This means arranging sections of your portfolio so that they show how you worked toward final pieces.

Collage or Hypertext. This is a form of arrangement that looks random but is arranged so that the reader can begin anywhere and go anywhere. The reader creates the order; you have simply laid out the pieces. You can suggest ways of moving through the portfolio, but you cannot be sure the reader will follow that set of pathways. It is a risky arrangement, as it can be a challenge to you and your audience.

The various formats we have mentioned are set out in the following table, which gives the strengths and weaknesses of each.

TABLE 8.2   Evaluating Conceptual Orders

Order	Strength	Weakness
Chronological	Focuses on change and growth	Frequently used; can show little change
Generic	Focuses on knowledge of literary forms	Can be repetitive
Historical	Focuses on knowledge of the course	Limited by the content of the course
Thematic	Focuses on ability to make connections among works	Can have forced connections and be unclear to audience
Critical Stance	Focuses on versatility as a reader	Limited by range of stances used
Medium	Focuses on creative versatility	Can be repetitive
Goals	Focuses on completing your plan; easy to follow	Can be fragmented or disintegrated
Practice to Performance	Focuses on the creative process and strength as a reviser	Can have too much material and take attention away from final performance
Collage or Hypertext	Focuses on the audience	Can be hard for the audience to focus on and may be seen as lacking coherence

Each of these arrangements, then, has some strengths and each presents some challenges for you as you think about the structure of your portfolio. The conceptual order needs to be balanced by the logistical order.

Establishing a Logistical Order

As you decide on how to shape your portfolio, you will need to contend with the physical and technical aspects of arranging it. The presentation context—the reading and viewing situation—is very important. Since any portfolio is designed for an audience, that audience's ease must be considered.

If you have a portfolio with nothing but writing—essays, poems, and stories—you will not give your audience too much of a problem. All they have to do is leaf through the material and read it. Let's suppose, however, that in addition to some things you have written, you have a couple of audiotapes of discussions you have been involved in and another audiotape of some music you picked to show your response to a set of poems you have read. You will want to make it easy for the audience to do all their listening at one time should they so desire, but you also need to make sure that when they listen to the music tape, they are also reading the poems. Therefore you will want to make sure that the two sets of tapes are recognized as being distinct. Besides labeling each tape clearly, you may want to put the music tape on the opposite side from the discussion tapes, or even use two separate tapes. The music tape needs to be cued to the poems or somehow attached to them—meaning that you must include the poems themselves as well as your response to them. The taped discussions can be introduced by whatever reading or auditory material you want.

To make matters more complicated, let's go on to suppose that your portfolio also includes a video of a scene that you created for a class presentation of the witches in *Macbeth*. Where should that go in relation to the other tapes and the writing? And perhaps you also have some illustrations or a cover for a novel you read. You now have visuals, papers, audiotapes, and videotapes. Is there a best order for these?

Some media require more elaborate set-up than others, and some are best seen by a group rather than alone. Shifting back and forth among media may be clumsy for your audience, and worrying about technical glitches may distract them from appreciating the quality of your work. One solution that may be available to you is the use of a hypermedia package. This requires having a powerful computer, a scanner or a recorder, and the software to integrate the various materials that you have produced. The resulting portfolio format can be a section on a hard drive or a CD-ROM that has your work on it in a variety of media. The final package can be arranged so that you either give your audience an order to follow or have them click to various parts on their own.

If you do not have the equipment to create a hypermedia package for your portfolio, you will have to make other kinds of choices about how to display your works. There is no one simple answer as to how best to manage the different media. We have found that it is often best to establish an order in which the most complicated medium comes first, followed by a simple one. This might mean that a videotape would be followed by some written compositions. Another alternative is to keep each medium separate so that all the video is followed by all the pictures and then by the compositions. This order, however, clearly will not work if a particular project uses more than one medium, as in our music-poetry example above.

We do not think that you should allow technical considerations to outweigh every other one. You will need to weigh the logistical issues against the conceptual ones, and we can only leave you with a few simple guidelines:

- *Remember your audience and what will be most suitable for them.* If they are used to handling a variety of equipment, you can expect more of them than you might of an audience of relatively inexperienced people.

- *Make sure that the technical problems are kept to a minimum.* The audience needs to focus on the substance of your work. You do not want to burden them with directions to do a lot of fast-forwarding or skipping around on a CD-ROM or floppy disk. You also do not want them to have to shift from one kind of equipment to another.

- *Make sure that your audience has time and space to reflect on what you have done.* You should not have a technical set-up that bombards them with material nonstop. Remember that they need to reflect on your work and not simply get through it as if it were a dish of badly cooked vegetables.

- *Remember that your portfolio is primarily a portfolio showing how well you can read, understand, and comment upon literature.* It is not a showcase of your technical skill as a film editor or sound mixer. You should work to the best of your technical ability, but the substance must come before the pyrotechnic display. Make sure you do best what you were asked to do in the first place.

- *The whole should be more than the sum of its parts.* Just as a pile of ingredients is not a meal, a hodgepodge of papers and tapes is not exactly a portfolio.

With these considerations in mind, together with the conceptual considerations we have outlined, you are ready to arrange your work into a portfolio that will have conceptual integrity and will also be relatively easy to manipulate for whatever sort of audience has been selected to view and judge it. Your portfolio can be like a professional's résumé: it can be tailored to suit a particular audience for a job or other opportunity.

Slotting in the Pieces

Now that you have selected and established the arrangement of the pieces for your portfolio, all you have to do is drop them in the slots you have chosen, right? Almost, but not quite. It makes good sense to take a closer look at the condition of the pieces. Some of them may be fresh, but many may have been gone over by your teacher or by classmates or someone else. Are those the versions you want to put in the portfolio?

We suggest that you take one more look at each item you intend to include. If it is a text piece, something you have written, you should decide whether to make a final revision. If it is a tape, you need to decide whether to edit it. If it is some other kind of work, you should determine whether it is in the best presentation format.

It is possible that your instructor will have laid down some rules about how you are to handle material that has been graded before. Some instructors like to have it redone for the portfolio; others like to see the version they have already marked up and commented upon. It may also be the case that instructors will want to see some draft material as well as the finished product. If you are including material that has been done for another class, some instructors will want both the original done for that class and the revision you have made. When in doubt, check with your instructor.

A good way to do a final review of your material is to enlist the aid of classmates who will go over your material in exchange for your going over theirs. It is handy to have a checklist like the following to help in reviewing each item:

Title or description of item:
- **Easy to read/play/see?**
  Suggestions for presentation:

- **Clear and understandable?**
  Suggested corrections:

- **Place in the portfolio clear?**
  Suggested commentary/introduction/explanation:

- **Effect or dominant impression:**

This sort of checklist can tell you about the work itself and whether its place in the portfolio is clear. Once you have used it and gone over your selections to make them easy to read, view, hear, and judge, you are ready for the final assembly.

Adding the Final Touches

Packaging. The packaging of your portfolio can take many forms. You can use an old-fashioned cardboard folder or portfolio, a box, or some sort of elaborate container; and any or all of these can be used in conjunction with a hypermedia set-up. The arrangement of the materials in the package we have dealt with, but the outside of the package is important as well. The outside is what people will see first, and our experience is that people do indeed judge books—and portfolios—by their covers. The cover should be attractive and also say something about you and your qualities as a student of literature. An appropriate cover can be created with a photograph, drawing, or collage; it can also be done with text and type.

Introduction or Self-Statement. Equally as important as the cover is the material that you use to frame your portfolio. In some classes, this material is an introductory essay describing yourself as a student and pointing out to the reader or viewer what is in the portfolio and what it shows about you as a student. In other classes, it is a brief preface followed by an elaborate table of contents or a written introduction to each piece. Self-statements such as these are the way you orient your readers to the portfolio, to get them to look at things the way you want them to.

Since you have already decided on your conceptual arrangement and your approach to the materials in the portfolio, one of the functions of a self-statement is to make those things clear to the audience. You will have to decide how much needs to be explained. You can use a form like this:

> This portfolio is arranged as follows: _____.
>
> The first section shows what I _____.

Or you can start like this:

> This portfolio demonstrates some of the things I have learned in this course. The first selection gives an example of the kinds of _____ I have developed this year.

Still another way of presenting the material is to write a general introduction concerning yourself. Here is the introduction to one student's portfolio assembled for a poetry class:

> This portfolio is an introduction to my personal response to poetry, the world, and creativity. It is an image as seen from my eyes.

When I first entered this course, my goals were to be able to read poetry properly, to be able to understand different styles and uses of symbols, and to upgrade my writing. Mission accomplished! I feel that my goals were definitely accomplished and that they are reflected in my work. The portfolio exercise was new to me, and made me a little nervous at first, but like everything else, once I wrestled with it, things fell into place. I have actually enjoyed this class more than any other because it has allowed me to work "hands on," and to explore the literary world. I have grown not only as a reader and a writer, but also as a thinker.

"A Needle in a Haystack" is a presentation of what I consider to be my greatest work. Some of the poetry has been revised, which is a new experience for me, because I have previously held the belief that the primary draft is the essence of what my inner being is trying to convey. A few of the samples, however, have been left unedited, in their original form. They speak a language I am unable to penetrate; a verse all their own. The title itself was derived from the personal meaning each piece holds. The poems are like a needle lost in the monstrous environment of my mind. They escape once in a great while for others to read, including myself.

—Michelle Tracy

Whatever approach you choose, you should let the introductory materials guide your audience to what you want them most to notice about you as a student of literature. And you might even do more. You could follow each entry in your table of contents with a brief summary of the item's purpose. Notes like these can guide your readers, orient them to what you want them to notice about each of the pieces. You could establish a metaphor that connects the portfolio elements. You could even create a thread connecting each of the pieces and end with a summary statement of what you want the audience to get from your portfolio. The danger of using this last approach is that you may lose your audience on the way. Unless you can keep their suspense level high, it is best to set the orientation at the beginning of the portfolio rather than hold it for the end.

PORTFOLIO ACTIVITY

Assemble the Parts

Decide on the most effective way to assemble your portfolio, keeping in mind your goals, audience, and purpose. Consider as well your ideas—or your instructor's requirements—for packaging, introductory material, and the like. Then take a deep breath and put the whole thing together into a pleasing, accessible, and meaningful package.

STEP 3: PRESENT THE FINAL PORTFOLIO

There are a number of ways in which portfolios are presented. Some are simply handed in to the instructor; there is no more ceremony than sliding a paper under the instructor's door five seconds before the last possible time for handing it in. We don't have much advice for that sort of presentation except to try to beat the rush and get yours in early, thus winning the approval of your instructor.

But often there is a public presentation or display of portfolios. This is a performance. Sometimes it occurs in a classroom with your fellow students, sometimes in a larger hall with an audience as large as that for any sort of public lecture. In some presentations we know of, each student has ten or fifteen minutes to present a portion of the portfolio or one of its major works to the whole assembly and then the rest is there for people to look at on their own.

Evaluating Your Portfolio Presentation

We don't know what criteria will be used to judge your portfolio presentation, but we can suggest some criteria for you to use to judge your own—*before* you present it. If you're satisfied that your presentation will fulfill these criteria, you can be pretty confident that your work will measure up to anyone's expectations. You can rate your own portfolio presentation or work with a classmate to exchange reviews.

Here is what you need to do. Using a scoring range of 1 to 6, rate the presentation according to each of the four criteria listed below (assume that a rating of 3 or 4 is about average). After each rating, write a brief comment that shows why you chose that rating. Then, using these ratings and your comments as a guide, give an overall rating for the presentation. In this step, your reflection is as important as your arithmetic. You may wish to make an overall rating that falls between numbers, such as 3.5.

The assessment criteria are as follows:

- *Depth of insight:* the range and depth of understanding the presenter reveals about his or her own language abilities— includes connectedness to goals, precision of language, focus on performance, use of evaluation criteria, scope of the assessment, specific nature of claims
- *Strength of evidence:* the quantity, power, and relevance of the evidence supporting claims of growth and achievement, as well as the strength of the warrants that connect data to claims
- *Elaboration and completeness:* the amount of data used to support claims; the extent to which claims are *proven* rather than *stated*, or *shown* rather than merely *told*
- *Clarity of expression:* the fluency with which the presenter expresses a case—involves organization, diction, sentence structure, transitions, other elements of style, and elements of spoken presentation

You will notice that the terms *claim, warrant,* and *data* are used in the criteria. Here is how they would be used in writing your comments. As you assess a portfolio presentation, it is important to consider the strength of all three elements:

- A **claim** is an assertion, interpretation, or conclusion based on evidence. Example: *I am an accomplished reader.*
- The **data** is evidence presented in support of the claim. Example: *My work is with varied forms and styles: editorials, poetry, expository pieces, and short fiction.*
- The **warrant** is justification or reasoning linking the data to the claim. Example: *One of the marks of an accomplished reader is versatility.*

PORTFOLIO ACTIVITY

Assess a Presentation

Be your own evaluator (or ask a classmate to be an outside evaluator) and assess your presentation according to the four criteria listed above. Follow this format for each criterion.

Rating: 1   2   3   4   5   6
Comment: _____
_____
_____

Anticipating Instructor Response

As we indicated earlier, we do not know the particular criteria of your class or instructor in evaluating your portfolio. But we do know some of the things that instructors often look for. Most literature instructors are also writing instructors, so they consider the various aspects of writing and presentation in a literature portfolio. If you are working in media other than writing, they are not necessarily looking for artistic merit in those media but rather for quality in the content and particularly in the way you put forth your understanding of the literary works, the course themes, or the other concerns of the course. Essentially, they will most likely be judging your portfolio according to the goals of the course and their weighing of the three main aspects: what you show that you know about the content of the course, what you show that you can do as a reader and critic of literature, and what habits of reading, writing, and being a student you display.

But they will also be looking to make sure the portfolio is well-organized. They will be impressed by the degree to which the material is interestingly portrayed. They will like something left to the imagination, but they will not like trying to imagine what you were trying to do. They will like an easy prose style, and they will dislike sloppy spelling, grammar, punctuation, and other aspects of presentation. Being writing instructors for the most part, they can't help noticing these aspects of your portfolio, particularly if there is something glaringly wrong. They are less likely to praise your good spelling and grammar and punctuation; people don't, just as they don't notice if all your buttons are buttoned—only if one is unbuttoned.

Writing a Grade Proposal

In some cases, you may be asked to propose a grade or a rating of your portfolio. In this case, we recommend being honest about yourself and your work. Most of the students we have worked with over the years have an accurate sense of how they are doing with respect to our expectations and goals. They do not inflate their grades, nor do they underestimate them. We suspect the same is true of you. So, if you are asked for one, make an honest estimate of who you are as a student of literature and what your portfolio shows about you. You will need to present a legal brief, not a letter to Santa Claus. Here is one approach you can take. Even if it doesn't serve your instructor's purposes exactly, it will give you a good idea of how you have fared in the work of the course.

Do a Final Self-Assessment. In Chapter 2, you did a preliminary self-assessment based on the goals you set for yourself, and in Chapter 5, you did a midstream assessment to see how well you were fulfilling those goals. Now you should reflect for one final time on what has changed, on how you have grown. Review pages 62–67 of Chapter 2 for self-assessment directions and take a look at your two earlier self-assessments to see what has changed.

Here are some examples from one student's cumulative self-assessment for you to look at. (Remember that a rating of 6 represents the level of the average high school graduate; 9, the average college graduate; and 12, an outstanding professional.)

> *Language Purpose:* reading for critical analysis and evaluation
> *Typical example:* I can apply criteria for evaluation in different situations, and I can also generate criteria appropriate to a specific task, as I did in my book review.

					Range						
least——————————————XX——————————————most
1	2	3	4	5	6	7	8	9	10	11	12

> (I can use four or five perspectives with almost any kind of work and fashion my interpretation from one or more of them, as I did in the story about the king's soup.)

Flexibility

least————————————————————XX————————————most

1   2   3   4   5   6   7   8   9   10   11   12

(Now I have done reviews, analyses, and interpretations for a variety of adult audiences.)

PORTFOLIO ACTIVITY

Final Self-Assessment

Now complete your final self-assessment based on your work in this course. Once again, here are the four language purposes that you will be considering:

- reading for information and understanding
- reading for literary and aesthetic response
- reading for critical analysis and evaluation
- reading for social interaction

And here are the five criteria you will use to assess each purpose:

- range
- flexibility
- connections
- conventions
- independence

For each rating for each language purpose, give a typical example from the activities you have completed. Rate your usual performance on each scale and give an explanation of each rating in a sentence or two, as in the example above. The result will be a total of twenty ratings, five each for the four language purposes.

Draft the Proposal. Now make a case for the grade you believe you deserve for your work. Develop each reason you have for the grade you propose by connecting your assessment (the claim) and the evidence from your work (the data) with your justification (the warrant).

In addition to the information you came up with in your self-assessment, consider also such questions as the following:

- What else have you done that is noteworthy? In what ways have you gone beyond just doing your instructor's assignments and developed and completed your own? What evidence do you have, and what does it mean?
- What have you contributed to the classroom as an academic community, to the development of others in the class? What were the consequences, results, or benefits to anyone? What evidence do you have, and what does it mean?
- Besides specific accomplishments and contributions, what else should be considered? What evidence do you have, and what does it mean?

Now draft a three- to four-page paper that makes a case for the grade you propose. Read and add. Pay special attention to the warrant and data for each claim you make. Read again and cut ruthlessly. Finally, select your most powerful arguments and evidence and complete a position paper of two pages or so. Think density, not volume. Then turn your paper in to your instructor.

Once you have done all this, the ball is in your instructor's court. But we expect that you will do well. After all, it is your reading and writing, your performance, your life as a student that is on the line. We think that if you followed much of the advice in this book, you can't help but be a success.

STEP 4: WAIT FOR A RESPONSE

You have arranged your presentation portfolio, put in the various pieces, and written and produced your summary statement, your rationale for the portfolio, and maybe even a grade proposal. You have turned in your work, either by making a group presentation or by simply placing it on someone's desk or worktable.

Before you handed it in, you made sure to put your name on it. You made sure that everything was spelled correctly—even the name of the instructor. You made sure that all was in the order you wanted and there were no missing pages. You made sure to keep a copy in case any-thing went wrong.

It is all over. You only have to wait for the reviews and the grade to come.

FINAL REFLECTIONS

We're almost out of questions, but we still have a few left for you to consider:

- What is literature—now? In Chapter 1, you wrote some early notes in response to this question. Before you go back and review your early answers, write your new answers to these same questions:
- What is literature? What does it mean to you? To other writers and readers? To society?
- What is meaning, anyway, and where is it?
- What is it for? Who is it for?
- When it's good, what makes it good? What do you like about it? Why do you care?

Now go back and compare notes. See where you came from and where you're coming from now.

And the last question is: So what? What about your work in this course? What about you as a reader? What's next for you? What's in store for you in the way of lifelong learning?

Write your final reflection as a reader. Make this one freestyle. Say what you want, how you want.

ACKNOWLEDGMENTS

Auden, W. H.: "Law Like Love" from *The Collected Poetry of W. H. Auden.* Copyright © 1940 by W. H. Auden. Reprinted by permission of Random House, Inc.

Dawe, Bruce: From *Sometimes Gladness: Collected Poems: 1954–1978* by Bruce Dawe. Reprinted by permission of Longman Australia.

Frost, Robert: "Nothing Gold Can Stay" by Robert Frost from *The Poetry of Robert Frost* edited by Edward Connery Lathem. Copyright © 1951 by Robert Frost. Copyright 1923 © 1969 by Henry Holt and Co., Inc. Reprinted by permission of Henry Holt and Co., Inc. and Jonathan Cape Ltd.

Gallo, Diane: "Two Dollar Mommy" by Diane Gallo. Originally appeared in *Capital Magazine,* July 1990, reprinted by permission of the author.

Gluck, Louise: "Gretel in Darkness" from *The House on Marshland* by Louise Gluck. Copyright © 1971, 1972, 1973, 1974, 1975 by Louise Gluck. First published by The Ecco Press in 1975. Reprinted by permission.

Gomringer, Eugen: "Silence" from *The Book of Hours and Constellations: Poems of Eugen Gomringer* presented by Jerome Rothenberg. New York: Something Else Press, Inc., 1968. Reprinted by permission.

Herbert, Zbigniew: "Armchairs" from *Selected Poems of Zbigniew Herbert,* translated by Czeslaw Milosz and Peter Dale Scott. Translation copyright © Czeslaw Milosz and Peter Dale Scott, 1969. Reprinted by permission of Penguin Books Ltd.

Hughes, Langston: "Dream Deferred" from *The Panther and the Lash* by Langston Hughes. Copyright © 1951 by Langston Hughes. Reprinted by permission of Alfred A. Knopf, Inc. and Harold Ober Associates, Inc.

Plath, Sylvia: All lines from "Mirror" from *Crossing the Water* by Sylvia Plath. Copyright © 1963 by Ted Hughes. Originally appeared in the *New Yorker.* Reprinted by permission of HarperCollins Publishers, Inc. and Faber and Faber Ltd.

Porter, Bernard H.: "Test" from *Found Poems* by Bern Porter. New York: Something Else Press, Inc., 1972. Reprinted by permission.

Roethke, Theodore: "Child on Top of a Green House," copyright 1946 by Editorial Publications, Inc., from *The Collected Poems of Theodore Roethke* by Theodore Roethke. Used by permission of Doubleday, a division of Bantam Doubleday Dell Publishing Group, Inc. and Faber and Faber Ltd.

Swenson, May: Reprinted with the permission of Simon & Schuster Books for Young Readers from *The Complete Poems to Solve* by May Swenson. Copyright © 1993 by The Literary Estate of May Swenson.

Welburn, Ron: "Once to Run" by Ron Welburn from *Council Decisions* (American Native Press Archives, 1991). Reprinted by permission of the author.

Welburn, Ron: From "Seeing and Listening: A Poet's Literacies" by Ron Welburn from *Multicultural Literature and Literacies: Making Space for Differences* by Suzanne M. Miller and Barbara McCaskill, 1993. Reprinted by permission of the State University of New York Press.

INDEX

Instructor's Manual

Creating the
Literature
Portfolio

A Guide for Students

Alan C. Purves
Joseph A. Quattrini

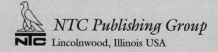
NTC Publishing Group
Lincolnwood, Illinois USA

Contents

Introduction

ABOUT THE TEXTBOOK

Now and then, instructors from universities and secondary schools work together. *Creating the Literature Portfolio* was a result of such a collaboration. After working together in a portfolio research project sponsored by the National Research Center for Literature Teaching and Learning at SUNY Albany, we joined efforts on a number of publications and presentations. The work that most directly influenced this book was *Creating the Writing Portfolio,* through which we became convinced that portfolios in literature can be as exciting, powerful, and productive as portfolios in writing.

Underlying this conviction is the belief, based on our experience, that you make yourself as a reader as surely as you make yourself as a writer. Our students have further convinced us that *how* you read is as important as *what* you read and that *more* is almost always better— more works, more kinds of works, more kinds of activities with works, more perspectives on works. Increasing one's repertoire as a reader is not just a matter of checking off more titles read, in a way that a sharp shooter might mark more notches on a belt or a bomber pilot paint more hits on a fuselage.

Writers have said, in one way or another, that an author's job is to shape the reader as much as it is to shape the characters. We would like to help readers be aware of the kinds of shaping going on and then to take charge of the process for themselves, making themselves into the kinds of readers they want to be.

The student text is, in a way, our portfolio for you. It contains hundreds of literature-based activities. Except for the goals and self-assessments, no one activity or group of activities is critical to success. What seems critical to us is that students help to direct their own learning in the broad categories of knowledge, practice, and habits; that they negotiate goals, plan activities, and conduct self-assessments; that they present their discoveries and their products to the classroom community.

Ideally there should be a current that runs through the course, from goals as its source to the portfolio presentation as its confluence with the larger community of readers.

ABOUT THE INSTRUCTOR'S MANUAL

The intent of this manual is not to tell you how you must do literature portfolios. Our own research and experience have convinced us that there isn't any one best way. We might assume, if you are with us this far, that you want to use portfolios in literature and that you believe they can be effective vehicles for learning and communicating that learning. Perhaps you have used portfolios in other areas, such as composition. Perhaps you have seen that instructors using portfolios are having more fun than you are, and you want to get in on the fun. Perhaps you are working on your teaching portfolio and want to give students an opportunity to work on learning portfolios.

The array of activities in the textbook is meant to offer you, as instructor, the same wide range of options available to students. Portfolios are about making choices, and we have tried to leave them for you to make. Your choices will be guided by features and by the needs of your own instructional context (the usual suspects, we suppose).

Probably the most important choice you will have to make—and you will make it many times—is this: *Who* will decide what needs to be decided? How much latitude will you give students in making *their* choices? More on this in Chapter 4 of this manual.

Organization of the Manual

Here is an overview of what you can expect to find in each chapter of this manual:

Chapter 1: The Portfolio Approach to Teaching
- Introduces the problem of assessment of literature instruction
- Discusses the representativeness of the assessment task, the students, and the ratings
- Offers the portfolio approach as a solution
- Examines the classroom context as a portfolio, a community, and a hypertext

Chapter 2: Using the Student Book

- Explains the overall structure of the student text and general chapter features
- Gives chapter-by-chapter summaries and suggestions for using chapter activities

Chapter 3: Techniques for the Portfolio Classroom

- Discusses the importance of working collaboratively with students in a portfolio context and provides a real-life example
- Gives information about various classroom techniques suggested in the student text
- Explains formative, summative, and reflective evaluation
- Discusses practices for keeping track, checking up, and finding out
- Compares evaluation designs and rubrics (analytical, holistic, and primary trait)
- Outlines some options for grade proposals
- Includes reproducible masters for preliminary and cumulative assessments

Chapter 4: Difficulty in Literature and Its Teaching

- Explores difficulty of works and of the task of interpreting them
- Categorizes traditional literature approaches as knowledge, practice, and habits
- Redefines literature learning as the intersection of these three
- Gives guiding questions about assumed knowledge, ideal understandings, and appropriate expressions of those understandings

Chapter 5: Examples of Student Performances on Assignments

- Shows samples of student work on assignments found in student text
- Provides samples of a self-assessment, grade proposal, literature definition, response to a literature selection, and criteria for a good novel

Chapter 6: Mini-Lessons for Special Problems

- Provides eleven mini-lessons on common literature class problems, including such things as getting started, reading between the lines to understand works, and metacognitive activities to enhance understanding
- Includes both techniques and specific directions for students

1 The Portfolio Approach to Teaching

THE QUESTION OF ENGLISH ASSESSMENT

In thinking about literature, texts, readers, writers, assessment, and teaching, we need to start somewhere. One place to begin is with assessment. After all, what we measure is what we teach. Testing is the tail that wags the dog.

Testing, particularly testing of literature understanding and writing, is generally not done well. But people still think that they can be scientific, make generalizations, and treat writing assessment as if it were a multiple-choice test. They forget the problems with multiple-choice tests and the problems of psychometrics.

The major issues in the assessment of literature and writing include the following.

How Representative Is the Task?

Is what we are asking the students to do related to what we think learning in literature is all about?

What is a representative task in literature? We would argue that it is difficult to define a literary work or a writing task that is typical. Which poem would you select to represent students' ability to read poems? Which short story? Which piece of African American literature would you use to say that a student "knows" African American literature? We typically ask students to demonstrate their knowledge through their writing, but writing tasks vary in a number of ways:

- In the cognitive demands placed on the writer
- In the functions of writing that dominate

- In the subject domain
- In the audience
- In length
- In genre
- In style
- In voice
- In rhetorical effect

Since each writing demand combines with others to produce specific, often unique results, it is difficult to find anything that represents generic writing. This is why people need multiple tasks to get any sort of fix upon a person's writing performance. Otherwise the judgment is only valid for the specific exemplar. The statistical optimum is nine tasks—provided they vary sufficiently. But what is sufficient variation?

How Similar Are the Students?

When we assess the writing performance of a given student, to what extent can we say that that student is really typical of students within the tested group? Are we allowing the student to show his or her individual characteristics, or are we treating all students like machine-stamped pieces of goods?

We realize that there are statistical sampling techniques, and we have been involved in a great many studies that used these techniques. But most sampling experts we know would agree that there is always error and that the error defines the unique properties of Mfwane as opposed to Birgit. Mfwane hates computers, writes in longhand on yellow pads, and then gets his sister to type the paper. Birgit works on the computer all the time and can program hypermedia presentations. Both like to write. Both produce what their instructors call good writing.

Should they be tested in writing in the same fashion? Is there any reason they need to be? Why should all English and writing assessment be a matter of timed longhand drafts in a large common room? There is also the question as to why one wants to aggregate from Mfwane or Birgit to X students in Y school.

How Fair Are the Ratings?

How do we know whether our judgment is a reliable one or just idiosyncratic? In literature and writing, assessment involves human judgment of cases. We know that such judgment is not particularly reliable. We know that it is bound by perceptual frames and that these frames are subject to culture, nurture, training, and all sorts of other conditions. We can train people to agree for a moment (that's what they do in holistic writing evaluation). But then people go away and change their minds.

We will simply summarize the research on judging by saying that across—and by extension within—national groups of raters, there are systematic group rater effects, so that a group of raters typically forms a community of judges with a particular bias as to what constitutes good writing. Anyone who watches Olympic competition knows that this sort of bias exists. Why should it be different in education? Despite the most elaborate training that could be devised, the bias will continue to exist. The same is true of juries in other performance measures.

Interpretive and writing communities, which are relatively small, have distinct sets of criteria. Attempts have been made to create broader sets, but their success is dubious. Writing is always specific to a given community, and so is its evaluation. What appears as meaningful writing in the world of astrophysics is not meaningful in the world of literature, and what is meaningful in television on-screen text is not meaningful in pulp fiction.

School writing is the writing of people learning to be members of a specific community and its subcommunities. It begins as a general form of text production with parameters determined by the kind of paper or screen and the kind of markers or keyboard used. It slowly becomes divided into kinds of writing appropriate for certain academic subcommunities. By the end of twelve or sixteen years of schooling, a student becomes an expert in a few narrow forms of writing.

Since we are focusing on literature in this volume, we know that writing well about literature is not the same as writing well about history and science. There are certainly differences of opinion about what constitutes good writing about literature, as there are differences about what makes a good dramatic reading, a collage, or any other performance involved in literature learning. That is why we wrote this book: to help students see something of the variety of possible ways they can be effective learners in the eyes of an instructor or some other academically oriented audience and to help them understand how they can succeed within various systems.

To our minds, the solution lies in the portfolio.

THE BENEFITS OF PORTFOLIOS

Portfolios are becoming more and more commonly used in the teaching and assessing of writing. They are also expanding into literature evaluation, not to mention evaluation in other subject areas. One reason for their growing popularity is that portfolios allow assessment in ways that more standard evaluation measures do not.

A portfolio in its simplest form is a carrying case. In it are various works (if it is an artist's or writer's portfolio) or commands, rules, and orders (if it is a ministerial portfolio). Portfolios have been around a long time under various guises: collections, promotion and tenure files, library shelves, anthologies, writing folders, bodies of work, oeuvres.

Connections within and among Portfolios

If you are a computer person, you might agree that portfolios resemble a hypertext. A hypertext consists of a number of texts linked in a network or web by the author. An interactive hypertext allow readers to take the texts and make new connections, to add new texts, and to add to existing texts.

A portfolio is a hypertext in that it comprises a number of text or artifact spaces created and arranged by the author, who is usually the student. The student seeks to have the portfolio represent him or her by creating a network that shows a relationship among the artifacts. But viewers may rearrange the artifacts, make different connections, and comment on one or more of the artifacts or the ensemble. They may make a different web—just as the readers of a catalog make a different document than did the authors, just as the readers of a comic make different connections among the frames or text spaces.

Because portfolios contain samples of student-selected work over an extended time period, they throw the emphasis on students as individuals, showing the class and the world who they are and what they can do. Within a particular classroom, the portfolios of the individual students also show something of how those students function as members of the classroom community. A community, since it is made up of a number of pieces that may be connected in a number of ways, may be seen as a human embodiment of a hypertext. It is a connection among individuals that is neither linear nor hierarchical; it respects the individual and yet finds common ground.

If you were to look at reactions to a large-scale assessment program you would find that the public has tended to treat individuals as clones or would-be clones, all of whom would spew forth the same answers or the same essays. This is the nature of standardized assessment. When the public looks at results, it seeks to treat individuals not as if they were spaces in a hypertext, not as if they were parts of a community, but as if they were interchangeable pieces in a machine-made world.

Using portfolios for literature and writing assessment lets students be seen as individuals and as community members, to get around the clone mentality. The novelist and poet Wendell Berry establishes an opposition between the community and the public that seems pertinent here. The public is an abstraction, perhaps a fiction. The community, on the other hand, is (or can be) a palpable ideal. Some other differences may be seen in the following:

Community	Public
Shared	Hierarchical
Limited in size	Mass
A writer and his or her readers	The writer
A text and its audience	Readership
Respects individual	Denies individual
Evanescent	Permanent
Dynamic	Static
Love	Fear
Hypertext	Taxonomy
Independence	Dependence

Within the portfolio community of the classroom, then, students can grow as individuals, nurturing themselves and each other as they develop as literature readers and as writers.

The Classroom as a Community, a Hypertext

Let us consider some of the implications of the classroom-as-hypertext analogy. In a given classroom, students who create portfolios are themselves like spaces in a hypertext. Each student is an individual, having created a portfolio that expresses the sum and substance of what he or she has accomplished as well as what each thinks of himself or herself as a writer. As an instructor, you may make connections among students, but at the same time you know to respect the differences. The connections among student portfolios are as complex as any hypertext web and as dependent on the author or reader. The class is a class, but it is more truly a community.

The students may work on similar assignments or topics. Their portfolios may contain items that look on the surface to be similar—a poem, a literary analysis, an autobiography. But the arrangements of these items within the portfolio—as well as, of course, their surface features—tend to give them individual character. The connections among students are in part made by the fact of the portfolio; they are also made by you, the instructor-reader, who creates a new set of links among parts.

Why should we look at a student, a student's portfolio, or a community and try to make any of them into a generalization? The portfolio is the student's presentation of himself or herself to the world. It, like the student creator, has an individual life and integrity. But so does the class, the community of which each instructor and student is a member. The importance of communities is that they restore us to that important state of union or communion with the other—human and divine—that we have lost in our misguided attempts to think only about individuals.

We think portfolios help develop both the individual and the community. That is why we have invested the time in this book. We hope you will invest the time in your students, each of them separately and as members of the community you have helped bring into being.

2 Using the Student Book

ORGANIZATION AND CONTENT OVERVIEW

We will begin here with an overview of the book and chapter "architecture" and then go on to give a more detailed synopsis of the content of and activities in each chapter.

Book Framework

The book guides students from an understanding of portfolios as communication vehicles through the development of a working portfolio to the assembly of a final, presentation portfolio. The current that runs through the book goes from

- self-assessment as reader/interpreter to
- establishing reading goals to
- building a repertoire—that is, a working portfolio—to
- presenting the portfolio to
- final reflections and assessments

Chapter Framework

Each chapter contains these features:

- *Looking Ahead:* a chapter preview of important concepts and activities
- *Text, models, and "For Your Portfolio Notebook":* main text and developmental activities
- *Building Your Portfolio:* activities/assignments based on chapter concepts and developmental activities

- *Reader's Forum:* an opportunity to present activities, selected by you and/or students, within the class community

- *Portfolio Progress Report:* a cumulative summary guided by three questions about knowledge, practice, and habits. When it's time to put together a presentation portfolio, this section summarizes for students the materials they may draw from, thus ensuring that the presentation portfolio will be more than a list of works read. The ongoing formative and reflective evaluation required in this section will also be useful when students actually present their portfolios and for the final evaluation by you and/or students.

- *Moving On:* a transition to the concepts and activities of the next chapter

CHAPTER-BY-CHAPTER GUIDE TO ACTIVITIES AND FEATURES

What follows is a comprehensive overview of each chapter of the student text.

Chapter 1: Portfolios, Literature, and You

In this chapter, students are given a general introduction to portfolios and are asked to ponder, through a discussion of its basic elements, what literature itself might be. They are shown, in simple form, how critical readers of texts fill in "gaps," and they begin to see how this knowledge carries over into creating a strong literature portfolio.

"For Your Portfolio Notebook" Activities

- *Name the Portfolio Owner* (page 5): Besides suggesting the variety of materials that portfolios may contain, drawing conclusions about three portfolio-makers by looking at the contents of their portfolios also gives students some insights about how their own efforts will be judged.

- *Your Own Literature Definition* (page 10): In creating their definitions, students may wish to react to the various definitions the chapter has provided. Portfolios often feature "before and after" pieces, and this activity can be one if you come back to the assignment later in the course.

- *Fill in the Gaps* (page 17): This activity asks students to create contexts to precede and follow one or more single sentences. If you have a number of teams working from the same sentence, you can mix and match the results and see in how many directions "readers" were going.
- *Finding Ironies* (page 20): You may want to discuss the quotations in this activity before sending students out to find their own ironies. A very effective way to learn to read irony is to try to create it in writing.
- *Twenty-Seven Ways of Looking at What You Are Looking At* (page 26): Reading and reacting to the poem in this activity might be a good assignment to have students do as a rather formal piece of writing, a first-response experience. The results make for an interesting discussion about what happens (and what doesn't happen) when we read.

Building Your Portfolio

The self-assessment, general goal setting, and development plan asked for in this activity will be useful for Chapter 2, when students articulate more specific goals.

Reader's Forum

For this chapter, a "Great Moment in Literature" presentation is recommended. This oral activity is an easy way for students to talk semiformally about literature, something between a casual conversation and a full-scale presentation.

Portfolio Progress Report

Here, as in every chapter, students are asked what they know, *can* do, and *do* do (knowledge, practice, and habits) as a result of working with this chapter. This self-assessment may be the most important activity in the chapter.

Chapter 2: Keeping Tabs on Your Reading

Students go from analyzing their own reading practices to categorizing types of critical responses and the kinds of portfolio organizations they might lead to. They then write specific portfolio goals based on their assessments of their reading needs and interests.

"For Your Portfolio Notebook" Activities

- *Your Reading Autobiography* (page 41): Students may find the model directly preceding this activity helpful in determining the kind of specificity they should aim for. The completed autobiographies make for powerful presentations and immediate connections between literature and students' own experiences.

- *Making Music* (page 44): Students may want to share the results of this activity to see how much variation there really is in people's response to music and musical performers. The analogy to varying literary tastes should be obvious.

- *Your Own Response* (page 52): Using the response sheet and categorizing responses is a step toward developing one's own reading method. If students are interested, you may want to reapply the activity to "Mirror" or other poems.

- *Design an Anthology* (page 58): This activity should help students learn to personalize their classifications of literature types. It should also point out the unavoidable inconsistencies in such classification—selections don't always fit neatly into groups.

- *Preliminary Self-Assessment* (page 64): This important baseline activity is a new experience for most students. You may need to have students review the example of typical performance (pages 62–63) to remind them to describe their usual performance, not their best ever. You can use the reproducible masters from this manual (page IM-44) to provide copies of assessment shells for all students.

- *Write Goal Statements* (page 67): This will also be a new experience to many students, and it is more demanding than the self-assessment. Each goal needs to specify an achievement (not a grade), some activities to get there, and a means of measuring the degree of achievement. These goals are important to students' ability to work independently later in the course, and so they often need to be revised two or three times until they are sufficiently articulated. Studying the model on page 66 may be a good start-up activity.

Building Your Portfolio

The activities in this section represent various ways to respond to a text.

- *Response Journal* (page 68): This is the simplest activity of the four, requiring only that the student make some sort of ongoing written response to materials being read. It is a good activity to start students on the critical-reading road, either for a work all will read or for different works.

- *Dialogue Journal* (page 69): This device allows for a written conversation about a student's response, changing the focus of the discussion from the work to the readers of it and of their sometimes conflicting responses.

- *Burke's Pentad* (page 70): In this activity, a literary work is looked at in terms of five basic text features. This is a good activity to assign to all, as several later assignments are built on it.

- *Study Guide* (page 71): Another device for mapping out some essential features of texts, a study guide is particularly useful for exam or paper preparation. Students working in a study group will sometimes write one each and then share these.

Reader's Forum

Here, as in all subsequent chapters, two options are presented: either students may select one of the chapter activities that they have completed and present their work orally to the class, or you may choose an activity for them.

Chapter 3: Perspectives for Interpreting Meaning

In this chapter, students are given practical tips on reading a text critically, including the use of the claim, warrant, and data system. The discussion culminates in the presentation of four specific critical perspectives to use in analyzing a work.

"For Your Portfolio Notebook" Activities

- *Applying the Method* (page 78): You can use the poem in this activity to introduce the powerful interpretive concepts of claim, warrant, and data.

- *Making an Interpretation* (page 82): In Chapter 1, we asked students to "read" three different portfolios; here, in an effort to demonstrate the informing power of context, we ask them to give three different "readings" of the same event.

- *Your Own Interpretation* (page 89): The demonstration of three possible ways to mark up and read Andrew Marvell's "To His Coy Mistress" that precedes this activity should have motivated students to mark up the text to create their own reading.

- *Creating Warrants* (page 89): Here students are given options for an expository and then a more creative response to a short selection. You could create the group's first class portfolio by having students respond to various questions and activities from this two-part exercise.

- *Analyzing a World View* (page 92): Earlier activities ask many questions about one work; this one asks for a larger inference, a world view, about a group of Stephen Crane poems. The activity constitutes an early step in reading an *author* rather than just a work or series of works.

- *Using the Guides* (page 97): Following a presentation of several "guides" to critically reading a work, students are asked to apply one of the perspectives to one or both of the poems. Although the guides are named by areas of interest that will be familiar to students, some traditional critical perspectives are actually represented. It is interesting to assign groups of students to each perspective and then report findings to the class, noting what issues are backgrounded and foregrounded by each perspective. In the two poems in the activity, we have something old, something new. Reports on findings are good opportunities for Reader's Forum.

Building Your Portfolio

As in all subsequent chapters, this section presents various activities that students may elect to use to create portfolio pieces.

- *Correspondence Course* (page 100): By asking students to write to a character in a work they are reading and also to create that character's response(s), this activity encourages students to articulate the reader's connection with a character.

- *Extending the Action* (page 100): The activity of creating a brief prequel or sequel to a work calls attention to the gaps readers fill in as antecedent and consequent action.

- *Changes in Meaning, Meaning in Changes* (page 100): The reading record of changes in a work that this activity asks students to keep helps them to go beyond the plot, to notice what they're noticing.

- *"Your Notes"* (page 101): To this activity of creating a guide-book for a chosen work you might add the direction to design an appropriate cover for the completed guidebook.

- *Making a Storyboard* (page 101): Joseph Conrad said writers make us *see*, and the storyboard offers an opportunity for readers to think cinematographically.

- *Kinesthetic Approaches* (page 103): Constructing a representation for a character involves some of the same analyzing, selecting, organizing, and presentation processes required to produce a portfolio. You might start this activity by photocopying a face-sized generic mask or a plain picture frame. Students can build on or cut away from these representations, or they may choose an entirely different kind of construction: a closet or costume or vehicle or burial vault.

Chapter 4: Using the Language and Devices of Literature

In this chapter, students refamiliarize themselves with figurative language and the importance of word choice. They also learn some specific terminology for writing about literature and are given some practical help with writing a good essay, either for a portfolio or in a testing situation.

"For Your Portfolio Notebook" Activities

- *Analyzing Figurative Language* (page 116): This activity provides an important culminating application of terms discussed to this point in the chapter.

- *Working with a Conceit* (page 116): First analysis, then synthesis are afforded in this two-part activity. Students should enjoy the chance to play the poetic game and express one thing in terms of another. Although some of the conceits they create will turn out to be mechanical, others will be discoveries, demonstrating that poet equals maker, not just rhymester.

- *Analyzing Connotations* (page 119): Noting connotative language in materials students themselves find is a good way to develop sensitivity to diction.

- *Initiations* (page 121): This activity will help students bring the initiation archetype into sharper definition by working inductively, noting treatment of the archetype in several narratives.

- *Your Own Ladder of Abstraction* (page 123): Good readers are aware of levels of abstraction and levels of interpretation. "Constructing" a ladder for an item commonly used as a literary symbol helps students develop an awareness of these levels while reading.

- *Using the Pentad for Interpretation* (page 131): Completing a claim based on some aspect of Burke's pentad will integrate applying a literary term, interpreting a work, and supporting assertions of meaning.

- *Write Using an Essay Response Plan* (page 137): An activity, as it were, rendered unto Caesar. There will be tests and there will be time limits, and getting practice with the essay response plan will help some students do what they do more efficiently.

Building Your Portfolio

(These untitled portfolio activities begin on page 141.)

- *Noting the figures in a poem:* Pairing this analysis of a student-selected poem with the next activity makes a reading/writing connection.

- *Writing your own significant figures:* Some of the responses will actually look like poems, even if the figures are labored. You can show students how to throw out the dead stuff and work with the interesting figures.

- *Writing more essay responses:* Though this activity is designed to provide additional practice in responding to typical essay questions used to measure ability with literature, the responses students create can certainly be used as portfolio pieces.

- *Inventing a character/analyzing a plot:* Either activity—creating their own plots or analyzing an existing one—will give students practice with archetypes. Another possibility is to show part of the film *Cool Hand Luke* and have students analyze it for archetypes. If Gulliver is right, then things are best understood in comparison with other possibilities.

- *Working with a monomyth:* This rather challenging activity requires understanding the separation—initiation—return pattern as described by Campbell and then writing or interpreting a work based on it. Campbell mentions several examples that students can flesh out as well as a few that he recounts in detail. Skimming through the prologue and other portions of the book will yield other examples of the pattern, which can then be used for analysis or to generate a writing.

- *Mapping a work on the pentad:* This activity offers a way to find a number of starting points or ways into a new work, as well as practice in using literature terminology.

- *Creating another Your Notes:* Here students are given another opportunity to create a guidebook for a work, with the added twist of making their guidebook a parody.

Chapter 5: Dress Rehearsal: A Portfolio of Portfolios

This midpoint chapter is devoted to providing students with a wealth of activities that they can develop for their portfolios. It also asks them to formally assess their progress toward the goals they set earlier.

Building Your Portfolio

This section comprises virtually the whole chapter. Each subsection within it contains several related activities.

- *"Law Like Love"* (page 146): Reading and responding to this W. H. Auden poem is a good starting place for a class performance, as all suggested activities are based on the one work. The activities include analyzing the use of words from the title in the poem itself, a dialogue between two of the speakers or between a speaker and the reader, a biographical and a formalist response. Activity 7, an oral reading of the work, is an easy way to break the ice for class performances.

- *Round Table of Critical Perspectives* (page 151): The four critical guides from Chapter 3 are here the basis for a critical discussion. The round table format gives equal time to each perspective, preventing the rush to judgment—that "Ah, here's how to look at it" feeling—that sometimes comes too early and cuts off further exploration.

- *"Something Wicked This Way Comes"* (page 152): The twenty suggested activities provided here range from writing obituaries for all the dead characters in the play to a grand jury investigation of the murder to designing sets and costumes for a scene or two. This can be an enjoyable and productive series of assignments in classes, offering an entry for students at many levels of ability and understanding. A number of the activities could be videotaped for future *Macbeth* students.

- *The Literary Canon and the Coffee Shop* (page 154): Some of the best (and worst) arguments among students have been provoked by this role play among characters and authors of various times and cultures. The activity has worked best when each character prepared some opening remarks as well as comments in response to anticipated statements of others. You might want to appoint a moderator to keep things rolling. The opening dialogue tends to get participants warmed up pretty well.

- *Eighteen Things to Do with a Poem* (page 155): This series of generic activities, based on work done by language arts instructors working in a Goals 2000 grant program, may be used in conjunction with any work you or students wish to explore in reading, writing, and beyond.

- *A Pairing:* The Things They Carried *and* Song of Solomon (page 157): Here is an opportunity for students to direct their work toward a central question set up by someone other than their instructor. If you and students use instructor Noreen Benton's central question and evaluation activities (also derived from a Goals 2000 grant program), you will have the experience of preparing a portfolio to meet someone else's standards, not an uncommon situation.

- *A Hypertext on* Mansfield Park (page 160): The hypertext shell presented in this activity can be adapted for use with many works. Keeping a disk and paper copy of the hypertext your classes produce would create a model or example with many points of entry for future students in the same course.

- *Your Way* (page 163): In the original portfolio project students devise for this activity, teams can compete to come up with the most interesting proposal, which the whole class would then work on. Or students can design and complete their own projects.

Portfolio Progress Report

Unique to this chapter, students perform two "For Your Portfolio Notebook" activities in this section as a way of assessing their progress to date.

- *Cumulative Self-Assessment* (page 165): Students here refer to their preliminary self-assessments and attempt to measure progress and growth. Students' "typical examples" should have changed; if they have not, at least students should be able to give evidence of more progress along the measurement scale.

- *Goal Reevaluation* (page 166): Reflection and revision are to be desired at this point in the process. Perhaps because they have had so little experience at it, goal-setting is not most students' forte. Here is an opportunity to rethink and reshape.

Chapter 6: Making Connections

In this chapter, students are shown how to make use of connections within and between works as well as connections with other readers and with their own experiences. They are then given a selection of portfolio activities that apply those connections.

"For Your Portfolio Notebook" Activities

- *Your Own Contexts* (page 173): By having students stop at an arbitrary point in a reading to project—and then defend—an ending for it, this activity demonstrates that story lines can have different kinds of integrity. A recurring motif or symbol can be as much a driving force as can a powerful motive of a character.

- *Do Your Own Readaround* (page 175): Remind students that during the readaround they can both give responses and take notes on ideas they want to pursue. You may eventually want to try this technique when students are reading different works.

- *Write Comparative Claims* (page 177): Remind students that comparative claims deal not only with similarities but with differences within those similarities. If it suits their portfolio purposes, students may decide to create full-blown critical pieces from one of their claims.

- *More Connections* (page 181): The answers to these modern retellings are as follows: 1. (a); 2. (a); 3. (b); 4. (b); 5. (a); 6. (c); 7. (b); 8. (a); 9. (d); 10. (b). The activity is a good conversation starter about the usefulness of such knowledge and the validity of such tests.

- *Seeing Cultural Connections* (page 185): This activity provides an opportunity to "read" an author through one of his poems and then read the author's "reading" of himself through his personal essay.

Building Your Portfolio

- *Connections within a Work* (page 192):

  1. Seeing connections through patterns: This is a formalist activity that requires determining patterns within a

work and then basing an analysis on them. The activity could also be expanded in scope to look at patterns in a body of work.

2. Analyzing movement and change: A series of ordered criteria guides students through understanding the how and why of character changes.

- *Connections between a Work and Your Experience* (page 194):

3. Using a reader response guide: This guide, a la theorist Wolfgang Iser, gives students practice in criticism from the phenomenological perspective that what happens to a reader is what a work "means."

- *Connections between and among Readers* (page 195):

4. Writing from a dialogue journal: When this activity works well, writings should demonstrate how other readers have pushed the student to articulate ideas beyond vague impressions and simple "I like/I don't like" responses.

- *Connections between and among Works* (page 195)

5. Comparing two works: Though this activity suggests several approaches for a comparison and several pairings of works, the ultimate choice is left to the student.

6. Writing comparative claims: Both activities give more practice with the claim device, one by directing it to each area of the pentad, the other by focusing it toward one of the critical perspectives in Chapter 3. The suggested end products, a hypertext and a critical paper, also differ.

7. Making a mini-anthology: Here students get to create and organize their own collections of favorite or perhaps influential works. A good follow-up is to ask for cover designs.

8. Build a chrestomathy: Although similar to the previous activity, the focus here is instructive and more wide-ranging—to demonstrate the tenor of the class through a range of literature-related artifacts.

- *Connections between and among Cultural and Literary Contexts* (page 197):

9. Planning a multicultural study: Although involved with selecting works a la the mini-anthology, this activity leaves the options for presentation open.

Chapter 7: Evaluating and Judging Literature

This chapter takes students beyond critical analysis of literature to the actual judging of it and offers several criteria for use in making judgments. It also discusses what kinds of judgments are factors in establishing literary canons.

"For Your Portfolio Notebook" Activities

- *Classify a Play* (page 203): Besides probing "willing suspension of disbelief," this is a good activity to start a discussion about what can be inferred and what can be assessed from such a small bit of text.

- *Make Your Own Judgments* (page 206): Ranking the three poems about death forces articulation of underlying content-evaluation criteria, especially those regarding emotional impact and "importance."

- *Your Own Judgments Again* (page 211): This unusual poem offers an interesting challenge, including some tensions among "Do I like it?" and "Do I *get* it?" and "Is it any good?"

- *Saving "Little Libbie"* (page 215): Here students get a chance to redeem a (perhaps unredeemable) poem using any of the criteria discussed thus far. Responses should be interesting!

- *Judge the Reviews* (page 216): Besides providing lovely models for nasty reviews, this activity provides practice in inferring the warrant from the claim and then continuing the review.

- *Write a Review* (page 219): Some student responses here may be worth sending to an outside audience such as the local paper or library newsletter.

- *Review Literary Canons* (page 221): This is a good activity to point out how some things change over time, even supposedly timeless classics or lists of classics.

Building Your Portfolio

(These untitled portfolio activities begin on page 221.)

- *Listing criteria for a good novel:* Students' ideas here are good jumping-off points for arguments in Reader's Forum.

- *Writing two book reviews:* It can be interesting to discuss whether writing the longer or the shorter version of the review was more difficult.
- *Choosing ten books for a desert island:* Ask students if the task changes when you vary the location—say, ten books to take to prison or Mars.
- *Creating one's self-portrait as a reader:* An interesting discussion might ensue if responses here are notably different from students' reading autobiographies.
- *Writing bad earlier drafts:* This is a backwards way to get at personal criteria of good writing. Bad drafts of one poem by six different people should feature a variety of "mistakes."

Chapter 8: Putting It All Together

In this chapter, students assemble their presentation portfolios. Various kinds of order are reviewed, and students are helped with actually presenting their work. The chapter concludes with students doing a final self-assessment and preparing a grade proposal.

Activities

- *Step 1: Review Your Working Portfolio* (page 226): Students should write their answers to the questions and complete the chart in this section, as their responses will lead them toward assembling the portfolio and making the final reflection.
- *Step 2: Assemble the Pieces* (page 231): Although students may have had several logistical and conceptual plans in mind as they continued through the course, they must now evaluate the pros and cons of each to decide on their final portfolio arrangement. The peer review checklist on page 237 can help them get another's opinion on the works they are considering including.
- *Step 3: Present the Final Portfolio* (page 240): As students do a final assessment of their progress and consider possible instructor response to their portfolios, they are ready to think about their final grades. Writing the grade proposal requires students to present legal briefs to persuade you to accept the grades proposed. Proposals offer you a chance to respond to their work and to their evaluation of their work.

3 Techniques for the Portfolio Classroom

The student text, as its contents makes clear, offers a fairly systematic approach to portfolio development, even if the particulars of each class vary. This chapter will give you some insights into what might happen when you take portfolios to heart. It also offers some nuts-and-bolts suggestions for making the portfolio approach work.

SEEING THE PORTFOLIO AS PROCESS

As we use the term, a portfolio is more than a writing folder. It is more than a collection of works or textual artifacts. As noted earlier, we strongly believe that a portfolio consists of the people, the activities, and the products of a working community, in this case a discourse community: your classroom.

There is a process involved here, and it is recursive. The route from preliminary assessment to goals to completed activities to portfolio presentation may look linear, but it isn't that simple. Like mental time when reading, the portfolio involves at any one point a mix of past, present, and future. Just as there are recursive stages in composing a single writing, there are broader, deeper, and messier stages in composing oneself as a reader through a literature portfolio.

Consider how you became as accomplished an instructor as you are. Did you learn X quantity of new things each year? Did you get Y percent better every month? Or did you progress in uneven and unpredictable ways, with epiphanies of understanding that made changes in breadth and depth at the same time?

If we have any useful advice here, it is this: Accept the ambiguity and the messiness of creating a portfolio at the beginning, and help your students to accept them. You will have some students who, up to this course, could whip out a calculator when a graded quiz was returned and recalculate their course averages to seven significant figures. But those figures are not so significant in a portfolio. It will take some time and work for students to give up the calculating and take on the responsibility for the important things: planning, conducting, and evaluating their work and themselves.

THE CLASS AS A DISCOURSE COMMUNITY OF COLLEAGUES

In a discourse community, the people and activities are more important than the products. We have all been to professional conferences that were productive experiences *even though they did not produce new text artifacts*. There was no assignment, no homework, no term paper at the end. Communicating with colleagues was the point, and you had to be there to understand the value of the experience.

And so the importance of establishing a context—specifically, a portfolio context—in the classroom and of turning your students into your colleagues. Here *colleagues* does not indicate those who have the same credentials or job descriptions as you do. Rather, it indicates the people you work with in your classroom, whose work and works you come to know well, whose accomplishments might be the best and most telling measure of your accomplishments as an instructor.

We are going to suggest some guidelines for dealing with students as colleagues in the discourse community of your classroom. Neither a bill of rights nor a set of commandments, the list that follows suggests what has produced the most outstanding work by students and the most fun and learning for us as instructors:

- Give colleagues every resource at your disposal: instructor's editions, methods of inquiry, evaluation criteria, models, notes, rubrics, and anything else you need to do your work. If you need it, they need it.

- Drop all activities whose sole or main purpose is to produce a grade or to be able to say "We covered that."

- Admit that all assignments, activities, and assessments are subjective matters. If humans make them, do them, or score them, they are subjective. Then use that subjectivity to celebrate differences.

- Be ready to negotiate almost everything. Academic standards should be explicit agreements.

- Allow revisions until a real deadline (contest or publication) arrives or until a marking period ends. In language arts, we are revising ourselves as language users more than we are revising any one piece of work.

- Use class time as laboratory and meeting time for the important work of the course.

- As you must keep your goals in harmony with curricular demands, students must keep their goals in harmony with yours. Think of the curriculum not as a box of stuff but as a group of paths or vectors, all possibilities.

- Set a context for risk-taking, theirs and yours.

- Hold the conversations you want to have about literacy and literature and pedagogy in the classroom, not just in the faculty room or office.

- Do real work and use colleagues' work fairly in activities that allow coauthorship or copresentation.

THE WORK OF ONE CLASSROOM DISCOURSE COMMUNITY

To show what it's like to work with students as colleagues in a portfolio context, the excerpted article that follows offers the views of the instructor as well as those of five students who worked in such a context in several courses. This piece, first published in the *Ohio Journal of the English Language Arts* (Volume 35, Number 1, Spring/Summer 1994), is itself an example of the collegiality we refer to. It was real work for a real audience. It was written under the usual time constraints. The process was exactly like professional collaboration or coauthorship, not so different from the process that produced the student text and this instructor's manual. The student sections in particular provide interesting insights into how students respond to some of the activities and procedures suggested in the text.

A Wholly Different Circumstance . . . Power and Portfolios

by Ryan Blothenburg, Kelly Buckley, Sarah Leonard, Matt Parker, Joseph Quattrini, and Austin Willoughby

What a Portfolio Isn't

It isn't just a new name for what we've always done. First, it's not a new name, and, second, we haven't always done it. Not in American language arts education, anyway, and not in any organized way. Neither is it only the latest buzzword. "Shared decision making" and "empowerment" are buzzwords; using portfolios is a way to actually achieve shared decision making and empowerment.

Neither is a portfolio a glorified writing folder, or some other collection of one-shot writings stored in folder or foot-locker, on temporary reprieve from the wastebasket. Glorified writing folders are easy to spot. Only the cover or folder or jacket has been jazzed up. The insides remain untouched, unread. Ballast, really.

A portfolio isn't just a different angle on traditional instruction. Collaborative learning, as it is often practiced, is a different angle. I sat in a workshop where we teachers were all trained to work in groups of three to memorize 20 meaningless symbols. (It was explained to us that in our classes we would have students do something meaningful, like memorize 20 dates or ingredients or authors or body parts.)

And a portfolio isn't just a paradigm shift, either. In the U.S., integration of the language arts is a paradigm shift. In New York State, for example, an earlier revision of the language arts curriculum shifted the paradigm from five "strands" to three: from reading, writing, speaking, listening, and literature...to reading, writing, and speaking and listening. (The most recent revision is quite a different matter.) Often, the term "paradigm shift" means another way to look at something. Without some internal or external demand *to do something different,* only the look need change.

So, a portfolio is more than a new word, more than a new name for an old thing, more than a different shuffle of the same old deck, which may not have been a full deck in the first place.

* * * * *

Our research has led us to some conclusions about some differences between use of portfolios for individual assessment and for large-scale assessment. This research, directed by Alan Purves of the National Research Center on Literature Teaching and Learning at SUNY Albany, yields these conclusions about individual assessment:

- A portfolio has a rhetorical purpose, to perform and persuade, and should present the individual student to the outside world.

- The portfolio should reflect the range and depth of the student's work in and beyond the curriculum, with the distinction of the individual the primary concern.

- Selecting, organizing, and presenting the material in the portfolio should be the student's responsibility.

- There are always two portfolios: the *working* portfolio is part of pedagogical practice, and it involves formative and reflective evaluation; the *presentation* portfolio involves summative evaluation.

. . . and these about large-scale assessment:

- The rhetorical purpose is to inform the public about the learning of a particular population, so large-scale assessment focuses on the performance of groups, not individuals.

- Large-scale assessment should be curriculum-based (expert consensus of the domain), confined to school activities, and accompanied by an index-of-opportunity to learn.

- Primary concerns are comparability across sites, centralized planning and scoring, and reliability of measurement.

- Large-scale assessment is summative.

Table 3 from the appendix to this research highlights the differences:

Assessment of the Individual	Large-Scale Assessment
Selects from the domain	Covers the domain
Seeks unique accomplishment	Strives for comparability
Focuses on the whole individual	Focuses on school effects
Is the responsibility of the student	Is the responsibility of the assessor

To these I would add:

Is grounded in context	Is isolated from context
Is the site for a conversation	Is the site for an observation
Is student-centered and -owned	Is assessor-centered and -owned
Is first-person, active voice	Is third-person, passive voice

* * * * *

What a Portfolio Can Be

What can the portfolio be? It can be a methodology for learning, one that turns traditional practice inside out, upside down, or out the door. It can be a philosophy of education whose focus is learning and growth, rather than teaching and testing. Whose point of comparison is one's later to earlier selves, not one's standing on a bell curve. Whose articulation is not of an empty field, but of living players' levels of play.

It can be a context for working: a network of relationships among the people, activities, and products of a discourse community—your own classroom.

* * * * *

Who makes the decisions about learning and assessment? The answer should be "teachers and learners." If students can't make *all* of the decisions, they can at least do *some* of all of them, and *all* of some of them. In the pages that follow, five students will explain what they do, how it feels, why it works, how it works.

So, the right stuff is people. A portfolio isn't only about products or papers; it isn't only about artwork or artifacts. It's also about process and readings and artists and artisans. This defining context, because it isn't portable, seems to me to doom attempts at teaching reform through large-scale assessment with portfolios. If context is important, then you simply have to be there. Like most good stories once removed, something is missing in the retelling. It's about the kind of intertextuality that exists in every classroom as a kind of potential energy. If we can accept the inherent openness and instability of written texts—accept this from Rosenblatt and Barthes and Eco and Iser—we can consider the potential power of the openness of the classroom as text. Some corollary thoughts about the *who* question:

- Reading is always between the lines. It depends on where the lines are drawn, and who gets to draw them. Learners need to negotiate to draw most of them, or the usual gerrymandering will take place.

- There are more than two sides to any story, as many as the number of narrators who will get the floor. Each learner needs to, and deserves to, narrate her own learning story.

- The site of the conversation determines the participants. When a teacher responds to a student self-evaluation or grade proposal or portfolio, both student and teacher have voice, even if the teacher has the last word. In traditional grading, the student isn't in the conversation—it's an interior monologue for the teacher to "prove the grade." In the new large-scale assessment designs, there will be no conversation.

It strikes me that the point of our reading and writing, of our learning, of our very language and literacy, is not to finish a conversation, but to be in one.

Some Conclusions

The conversation continues with views from students. The rest of the writers you will see here were (and are) part of the CLTL portfolio research project. Originally in this study, we wanted to expand the definition of the portfolio by extending writing folders to literature and other elements in language arts.

What we developed was a definition that integrated not only our approach to language arts but also the text of the classroom community. Each of us produced a portfolio. More than that, we were all *in one* for the year.

* * * * *

Portfolio vs. Traditional Grading

Kelly Buckley

There are many ways of evaluating a piece of work, a project, or an understanding of a subject. Too often in high school, students are exposed to only one type of grading known as the traditional grading system because it is well known and accepted. But traditional grading has many flaws that have not been attended to, especially when in an English class. To me a portfolio method of grading is more effective and completely changes the environment of the traditional classroom as we, the students, know it.

I worked in a portfolio class my junior year and it was a new experience, one which I was not quick to accept because it was different. But I became convinced that, yes, it actually works, and now I wouldn't want to move back to the old way again. In fact, our class was given the option at the beginning of our senior year to return to traditional grading, and we rejected such a change for reasons which are clear to me.

The first part of portfolios was setting goals that would show improvement. Each of us set goals in different areas. But they weren't goals that could be met easily. They were goals that were worked toward the entire year, long-term goals that would produce long-term effects after we were finished with our English 11A class and would help us beyond the classroom. For example, one of my goals was to speak more relaxed and comfortably before a group.

Our goals were sensible goals. And basically portfolios allowed us to evaluate our progress. There were projects that the entire class completed, such as reading the novel *Dancehall* and participating in a National Endowment for the Humanities seminar. There were some extra projects that individuals chose in order to work toward their personal goals, such as the "Great Moments in Literacy" feature of our class, where we shared a particularly striking work we came across. These "moments" ranged from musical presentations to more traditional poetry. I read a passage from *The Autobiography of Malcolm X* for one of mine. These projects were not graded by our teacher, but evaluated by us based on criteria he set and what we as students tried to do.

Now you may wonder how grades were established for school purposes. And, actually, school purposes were the only reason we needed grades. We did not talk of grades within the class. It was not necessary. We were there to work and to learn, not to get bogged down in the difference between a 92 and a 94. And the reason is simple: There were no right or wrong answers in the work we did. English is not like math where there is a definite answer that can be proven correct. Much of the work we did was open to our opinions and ideas as long as we could back them up with supports.

At the end of each marking period we wrote grade proposals. And again, we selected the grade we proposed with our work and progress made that quarter. It was a long process that became greater in depth as the year moved on. Those who worked hard were rewarded by themselves.

Therefore there was great incentive to go beyond the classwork that we were involved in daily. Ideally, we prepared through the entire quarter for our grade proposals and to get closer to our goals. The goals were such that they could never be completely met. It wasn't that simple. The goals were an important part of the course because many decisions were made based on individual goals and progress.

I learned a lot last year about myself. I can recognize my strengths and abilities and yet I also know my weaknesses. That's so important to understand. Overall it was a lot of work, but I believe that it was worth it. With each grade proposal I came to different conclusions about my work, my writing, and my understandings, and things really pulled together. It was work that will help me through my life. While other juniors were preparing for vocabulary tests and such, we were beyond and above, doing something more practical and new.

The portfolios which seemed so new and odd are now so comfortable to work in. They make so much sense. I think if more classes attempted portfolios they would agree. I too had to be convinced at first.

After years of school I think students are the most reluctant to change. Teachers owe it to their students to try something new. I'm sure there are many ways to work with portfolios and that each class should do it in the way that works best for them. I don't see portfolios taking over throughout school systems, but gradually receiving recognition.

I may only be able to offer my opinion as a student, but aren't we the ones affected? The system was established for people like me. I also believe it should change to meet the needs of the students to receive the best education in the high school years—which should pay off later in life.

* * * * *

Motivation: from Goals to Grade Proposals
Matt Parker

As a teacher you may have asked yourself: How can I adapt my lessons to a portfolio system? I will try to illustrate one aspect of this conversion from a traditional grading method to the portfolio system. This aspect includes goals. What makes the portfolio system different is that it allows students to personalize specific assignments and even the entire course to fit the goals they wish to accomplish for the year.

How can this be possible in a room of 15 or even 30 children all working on different goals (or at least variations on the same ones)?

The traditional grading system with its rigid assignments and worksheets would never be able to accommodate even two different personalities and needs, much less 30. But with the use of open-ended assignments in the portfolio system this is a possibility.

Why would one want to bother with such a thing? My feeling is that by having students set goals and work toward them, they feel more in control of their destinies, rather than being in a curriculum that descends from some entity on high. In this system, students are more motivated since they know they are

1. working to improve their own products, and
2. working to improve themselves.

I'll try to illustrate with an example: The teacher assigns a book to be read over the spring break. Let's say it is *1984* by George Orwell. The teacher asks the students to return with a certain number of pages of writing and reminds them that the strength of their grade proposals depends on the effort they put toward their goals this quarter.

To begin the work, students submit proposals to the teacher saying what they want to accomplish through the project. The proposal states what form the writing (or other products or activities) will take. It need not be more than 4-5 sentences. If the plan is clear and complete, it is approved. If not, the teacher will confer with the student to develop a more useful plan for a course of action.

The goal of the teacher in this situation, ideally, is not to tell the student exactly what to do, but to ask questions and to suggest an array of activities. (It has been my experience that such conferences are not often needed.)

They all sweat a little knowing they must work toward their goals or it will reflect in their grade proposals and eventually their final averages. From this point, let's follow the progress of three students as they move from the teacher's open-ended assignment to their own specific self-tailored assignment using their goals.

Take Polly, for instance. Last year in class she was a faltering speaker who had trouble expressing her ideas and feelings to the class. This year two of her goals are to speak better in front of a group (for information and understanding?) and to write better for personal response. She decided that the best course of action for the assignment would be to write an essay outlining her feelings about the society described in the novel, and then to read it aloud in class.

A different approach to this assignment can be seen in the way Geoff completed it. At the beginning of the year he said he wanted to write better fiction and poetry. In keeping with his goals, Geoff read the novel and then wrote a poem that expressed some of the ideas shown in the novel. He also wrote a short essay that told how his work showed his understanding of the text as a whole and the concepts involved.

A third version of this same basic assignment can be seen in how Lisa approached it. She was unclear at the start of the year about exactly what she wanted to accomplish, but she knew she wanted to be able to read things that were more complex from different points of view. After some contemplation she decided that she would best accomplish her goal by telling the events of the story from the point of view of another character.

These separate projects are brought back into the conversation of the class in several ways. During the work, we might exchange papers and ask readers for responses to specific questions we have about the drafts we're working on. Later, after we present the works in a seminar, we have a round table discussion about how our goals and these projects have helped us personalize the course to fit our perceived needs.

So there you have it. Each student worked on what he or she wanted, according to individual goals, but building from the same basic assignment. No one was limited to one goal or one assignment. Each had several goals to choose from or combine to accomplish the assignment satisfactorily, and all the individual work comes back to the conversation within the class. It just requires creativity on the part of the student and the teacher.

* * * * *

Real-World Extensions
Ryan Blothenburg
My feelings concerning our portfolio-based class are many. It is difficult to portray our diversion from the traditional system in words. It's a feeling one has, both as a student and a person. I feel I now have the power and freedom to pursue the goal I choose— to take the road not taken. I think this want exists in everybody. A want, which when achieved in my case, left me all alone in a sense. Even the widest boulevard was nowhere in sight.

I soon found myself—able to make my own path. All I needed was one additional support. And hence the portfolio class. A place where justification is the "key to the city," so to speak.

This aspect of the class has taught me many things: responsibility, respect, and attention to detail. All of these are applied to my projects. In a portfolio class they must be.

My participation in this type of class has led me to a variety of special opportunities. Of these, the most notable would have to be my part in a presentation at a New York State English Council professional conference in Albany in October of 1993. Six students (and, of course, the teacher) held a workshop based on our "Great Moments in Literacy." This is a regular feature of our class where we are asked to uncover any particular texts within our daily reading and listening which we find striking in meaning or appeal. Our job is then to bring them in and present them to the entire class. At the conference, we set out to present various works to the audience which we felt struck fire in us as readers—and then to explain why. That's what we did, and it was a tremendous success, mostly because we could demonstrate our type of class firsthand and further the understanding of it by other language users.

Besides taking part in a "teaching" experience at the conference, I was also a part of a particularly influential learning experience. A fellow student and I attended other conference workshops and became aware of a "revolutionary" discussion technique. Seeing that it had many parallel ideas with our portfolio class, we decided to devise a similar project. In a nutshell, it was an experiment in heterogeneous grouping: we (two high school seniors) would read and later discuss a 3rd-grade level book with a group of 3rd-grades who also read the story. We videotaped the 45 minutes of discussion, showed and explained the tape to our AP English classmates, and later came to the conclusion that our experiment had been successful. It was successful because each student was entitled to an opinion, and no one hesitated to show justification for his or her thinking.

That's what I believe to be the basis and the sensibility of the portfolio class, and its advantage over the traditional program: the capacity to involve others through a claim, warrant, and data model where everyone can propose a valid opinion, not just one right or wrong.

* * * * *

What Teachers Need to Know
Austin Willoughby
Making a portfolio class work depends on the teacher's willingness to stray from the standard methods of teaching to a radical new style. The teacher needs to be ready to guide students into a new style of class, but also must not hold students' hands through the class, as traditional teachers have. The most significant changes the project makes is that students must find ways to work on their own, without a teacher there all the time telling them how to budget their time. They must take the initiative to assign homework, and prepare to rate their performance during the quarter to construct a grade

proposal, which will help decide the one grade the students receives in the quarter.

Another change this method requires of teachers is that they know how to allow students to work on their own with long-term assignments to be accomplished through the quarter. Teachers need to know how to involve response and rating sessions into the lesson plan so that students can ask other students questions about the work. In my class, we have portfolio groups. A portfolio group consists of three people who read each other's papers in what is called a read-around. After the ratings, responses and possible revisions, the work will be put into the student's portfolio, where it will be evaluated by student and teacher at the end of the quarter in the negotiation over the grade proposal.

Teachers also need to know when to have students working individually because this is a big part of the class. By working on their own, mostly on long-term projects, students can assign themselves the homework they need to do in order to complete the project by the end of the quarter. This allows students to work at their own paces and also allows as many revisions as the student wishes, making better, more insightful works.

The teacher needs to know how to budget the class's time. This is where long-term projects help because they allow the class to get more accomplished in a quarter. Long-term projects do this because we are not obligated to finish one project before beginning another. Having many projects being worked on at the same time forces the student to take out "homework insurance"—they need to work on every project nearly every night to insure that they will be able to finish the work needed for the portfolio by the quarter's end. Long-term projects may be coupled with a group project, another major difference in portfolio classes. In many of my other classes, we never have group projects, but in this English class we work in groups often. I feel that group projects work because they allow us to see points of view we may not have seen if we had not been in the group.

In most of my classes teachers frown on group projects. They claim that the groups don't work and are not worth spending the class time on, but through this portfolio-based English class I have found that the groups really do work.

The grading system for a portfolio class is also extremely different from what most students are used to in their other classes. The teacher must be able to deal with questions such as "How are my papers graded?" and "Can I make revisions to works I already put into my portfolio?" We asked these questions, and the answers came from our negotiated agreements in our class academic standards work:

1. "Your papers are not graded individually, but they are rated to help you see where improvements might be made. Your grade will be based on your work, as shown in the proposal you turn in at the end of the quarter."
2. "Sure. Any paper (or other project) done this quarter is open to revisions during the whole quarter."

So, our portfolio grading system is that there are no grades. Well, almost. There is one grade, a quarterly grade which is decided on by the student and the teacher. The student's part is the grade proposal. It is the most important paper the student will write all quarter because this is where the student attempts to prove the work he or she did all quarter is worth the grade asked for in the proposal.

In my other classes, I receive a single grade for every work I do. If I get 75 correct out of 100 problems on a math test, the teacher says the work I did is worth 75 in the gradebook, which will be averaged along with all the other daily grades for the quarter grade. Teachers need to know that it is time to leave this method of grading behind and enter the new era of grade proposals.

The grade proposal is different and better. It is better to let students have a say in the grades they will receive and to let them validate their opinions in a formal proposal. The grade proposal tells the teacher what grade the student deserves and why the grade is justified.

In the grade proposal I wrote for the first ten weeks of this class, I used the goals I had established as support for the grade I suggested. I chose three goals that I would work toward through English and other classes. I made improvements in the areas I worked in and put that to use as evidence in my grade proposal.

For example, I needed improvement on speaking to groups. Before I chose to work on speaking for personal response, I feared speaking to groups. When I did speak, I stumbled over words and fidgeted, not knowing where to put my hands. During the quarter I made two presentations to groups, one in French and another in English. In these I used suggestions made by others. I used a podium, which made me more comfortable and cut down on how much I waved my hands, and I used an outline instead of a script. This allowed me to have less trouble with words because I wasn't reading word for word. This is one example of how I justified the grade I proposed for the first ten weeks.

* * * * *

The Problem of Assessment
Sarah Leonard

I believe that using the portfolio as a measure of student academic understanding is a good idea. It is better than standardized tests. While they are okay for some purposes, they can sometimes classify students into categories they don't belong in, especially if the tests are used to determine which students go into accelerated courses.

The portfolio is a good idea, but without the proper assessment, it could be worse than standardized tests, such as Regents Exams, SAT and ACT tests. At least these tests have clear-cut answers to every question. Portfolios don't have this feature. They must be judged qualitatively. Some teachers may not like reading through and having to know how to make these kinds of judgments.

I agree that these decisions are difficult, but they must be made. Standardized tests provide an easy way to grade students' work and achievements, but the easy way is not always the best way. Students that may have horrible test-taking skills may also have very good writing skills. Students should not be categorized by tests.

Portfolios should be assessed by students and teachers together, perhaps by the student and teacher working together. The best way to assess portfolios might be to use a rating system. Grades are often set in stone by the teacher when they should be discussed by the teacher and the student.

One idea for assessment is a panel of teachers and students getting together and discussing ways to assess portfolios. They could use several portfolios as good and bad examples. They could set up a rating system for teachers to use. Also, they could make a list of things raters should look for. Raters need guidelines established to work from. When we rated each other's presentations in my English class, we thought about each of these criteria on a 10-point scale:

1. freshness of insights
2. elaboration and support
3. completeness and closure
4. assertion of significance

Student participation is essential. If students aren't involved, what's the point? Students should be a part of the assessment of their work. Teachers can't always be right, and students may be the best judges of each other's work.

By using students to help decide how to grade their work, new viewpoints and perspectives are brought to light. Students have very different points of view from teachers. There are vast differences in age and experience. How can adults judge teenagers' work? There are always some differences of opinion.

Portfolios are a grand total of what the students feels is his or her greatest work. Students need to be in on the assessment so they can know how to assess their work themselves. This assessment is something that is subjective, and that is why guidelines need to be established.

MAKING THINGS WORK

In addition to the suggestions in the preceding article, here are a few more ideas and aids for making a portfolio class progress effectively. You will notice that everything presented here is connected to activities found in the student text.

Using Reader's Forum

Reader's Forum is meant to be a confidence- and community-building activity that encourages students to share views. It avoids the unfortunate classroom dynamic of the dialogue between the instructor and the smart kid. It says to students:

- You are supposed to have an opinion.
- Don't wait for the instructor to ask a question.
- Every day is presentation day.
- You have to read and write and speak and listen your way to achieving your goals.
- Oxygen consumption is not the measure of brain activity here.
- Participation equals contribution, and what have you done for us lately?

You will probably have to train students to use Reader's Forum activities to engage each other. They may well be in the habit of waiting for their turns to speak but not so facile at responding to the speech of another by questioning, affirming, disagreeing, or somehow building on the speaker's ideas.

Establishing Portfolio Groups

In our own teaching, we have noticed that productive work seems to come when students are involved in independent, small-group, and whole-class activities. Like a good writing group, a portfolio group provides a forum, a workshop, an opportunity for response, a team for collaborative ventures, and a support group for needs that include and extend beyond language arts.

If there is anything to be learned from teaching, then group members learn as much when they are responding and advising as when they are speaking or asking questions. If we want students to become lifelong learners, then they also have to become lifelong self-instructors. The portfolio group offers experience that leads past knowledge to practice and habits.

The purpose of the group is not to "fix" the work of a member. Rather, it is to help set an agenda for rereading, perhaps by changing the site of the conversation or raising questions not thought of by one of the members. Each member needs to learn to ask specific questions before presenting a text or other work. "Do you like it?" and "What do you think of it?" are usually answered "Yes" and "I like it, it's good"— warm but not helpful responses.

Who chooses groups? Whether you choose them or students do, it seems important that the groups stay together for some time, probably most of the course. The benefits of the long-term work are trust and familiarity with goals, style, and methods of operation. If you have to keep switching rowing partners, it is hard to get any rhythm to your stroke.

Whoever chooses, groups should be formed on the basis of members' ability to work together and help each other. No instructor can (or should) read every word each student writes or hear every word each speaks.

Depending on the size of a class and the duration of your meeting time, groups should probably include three to five students. Responses tend to become speed trials and glosses if each member has only a few minutes with each paper.

RESPONDING, GRADING, AND ASSESSING

In practice, personal judgment is the basis for almost all the instructional and assessment decisions we as instructors make about students and their work. Such judgment is subjective. It has to be. Maybe it even should be. None of us has (or *is*) a machine that can read a paper and tell if it is an "82" or an "83." Like Hieronymo in *The Spanish Tragedy*, we sometimes wait for the answer to flutter down from the heavens: "Aha! *Now* I've got you!"

Nevertheless, in most classroom situations evaluation is required, and you must decide how to go about it. In *Portfolios in Language Arts*, Kathleen Blake Yancey outlines three types of evaluation and their products. *Summative* evaluation produces a final assessment, often in the form of a grade or rank of achievement. The evaluation of the presented portfolio, for example, is summative. *Formative* evaluation, done midstream, produces not only numbers or rankings but also useful diagnostic and planning information for both student and instructor. Every activity and response to it through the course can be part of this formative evaluation. *Reflective* evaluation, which is done by students, is perhaps the most powerful learning vehicle of the three, for it provides the most useful long-term insights about both their works and their work. Reflective evaluation is formative for the long run, and since it is first person, it is owned by the student. Each "Building Your Portfolio" activity in the student text is an opportunity for reflective evaluation. So is each "Portfolio Progress Report." So is the reflection at the portfolio presentation or the end of the course.

In *Expanding Student Assessment*, Vito Perrone discusses three types, or levels, of assessment. "Keeping track" is administrative work, keeping records of who is doing what (and who is not doing anything). "Checking up" includes most tests and quizzes that measure who knows what on a given day. He suggests that the third kind of assessment, "finding out," is the type least often practiced in secondary school and college—and also the most important kind to be done. Finding out means discovering who is learning what, and in what ways and to what degrees. Almost every activity in the student text will let you find out what students are able to do, individually and in groups, with literature.

If you use the general assessment framework and philosophy we espouse in the student text, you and your students will spend most of your time and effort finding out and then reflecting on what was found. You will be giving students the knowledge and practice and habits they need to be independent self-evaluators. You will also be giving them the evaluation criteria toward which to revise their work and themselves as they make themselves as readers.

Achieving this expertise will take some work on the part of students. We have seen students at all levels who have not taken a course which offers them so much of what is often the secret lore of evaluation. It is a shock to them to be presented with the methodology—and the responsibility—for assessment.

Understanding and Using Rubrics

Because growth in language and literature is so difficult to measure quantitatively, an intelligent approach is to use rubrics. There are three kinds of rubrics that may be used for evaluation (though most commonly used rubrics are really hybrids of these). An *analytical* rubric awards so many points for each aspect of a work—content, organization, style, and mechanics. Within each aspect, more specific criteria may be defined, and the point values indicate the evaluator's take on the relative importance of each aspect. Here is a sample rubric for an expository paper:

30 **Content**
Thesis is clear and unambiguous
Background is explored
Proof is relevant and substantial

30 **Organization**
Points made support the thesis
Each point is dealt with separately
Transitions are effective

25 **Style**
Opening paragraph is interesting and attention-getting
Sentence length and structure are varied
Personal voice is evident

15 **Mechanics**
Capitalization, punctuation, and spelling are correct
Run-on sentences are avoided

A *primary trait* rubric generally evaluates on the basis of several criteria that define the essence of the work. Points of focus are established for a work by defining traits such as:

- originality
- power
- control

A *holistic* rubric looks at an entire performance and describes the features of various levels of play. Often four to six levels are designated, from "incomplete" or "needs much instruction" up to "exceptional" or "demonstrates mastery." Within those levels the general attributes of content, organization, style, and mechanics are combined into one criterion.

The evaluation design we offer in Chapter 2 of the student text suggests a kind of holistic rubric that describes levels of performance for different language uses. Since a portfolio offers a long-range assessment of growth over time, this rubric gives you and your students a tool to assess interim progress as well as to help perform an end-point or summative evaluation of the finished product. Copies of reproducible forms containing the aspects of this rubric are found on the pages that follow.

The responses and ratings done during the course, as well as the self-evaluations called for in each chapter's "Portfolio Progress Report," can all fit within the framework of assessment. A vehicle to connect various kinds of assessments is the grade proposal. The student conducts a performance review—from goals to achievements—and makes a case for a grade for the quarter's or semester's work. The instructor responds to the grade proposal with an acceptance or a counter-proposal. This negotiation of grades leads to some interesting conversations, spoken and in print, about the nature of evaluation. The directions to students for completing a grade proposal are discussed in general on pages 243–245 of the student text, with specific instructions for drafting the proposal beginning on page 244.

Reproducible Masters for Self-Assessment

The masters provided on the next few pages may be used for preliminary, midcourse, and final self-assessments. Their use is explained in detail on pages 58–63 of the student text.

SELF-ASSESSMENT
θ **Preliminary**   θ **Midcourse**   θ **Final**

Language purpose #1: Reading for information and understanding
Typical example: _____

Range
least————————————————————————————most
1   2   3   4   5   6   7   8   9   10   11   12
Explanation: _____

_____

Flexibility
least————————————————————————————most
1   2   3   4   5   6   7   8   9   10   11   12
Explanation: _____

_____

Connectedness
least————————————————————————————most
1   2   3   4   5   6   7   8   9   10   11   12
Explanation: _____

_____

Conventions
least————————————————————————————most
1   2   3   4   5   6   7   8   9   10   11   12
Explanation: _____

_____

Independence
least————————————————————————————most
1   2   3   4   5   6   7   8   9   10   11   12
Explanation: _____

_____

SELF-ASSESSMENT
θ **Preliminary**   θ **Midcourse**   θ **Final**

Language purpose #2: Reading for literary and aesthetic response
Typical example: _____

Range
least———————————————————————————————————most
1   2   3   4   5   6   7   8   9   10   11   12
Explanation: _____
_____

Flexibility
least———————————————————————————————————most
1   2   3   4   5   6   7   8   9   10   11   12
Explanation: _____
_____

Connectedness
least———————————————————————————————————most
1   2   3   4   5   6   7   8   9   10   11   12
Explanation: _____
_____

Conventions
least———————————————————————————————————most
1   2   3   4   5   6   7   8   9   10   11   12
Explanation: _____
_____

Independence
least———————————————————————————————————most
1   2   3   4   5   6   7   8   9   10   11   12
Explanation: _____
_____

SELF-ASSESSMENT
θ Preliminary   θ Midcourse   θ Final

Language purpose #3: Reading for critical analysis and evaluation
Typical example: _____

Range
least——————————————————————————————most
1   2   3   4   5   6   7   8   9   10   11   12
Explanation: _____

_____

Flexibility
least——————————————————————————————most
1   2   3   4   5   6   7   8   9   10   11   12
Explanation: _____

_____

Connectedness
least——————————————————————————————most
1   2   3   4   5   6   7   8   9   10   11   12
Explanation: _____

_____

Conventions
least——————————————————————————————most
1   2   3   4   5   6   7   8   9   10   11   12
Explanation: _____

_____

Independence
least——————————————————————————————most
1   2   3   4   5   6   7   8   9   10   11   12
Explanation: _____

_____

SELF-ASSESSMENT
θ **Preliminary**   θ **Midcourse**   θ **Final**

Language purpose #4: Reading for social interaction
Typical example: _____

Range
least————————————————————————————most
1   2   3   4   5   6   7   8   9   10   11   12
Explanation: _____
_____

Flexibility
least————————————————————————————most
1   2   3   4   5   6   7   8   9   10   11   12
Explanation: _____
_____

Connectedness
least————————————————————————————most
1   2   3   4   5   6   7   8   9   10   11   12
Explanation: _____
_____

Conventions
least————————————————————————————most
1   2   3   4   5   6   7   8   9   10   11   12
Explanation: _____
_____

Independence
least————————————————————————————most
1   2   3   4   5   6   7   8   9   10   11   12
Explanation: _____
_____

4 Difficulty in Literature and Its Teaching

Many of us who have been concerned with the teaching and testing of literature have worried about the question of difficulty. When people choose selections to be used in a course or put in an anthology, they are often plagued by the idea of grade level.

- Should this poem be in my anthology?
- Is this story too hard for my class?
- How do I know whether this class is ready to read this selection?

Instructors and editors try to respond to such questions in various ways. People who develop literature anthologies and programs make up scope and sequence charts. College curriculum committees establish introductory, prerequisite courses that attempt to delineate what the preparation for studying literature in more depth should be. Individual instructors will try a poem with a class and then realize that it may have been too easy or too difficult. Test preparers, particularly those who develop state and national examinations, also worry about difficulty for the grade, age, or experiential level of the students as they work to determine what is to be tested and what shows that one student is "better" than another. Since examiners must deal with a psychometric world that seeks certainty and definition of answers, reliability in the rating of performance and the ability to rank students on a true scale from the able reader to the insensitive clod, they face a complex set of problems.

COPING WITH DIFFICULTIES

While we would not wish to postulate that there is absolutely no such thing as difficult literature, there is much to be said for the way a work is read and analyzed.

Factors Influencing Literature Interpretation

One of the findings of research is that often the difficulty of a particular piece of literature may have little to do with any quality of that piece all by itself. A poem like Blake's

> Tiger! Tiger! Burning bright
> In the forests of the night:
> What immortal hand or eye
> Could frame thy fearful symmetry?

does not have particularly difficult words; nor is the grammar hard. Yet it is not an easy poem for some people, who see it as a complex symbolic structure coming out of William Blake's particular view of Swedenborg and Christianity. The difficulty is not in the poem but in what surrounds it. The difficulty lies in the context, not in the text.

Recently, research in learning in English and other humanities has shown that there is no such thing as learning to be a good reader or writer or critic across the board. Learning in these areas and others is learning the rules of a group, or "interpretive community." This means that students in England may become different sorts of interpreters than students in the United States. It may even mean that learning in literature is learning to be a member of a small community, that of an individual classroom. There are two authors of this book: one of us teaches in college classrooms, the other in high school. Each of us probably has a different picture of a "good" literature student, and so we judge achievement or learning somewhat differently. Our students learn to play our game, to be good students in a specific context. But they may have trouble if they were transported to a class that the other of us teaches. Different things might prove difficult.

Directing the Curriculum

Traditionally, instructors, textbook writers, and examiners have focused on one of three aspects of the curriculum. The choice has traditionally depended upon which aspect has held sway within the profession and the schools:

- knowledge of texts and related information (e.g., biographical information and literary terms)
- performance in the critical and interpretive reading of texts
- attitudes concerning the reading of literature and particular texts

These are summed up in the student volume under the general headings of *knowledge*, *practice*, and *habits* (which we discuss with the students in Chapter 1). One or another of these has been prominent among different groups over the course of the history of English and literature teaching. We advocate a balance among the three, for each is important and each affects the others. What we know affects how we read and criticize; so do our attitudes and habits of reading. Our habits affect what we think it is important to know. So why not think about teaching literature as a blending of the three? A broad summary of the three appears in the following table:

Knowledge		Practice		Habits	
Textual	Extratextual	Responding	Articulating	Aesthetic habits	Choice of behavior
Specific text	History	Decoding	Retelling	Evaluating	Selecting
Genres	Author	Analyzing	Discussing	Valuing	Personalizing
Cultural allusions	Critical terms	Interpreting	Generalizing across works		

Under the first heading, we have concentrated on that body of knowledge that appears to distinguish literature as a separate and perhaps unique domain. Knowledge of texts can be contained in texts and myths and folk tales or it can exist outside of texts as part of the common core. Many people know about a "Romeo" without having read the play.

Under practice, the first level of response includes reading—or in the case of film, watching and listening. It begins with decoding or making out the plain sense of the work, moves on to envisioning or coming to some whole impression and re-creation of what is read, and should (but unfortunately does not always) culminate in the more detailed tasks of analyzing, personalizing, and interpreting. The second level of response involves articulating; that is, using a variety of means such as speaking, writing, and performing to communicate one's reaction to a work. Articulation is central to the curriculum in many ways because like any school subject, the study of literature involves public acts in which the student must be more clear and forthcoming about procedures, strategies, and conclusions than might be true if he or she were simply reading for pleasure outside of school. It is in the articulation as well as the display of knowledge that the student comes into contact with the community and is accepted into it. Ideally, the articulation of a response will come to influence the response itself.

In order to preserve the aesthetic nature of the text and to treat a work such as *Moby Dick* as literature rather than as a treatise on whales, certain habits of reading and of mind need to be developed. If literary works are to be read and talked about differently from other kinds of texts, students must learn how to perform a critical reading and must be encouraged to read this way voluntarily. One of the habits involved is to make aesthetic judgments about the various texts read and to justify these judgments publicly. Personal preference is not sufficient; students need to learn to give up "I don't like it" or "It sucks" in favor of "I think this is a poorly written book that deals with an insignificant subject in a pretentious manner."

Literature education is also supposed to develop something called "taste," or the love of "good literature," so that literature education goes beyond reading and writing and even specific, preferred habits of reading and writing. It generally includes the development of a tolerance for the variety in literature, of a willingness to acknowledge that many different kinds and styles of work can be thought of as literature, and of an understanding that just because we do not like a certain poem does not mean that it is not good. It can even lead students to distrust the meretricious or the shoddy use of sentiment. Experienced readers of literature can see that they are being tricked by a book or a film even when the trickery is going on—and they can enjoy the experience.

If we redefine learning in literature so that it involves the intersection of knowledge, practice, and habits and so that the standards for learning achievement are those of the interpretive community into which a given individual is entering, the nature of difficulty changes from the text itself to what students are asked to do with the text. Literature is a difficult subject because of what we ask students to become, not necessarily because of what we ask them to read.

Thus an interpretation of Shakespeare may be harder or easier depending upon the nature of the community and its standards and upon the intellectual distance an individual must travel to enter that community. Shakespeare can be a good and relatively accessible experience to a group of beginning literature students if they attend a film of *Romeo and Juliet* and then write what they like or didn't like about the film. It can be quite different if they are asked to write critical papers on the nature of Renaissance views of romance and honor as they affect the actions of the two major characters.

A Formula for Difficulty

Having said all this, we can even go so far as to give a formula for difficulty. The difficulty of a text (D), then, varies with the amount of knowledge (K) presumed sufficient by one's interpretive community to demonstrate an adequate (A) and appropriate (A1) articulation of a response to that text:

$$D = K (A + A1)$$

Thus no text is easy or difficult outside of the norms and standards of the community that determines (1) what is necessary and sufficient knowledge; (2) what is an adequately framed discussion of or generalization about the text within a larger discussion of literature; and (3) what is an appropriate aesthetic disposition towards the text.

We can illustrate this principle with, say, e. e. cummings's poem on Buffalo Bill as an example. In terms of knowledge, the difficulty of this poem depends upon the degree to which the community deems it important to know who Buffalo Bill was, the background and poetics of cummings, and cummings's place in twentieth-century American poetry. A group of students can show understanding of the text with a vague knowledge of each of these points. To demand a more precise knowledge immediately makes the poem more difficult.

As it is with knowledge, so it is with practice. The text could simply be presented to a group of readers with a request for a minimally articulated response, perhaps only to identify the author or the period or to read the poem aloud. On the other hand, the community may require an elaborated discussion of the style and structure of the poem related to an interpretation that deals with the death of a superstar and the views the American public had of Buffalo Bill, as well as cummings's ambivalence toward American heroes, the American public, and death. If the elaborated knowledge needs to be further integrated into an appropriately detailed essay with proof and counters to alternative interpretations, the poem takes on an additional layer of difficulty.

Similarly, if one were to demand, perhaps in addition to the other requirements, that the reader elaborate an aesthetic judgment of the poem that demonstrated an awareness of the norms of reading modern American poetry and a personal commitment to the habit of reading it for the delight the experience offers, the difficulty of the text increases. By contrast, if the reader were only asked to comment on a personal judgment as in "Did you like it?" the difficulty is not great.

The difficulty of a literary text that we choose to teach for a particular class, then, is only partially determined by various characteristics of the text itself. Much more influential are the demands of the classroom community regarding that text. The community may require a more or less elaborate articulation of the individual reader's knowledge and understanding of the work and may set detailed criteria to judge that articulation and the degree to which it satisfies the community's ideal of an aesthetic reading.

In short, a text's difficulty depends upon the nature of the understanding expected. For this reason, a poem like "The Wasteland" is difficult when a reader is expected to elaborate all of the interconnections, ambiguities, and allusions and make a coherent statement about the poem. The poem is complex because a group of readers has established the ground rules for complexity; by taking a more impressionistic view of how the poem is to be read, its complexity diminishes.

So what does this all mean for you as you work to develop your literature class and course? We think that it means that you must be careful to consider a number of questions as you plan the course and think about student performance:

- What kinds of knowledge are you assuming or demanding of your students? Where are they to get it and how?

- What do you define as an informed understanding of a particular selection? Have you communicated your view to your students?
- What do you see as an appropriate way of expressing that understanding? Will you allow for alternatives?

Some of the activities we suggest in the later pages of this manual may help you to answer these questions.

5 Examples of Student Performances on Assignments

The examples that follow were written by our students in response to assignments in the student text. We include these not as models of perfection but as illustrations of what responses might look like. We might mention that although these pieces have been edited for length, they were written by students without direction or assistance beyond the textbook explanations of what to do. We hope you will find them useful.

Example 1: Preliminary and Summary Self-Assessments (Jason Croston)

Examples follow of a preliminary self-assessment and a summary self-assessment from the same student. Jason writes about his range in the area of literary and aesthetic response.

Preliminary Self-Assessment:
Range
I rate myself a 4 here because the only way I have ever responded to literature was through a reading log, and I hate them. On my last project, I read the entire book first and then randomly picked pages for passages to write about. My entire viewpoint is colored by what happens in the end. Also, this means I can write just comments, and not questions, in my log. Thus they are dull, lacking any real thought or emotion. That's all I do.

Summary Self-Assessment:
Range

Some things have changed. Reading logs still annoy me because they force me to stop reading, but I have learned the value of capturing my thoughts and emotions as they are still raw and fresh; thus, I would rate myself a 10. This has led to my having questions and speculations in the log and to my being aware of having them. My logs are more interesting to read, and I think I read in a more interested way. Is that depth?

I can read a much wider range of materials because these questioning and commenting techniques work with any kind of reading I want to do (or have to do). Also, I have learned to write a book review, an extension of a story, a dramatic sketch, and fifteen other kinds of responses, so I suppose my range of response has improved, too.

Example 2: Grade Proposal (Amanda Klump)

Here is an excerpt from a grade proposal written by a second-semester junior in high school. The course she refers to is a college-level course using many of the activities in this book. Amanda proposes a grade of "A" for her work.

... In the literary expression and response category, my goal was to use language creatively and to use words and structures effectively to form images and communicate experiences in a way that expresses my feelings, attitudes, and ideas. Throughout the year I have progressed toward this goal and I feel I showed this progress during the 4th quarter. I drafted a cover letter for Sarah Jordan, revised my "parents" essay for *Woman's Day*, and wrote a review of the National Endowment for the Humanities book seminar. I believe the cover letter was an example of my flexibility. I feel I was successful in writing to a different audience, someone whom I do not know. My independence was displayed with my "parents" essay. I revised it again and again, on my own, until it met the criteria for the *Woman's Day* editor. I think I did a good job with the piece and the editors must have agreed, because they used it. I think writing the review about the book talk actually increased my range. This writing also helped me prepare for the [New York State] Regents Exam, for which I will use the books we read, *The Invisible Man* and *I Know Why the Caged Bird Sings....*

I have made some contributions to the class. I wanted to perceive the appropriate role for myself within the group and perform that role independently. I did a Great Moment in Literature on an Emily Dickinson poem, "Success." I not only gave the class a look at a rhyme scheme for their Writer's Notebook, but I also compared the poem to my own life (my reason for choosing it). I made the presentation at the Capital Area School Development Association's conference on assessment, and I developed, planned, revised, and performed my work without much outside direction. In that presentation I explained to the audience the features of our classroom community such as Great Moments, portfolio covers, and presentations. Then I led a discussion group of eight teachers and answered their questions about my experiences in this course.

Example 3: What Is Literature? (Jaime Sajeski)

Excerpts follow from Jaime Sajeski's response to the "What Is Literature?" activity begun in Chapter 1 of the student text. Toward the end of the course, she was asked the same set of questions.

Literature is a means of expression. With it you can say anything you want about yourself, the world, outer space, or anything else. You can write stories such as "Eveline," poems like "The Writer," or openings like the one for *Appointment in Samarra*. In one way, literature "means" what the author "feels."

For me, literature is a means of connection and a way to relate my experiences to those of others. It is kind of a shelter. With literature, I can assure myself that I'm not alone in dealing with my problems because the people who write the works I can relate to must have experienced these problems also.

For writers, literature is a way of reaching out, like in "Not Waving, But Drowning." The author of this poem is reaching out for help and, in a sense, is telling readers who feel the same to likewise reach out for help.

The writer could also use the work as a means of letting go of something. In the poem "The Writer," the speaker is letting go of his daughter, he is letting her grow up. . . .

Literature portrays meanings by the mood it is written in or read in. The story "The Laugher" was written in a sad, depressed, sentimental mood and that's how it came across to me. In listening to Diane Gallo read her poem "Two Dollar Mommy," the mood was painful, full of hurt and sympathetic to the mother. That is exactly how it made me feel when I listened to it being read. When the husband "punched her happy hello," the word "punched" gives such a violent gesture to the end of the piece. . . .

Example 4: Response to Poem and Personal Essay (Megan Kavanaugh)

Megan's essay shows a way to relate issues in Ron Welburn's poem to the biographical information in his essay.

Knowledge of Ron Welburn's "Native American and African ancestry," his "rural small town birth and upbringing," and his intrigue with irony and paradox allowed me a greater appreciation of . . . "Once to Run." . . .

The first stanza of "Once to Run" from a song by Buddy Red Bow most likely paralleled the stories of hardship Welburn heard from his grandmother, while the second stanza from a late Fifties pop song most likely represented feelings Welburn himself experienced. Thinking that Welburn was writing from a personal perspective caused me to give the poem further readings. I thought about the real discrimination generations of minorities have faced (and still face), rather than simply reading the words that were printed on the paper.

From Welburn's statement, ". . .Part of [my family's] ease about things lies in knowing who they were. . . . They were independent and proud but not arrogant," I recognized his own pride in his ancestry. Conscious of the "layers of masks" imposed upon Native Americans by recent society, Welburn uses his poem . . . as a tool to strip himself of his masks and maintain his heritage. Never does he want to find himself "lost on another continent."

The image of people being transplanted to another continent raises pictures of the slave trade. Welburn's poem . . . include[s] references to both displaced Native Americans and to African slaves; . . . "coyote chases his tail" and "we who worked jazz" seem to exemplify this. If I had not read Welburn's article, I think I would have found this imagery very confusing. Knowing the diversity of his upbringing also made it easier for me to understand lines such as "She ran and ran into and beyond/ the slave whip and the cotton fields/ and moved stealthily down Chicago streets/ to shuffle dance in a storefront sanctified church."

In the poem it seemed that although Welburn acknowledged his heritage and desired to preserve it, he was being forced into assimilating with American culture as society desired. I concluded that, with his realization of this irony, Welburn turned to writing poetry as a way to share his journey, portraying his ancestry more accurately than is done in modern stories such as "Rin Tin Tin." . . .

Example 5: Criteria for a Good Novel (Josh Tallent)

We include this final example as a sort of challenge, a little assessment problem for you. Although the assignment—list, explain, and justify your personal criteria for a good novel—seemed to call for a straightforward expository response, the writer has gone somewhere else with this, a place somewhat outside our expectations. An almost involuntary first response is, "That's not what I was looking for," followed by another, "This is more interesting." It's more interesting because the evaluative task required by the activity has been done, but in a powerfully and personally situated way. Somewhere we have said that writers don't come from Writerland, and readers don't come from Readerland. Josh is a *writer* reading.

See what you think. Would you hand this out to students as an example of a good way to do business?

This may be arbitrary, but so are most things. I think that the novel *The Shipping News*, by E. Annie Proulx, is a stunning example of literary achievement. (And the Pulitzer Prize would seem to reaffirm my conviction.)

Anyway—why? It's never good enough just to say (like a parent) "because I said so." There needs to be a reason, a "so what?" There needs to be a justification. Why after I had read the final page, and then reread it, and then read it again, did I have the distinct feeling that I was bearing witness to an amazing creation? Several reasons, I think.

At first it was the technique that so impressed me. The constructions, the descriptions contained within this novel are unlike any I have ever encountered before—the style is fascinatingly new to me, and as a result, captivating. Don't you, in your reading, desire to be shown something new and different, in the place of what has, forever, remained constant, changing only in name? Well, I'm shown something brand new this time, and it appears to be almost a revelation. Constantly, I found myself green, wishing desperately that I possessed the ability to duplicate, or even begin to approach, this level of success in my own writing. I do not often wish to do as another has already done, but here the feeling is inescapable. Sentences that demand such attention and respect that the reader is barely able to continue on with the work, and must choose between basking in the glow of a beautiful phrase or moving forward. And, of course, anticipation inevitably triumphs.

I read it once to see how it was written, and then found myself reading it again to ensure that I had heard what had been said. Whether or not I had the first time, I did the second. Generally, I find myself drawing parallels between facets of a work and my own everyday existence. However, I did not do so with this novel, the reason being that all I needed could be found within its pages. There is a vast difference, I believe, between detail—possible excessive detail—and effective detail. Detail in sure quantity does not ensure a clear, realistic description. Detail, rather, must be chosen carefully, in this instance resulting in descriptions so breathtakingly real that no questions in my mind remained unanswered. Characters seem nearly to live on the page, changing, evolving, or devolving—whatever suits them and their situation. And as I watch them change, I can't help but become personally interested in that change, and in the directions it will take them.

I have read a beautiful book, though not a pretty one. There are no kind descriptions or blurred images. There is only accuracy, clean and true—and all of the emotion, the feeling that accompanies it. Realism affects the reader in a very specific way. It breeds interest. It drags us, kicking and screaming sometimes, or sometimes willingly, into the depths of the work, from where we are afforded an entirely new view of the world as it is seen by someone that is not ourselves. And therein lies the beauty of this work—in experiencing the world of its characters, if only for the briefest of instants, we have seen something that we otherwise never would have dreamed, and thus become a bit better ourselves.

6 Mini-Lessons for Special Problems

When you see a number of students having similar problems dealing with literature, you might use one of these mini-lessons to offer them a solution strategy. This is not quite so simple as a troubleshooting guide (you can't just check to see if the student is plugged in), but the lessons are set up in a similar fashion:

- The Problem
- A Possible Cause
- A Solution Strategy

MINI-LESSON 1: GETTING STARTED

The Problem

It is a new class, the students do not know each other, and most of what you say seems to draw blank stares. You are not sure how to begin.

A Possible Cause

The students may not be well-informed about how to think about literature or how to respond to it. They may be unsure how to be good students of literature and how to share with each other. They may, in fact, be shy.

A Solution Strategy

To loosen the students up and get them to think about themselves as readers and responders to literature, try giving them the following questionnaire. Use some or all of the questions and then have students share their answers either in small groups of three or as a whole class. Remind them that there is no right or wrong, that what you are trying to get all of them to consider is the nature of the literary life of the class. Don't evaluate questionnaire responses individually, but have students draw up a class profile based on a summary of the answers. The first ten questions deal with how people read literature, the second ten with what sorts of readers they are.

Directions to Students

Answer each question that follows with a brief explanation or example to support your response. Ideally your example will relate to a specific work you have read or film you have seen.

1. Have you done something you would not ordinarily have done because you read about it in a story, poem, or play? (For example, when you were younger, have you dressed up as a pirate because you read a story about pirates?)

2. While you were reading a book, have you thought of yourself as one of the people in it?

3. Have you compared a person you met in real life with people you have read about? (For instance, have you ever called a strong person Samson?)

4. Have you been in a situation and asked yourself what some person in a story you read would have done in that situation?

5. When you read a novel or a story, do you imagine that what is happening in the story takes place in some town or city that you have seen?

6. Have you done something or gone somewhere, felt that this has happened before, and then realized that in fact it happened in a book you read?

7. When you read a story, how often do you imagine that the people in the story look like people you know?

8. When you meet a new person, how often do you compare the person to someone you saw in a movie?

9. How often do you think that the people you are reading about in a story are real people and not simply people in a story?

10. When you read a story or a play, do you try to remember something that happened to you that is like what you are reading about? Do you ever say to yourself, "Something like this happened to me once"?

11. How many poems have you written or read for your own pleasure in the past year?

12. During the past year, how many plays have you read or gone to for your own pleasure?

13. During the past year, how many novels have you read for your own pleasure?

14. When you choose a story or novel to read, which one of the following is most likely to be the reason for your choice?

    • Friends or parents recommend it

    • I have read other books by the same author

    • The title attracts me

    • I just choose any

    • other

15. How often do you reread novels, stories, or plays?

16. Have you ever tried to write an imitation or another piece based on a story or poem you have read?

17. Have you ever gone to a movie because you read the story in a book?

18. Have you ever read a book because you saw the story in a movie?

19. Have you ever read a book because you saw the story on television or heard the story on the radio?

20. After you have seen a play or movie, would you want to read a criticism of the work?

MINI-LESSON 2: WORKS SELECTION COMMITTEES

The Problem

Students are not participating as actively as you wish.

A Possible Cause

Accustomed to being the decided-upon rather than the decision-makers, they might be waiting for you to feed the course to them.

A Solution Strategy

Require them to make decisions about which works to read and how to help the class learn something about those works. To begin, decide how much time you have to spend on this activity. Then set the number of work groups you will want, the number and types of works students should read, and the approximate amount of time each group presentation should take. The directions that follow, set up for lessons on individual poems, can easily be used with groups of poems or with other genres.

Directions to Students

1. Elect/appoint/coerce someone to be a recorder for your group, someone to take notes on group activities and decisions made during planning. We will want to talk about your decisions and reasons for making them.

2. Select a poem to work with—one we have not yet read—and decide how to teach us the work. You will have (*amount of time*) for this lesson. You will need to decide

   • how to collaborate to develop the lesson

   • how to keep records of your activities and decisions in the group

   • what is important for us to "see" about the work

   • what reading, writing, speaking, and listening activities we should do

3. Come with everything you need to begin this lesson on (*date*).

MINI-LESSON 3: READING BETWEEN THE LINES

The Problem

Students think reading literature is a mysterious process and it scares them.

A Possible Cause

They may believe that you have to have a lot of esoteric knowledge before you can read a poem or a piece of fiction.

A Solution Strategy

We have mentioned reading between the lines in the student book. Here is a way of making that lesson apparent.

Take a four-panel comic strip such as *Peanuts* and make a transparency of it. Show the students the first two of the four pictures and ask them what happens between the two scenes. There may be a change of character or scene, a change of perspective, or a change in time. After students respond, ask them how they know. Do the same going to the third and then the fourth picture in the strip. They will have read between the panels and made sense of four things that could perfectly well be unrelated.

Next give them another strip, this time with the panels jumbled, and have them put the panels in the proper sequence. How did they know how to do it? Probably they were following the conventions of plot or sequence.

Now try them out with the first two or three stanzas of a ballad like "Sir Patrick Spens," "Lord Randal," or "Edward." You can scramble the stanzas of one of these as well. Have them fill in the gaps of the ballad to make a sensible story, and once again ask them how they did it.

Now move on to a poem that does not have an obvious narrative base, such as one of T. S. Eliot's "Preludes," or a Shakespearean sonnet. Discuss what gaps they have to fill here to make sense of their reading. Or try the same exercise with a story where the time line is not clear, such as a Hemingway story based almost entirely on dialogue and suggestion. How do students make a story out of that? What do they do to fill in the gaps?

MINI-LESSON 4: KNOWING HOW YOU KNOW WHAT YOU KNOW

The Problem

Students can work with literature, but they can't say how they do it. Interpretations "just happen," they think; a mystery occurs in their heads.

A Possible Cause

Many students do not have (and never needed to have) much metacognitive awareness.

A Solution Strategy

Ask students to project a poem from your directions, and they might better understand what happens when they read, what meanings they bring to texts. Begin by giving students the word "Journey" and explaining that it is part of the title of a poem. You will probably want to discuss students' responses after each of the steps below.

Directions to Students

1. Write about "journey" with respect to physical characteristics of journeys, their uses and purposes, the types or kinds, and famous journeys from history, literature, myth, religion, and your own life.

2. List your expectations of this work because it is a poem.

3. There are three parts to the work. Sketch out two different three-part maps that show relationships among the parts (time, space, logic, etc.).

4. What movement do you expect in the poem, leading to what ending?

5. Give both a straightforward and an ironic interpretation of your ending.

6. Reconcile those two interpretations so that they both "work."

7. List five to ten words or ideas you expect to find in this poem.

8. Give one important word you expect to find and explain its importance.

(Once they have finished their projections, give students T. S. Eliot's "Journey of the Magi" and ask them to see how much meaning resides in readers. See what they could "know" about a poem before even looking at the text.)

MINI-LESSON 5: INFERRING THE POEM

The Problem

On essays and tests, students write papers that are centered on the work but that do not answer the question posed by the task.

A Possible Cause

Students might be getting lost in the complexity of the work, thus ignoring the task or question. They do not get into clear focus what they are "hired to do" by the task or question.

A Solution Strategy

Create focus by asking students to generate a work by inference from an assignment based on it. Rather than do the assignment, students must write the work implied by it.

Have the poem "Storm Warnings" by Adrienne Rich available for eventual distribution. Give students the title and this task: "Show how the imagery and structure of the poem develop the literal and figurative meanings suggested by the title."

Directions to Students

1. Use the essay response plan to underline, count, and form into an outline the elements of the assignment.

2. Work backwards to imagine the poem you would need to write a response to the assignment. Write notes about the requirements for imagery, etc. Make sure you attend to all parts of the assignment.

3. Write a poem that includes the elements you need to respond to the assignment.

4. Now write your response to the assignment, basing your writing on your own poem.

5. Respond to the same task by writing about this poem by Adrienne Rich.

(As students complete these steps, you may want them to compare the original poems they write, as well as their responses to their poems.)

MINI-LESSON 6: UNDERSTANDING HOW WE READ A POEM

The Problem

Some students have trouble getting into a poem and understanding how to read it carefully.

A Possible Cause

Students may think they have to come up with a summary message, and they don't stop to think over the words. They think that they can skim to get the meaning.

A Solution Strategy

Present the students with a short poem—in this case, a nursery rhyme—a word at a time.

Using a transparency or the board, write first the word *gray*. Ask the students to jot down and share what comes into their heads as they see the word—associations, feelings, images. Let them be as diverse as possible. Then next to *gray* write the word *goose*, and ask them to do the same thing. Keep doing it until you have written out the whole poem:

Gray goose and gray gander,
Waft your wings together;
And carry the good king's daughter
Over the one-strand river.

The only words they might have trouble with are *Waft* (wave) and *strand* (it can mean "line," but its original meaning is "shore"). Pause after each word and ask what connections and pictures each reader is making. How do they change? How does the addition of each word narrow the images? (Or are we as readers doing the narrowing?) How does the whole poem come together? Is it the sum of its words or something more?

MINI-LESSON 7: GETTING THAT FIRST IMPRESSION

The Problem

Students pay insufficient attention to titles and opening passages, almost ignoring some of the most carefully crafted parts of the work.

A Possible Cause

Sometimes students are in a hurry to get to "the important parts," which they see as the main course of the reading.

A Solution Strategy

Give only the early part of a work and require an articulated response. Readers should learn to savor the appetizer.

Option 1 (Title only)

Give students the title of a work (*The Stranger*, for example) and ask for five minutes of writing about associations, expectations, predictions, questions, speculations, and anything else that comes to mind. Discuss the responses, and keep a list or concept map on the front board. This activity frequently touches many significant issues in a work—one class wrote just about the whole story of *The Stranger* before they had read anything but the title. For titles such as *A Clockwork Orange* or *The Effect of Gamma Rays on Man-in-the-Moon Marigolds*, give parts of the title separately and then ask for connections.

Option 2 (Title and first page or opening stanza)

Give the title and the first page or first stanza and have students take fifteen to twenty minutes to read and respond in the same ways as above. Then ask students to write four or five answers to this question: What is this work *about*, and why do you think so? The list of issues thus generated might create a good reading agenda, issues to track during the actual reading of the work.

MINI-LESSON 8: THE RHYTHM OF POETRY

The Problem

Students are unsure how to read poems aloud. What should they do at the end of a line? How should they treat rhyme or rhythm?

A Possible Cause

Students probably don't fully understand the principles of meter and rhythm. They may be able to define an iamb or pentameter, but the knowledge does not help them read.

Solution Strategy

Create an analogy to music.

Many students either sing or play an instrument. Those who can read music should explain to the others what a bar is (the space between two vertical lines that marks a rhythmical grouping and is given a beat). Then explain that traditional poetry was all sung or chanted. When people began to write down poems, they used a line as an attempt to write down what was heard as the basic rhythmical unit of a poem. The line was like a bar. Show a poem like

> How doth the little busy bee
> Improve each shining hour,
> And gather honey all the day
> From every opening flower.

> Isaac Watts, from *Divine Songs for Children*, 1715

Explain that in this poem each line is a bar, and the first and third bars are four-beat lines, while the second and fourth are three-beat lines. But the musical phrase goes beyond the bar, so that we tend to read the first two lines together and the third and fourth together as well. There is the smallest of pauses at the end of the first and third lines. A phrase that ends at the end of a line is often called "strong"; but a phrase that goes beyond the line sets up a kind of counterpoint rhythm. Show these lines from Keats's "To Autumn":

> Who hath not seen thee oft amid thy store?
> Sometimes whoever seeks abroad may find
> Thee sitting careless on a granary floor,
> Thy hair soft-lifted by the winnowing wind;
> Or on a half-reaped furrow sound asleep,
> Drowsed with the fume of poppies, while thy hook
> Spares the next swath and all its twinèd flowers: . . .

Have students note that the second and sixth lines end between verb and object and between subject and verb respectively. It makes no sense to pause, and so the phrase goes beyond the bar to carry over into a two-bar rhythm that alternates with the one-bar rhythm of the other lines. The pattern sets up a counterpoint.

Point out that when students read, they should notice the bars but read the rhythm of speech against that basic beat and not try to make everything fit into a strong line, sing-song rhythm.

MINI-LESSON 9: GETTING INTO DRAMA

The Problem

Students have trouble reading a play.

A Possible Cause

They may not be used to transforming a script into a literary experience.

A Solution Strategy

Students should first see that the script on the page, even for a Shakespearean play, is not a piece of literature any more than a score is a piece of music.

Have students read the following opening of a script. Then elicit the discussion points that follow it.

ONE NIGHT AT THE BORDER

a melodrama
by
Jay Reid Gould

CHARACTERS

GEORGE MERCHANT, an officer in the United States Customs Service. He is about thirty and is attractive in personality and appearance.

JACKIE HOLLIDAY, another customs officer some years younger. She is exuberant by nature.

FELICIA MCRAE, a young Canadian, daughter of a very rich man. She is sure of herself.

ARMAND DOUCETTE, a French-Canadian who isn't as unworldly as he first appears. He is middle-aged and amiable.

MITCH MCGUIRE, a New York restaurant owner in his thirties who looks and acts like the popular conception of the big-time gambler.

ANNA MCGUIRE, a withdrawn woman in her thirties; of foreign birth.

EVELYN GRIBBLE, a middle-aged woman of weak and ineffectual character.

DORIS GRIBBLE, her daughter, about seventeen, spoiled and petulant.

SONNY GRIBBLE, her brother, about eighteen, a match for his sister.

SETTING

The setting for this play is the waiting room of an American Customs Office somewhere on the eastern border between the United States and Canada.

It is near midnight, at the present time.

When the curtain goes up, it reveals the waiting room of an American Custom Office set somewhere on the eastern border between the United States and Canada.

The time is late of a summer night. The telephone is ringing vigorously and continues to ring until George Merchant enters from the rear. George is a young official in the United States Immigration Service. He is about thirty and personable. Before he answers the telephone, he goes to the outside door which is open and calls to someone.

GEORGE

Jackie!
(The phone continues to ring)

Jackie!

United States Customs, George Merchant speaking. . . . Oh, hello, Canada, how's your side of the border tonight? . . . Of course it's hot, what do you think? . . . Well, what's on your mind?

What?. . . .You don't mean it, here? . . . What do you think they're carrying? . . . Holy Smokes, that's plenty. Why didn't they pick a big place to cross over? . . . Well, I suppose you've got something there. What's the description on them? . . . You don't know? How do you expect Jackie and me to spot them then. . . . Yeah. Yeah. . . . Fancy names you Canadians have. . . . Oh, they're Americans. I beg your pardon. . . . O.K. Canada, thanks for the tip. Will do.

(Jackie Holliday is standing in the outside doorway before George finishes talking. When George is about to put up the phone and with his back to the door, he senses that someone is behind him. In one motion he replaces the phone, picks up a gun from the counter, and whirls around to face Jackie.)

JACKIE

Don't shoot, boss. It's just me. . . . What's the matter, George, the heat getting you?

GEORGE

I'm sorry, Jackie. The Canadian Customs just called. They've had word on that pair of diamond importers they've been trying to catch in Montreal—they think they're headed this way.

JACKIE
Well, why don't they catch them then?

GEORGE
They're leaving that to us. You can't do a thing about them leaving the country, but we can try to stop them getting across here.

Have the students look at the title and subtitle, and discuss what a melodrama is (an exaggerated story in which the good are very good and the bad very bad). Explain that all characters are to be played broadly with a bit of humor as well as tension, and the description of the characters suggests how the actors are to say the lines. George is going to be the hero and Jackie the slightly comic foil, so George should be read seriously, Jackie with a bit of humor.

Discuss the setting, having students see that it gives something of the mood and sets up the tenseness of the action that is about to follow. Note that the speeches rather than the description provide the real exposition to the audience. The directions to the actors are just that, and the actors need to practice saying the lines so that George is serious and Jackie just a little bit mocking.

From this bit of script, students should go on to another play. After discussing the character introductions and the opening stage directions, they should take turns reading the parts and trying out characters, stopping occasionally to see if they have the tone and the mood. The point of the oral reading is to try to make the play come to life, not to get through a reading assignment.

MINI-LESSON 10: MAKING A COLLAGE

The Problem

Students often hand in collages as a form of response to a poem or as an introduction to their portfolio, but the result is messy and unattractive.

A Possible Cause

They probably have not thought about the design of a collage.

A Solution Strategy

A mini-lesson on layout and design can help students make an effective collage.

Start with a definition: A collage is a visual compilation of different pieces to make a whole impression, image, or idea. The important ideas here are different pieces (pictures, letters, pieces of material, etc.) and whole impression. The viewer must see not the pieces as much as the whole that the pieces contribute to.

Many students will have too many pieces and they will paste them anywhere on the base board so that the viewer is simply confused. Point out that the viewer should not have to work too hard, nor should he or she have to concentrate on the individual pieces as in a "Where's Waldo?" puzzle. The impression has to come from the whole effect, and this means that there must be a central design element some place in the collage toward which the eye focuses so as to see all in a glance.

Students should also remember that the page does not have to be filled and that too much detail can obscure the message of the collage.

MINI-LESSON 11: READING INTERPRETIVE PAPERS WITH A CRITICAL EYE

The Problem

Students do not effectively revise their critical papers for content and organization.

A Possible Cause

Although they may edit well, most students are not trained to *revise*—to read for content, logic, and organization.

A Solution Strategy

Students should learn to read their own papers as a rhetorical critic would, for the structure of the argument.

Directions to Students

1. Divide your paper into episodes or blocks of content.
   Don't be fooled by your own paragraphing! An episode
   is a group of sentences dealing with one topic. Use
   brackets to show the divisions and label each by naming
   it in the left margin. What is each *about*?

2. Now look at each episode and decide what it *does*:
   - Does it state or extend a claim or thesis?
   - Does it support a claim or thesis by giving evidence or
     proof?
   - Does it suggest significance by
     - telling the effect on the reader?
     - showing how meaning is developed?
     - implying the writer's purpose?
     - saying "So what?" about the thesis?

   Label each episode by naming its logical purpose in the
   right margin.

3. Read the left margin to see a content outline of your
   paper as it is written. Do you need more ideas? Do you
   need to rearrange blocks or episodes?

4. Read the right margin to see the logic of your paper as it
   is written. Do you need a stronger claim or thesis? Do
   you need more evidence or proof? Do you need stronger
   significance? Do you need to rearrange existing episodes
   to construct a better argument?